AF594584

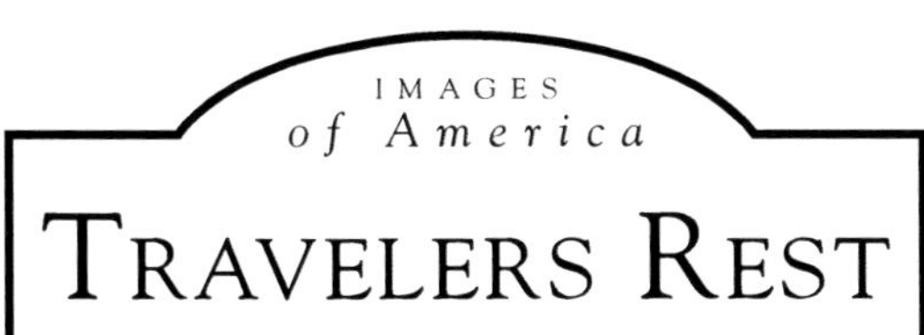
IMAGES
of America
TRAVELERS REST

On the Cover: This photograph of elementary school students (identified on page 53) was taken in 1942. The students are seated on the concrete-and-wooden bleachers located behind the high school wing on the steep bank beside the old football field. The bleachers are still used as seating for community activities, such as festivals, concerts, and Little League games. (Travelers Rest Historical Society.)

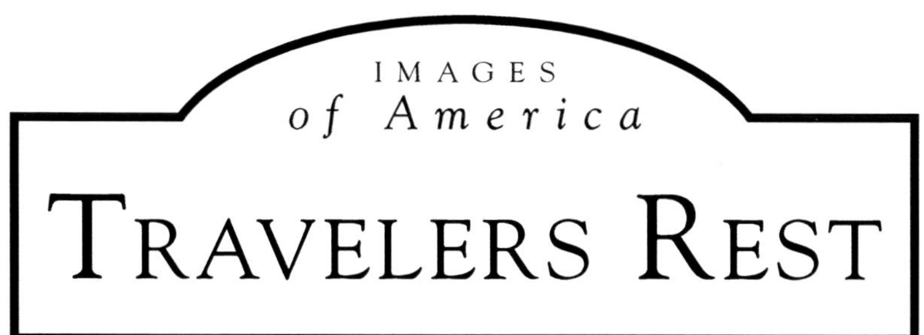

Travelers Rest Historical Society

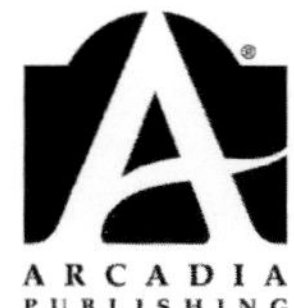

ISBN 978-0-7385-8219-1

Published by Arcadia Publishing
Charleston, South Carolina

Printed in the United States of America

Library of Congress Control Number: 2010938396

For all general information, please contact Arcadia Publishing:
Telephone 843-853-2070
Fax 843-853-0044
E-mail sales@arcadiapublishing.com
For customer service and orders:
Toll-Free 1-888-313-2665

Visit us on the Internet at www.arcadiapublishing.com

In Memoriam
JoAnn Elizabeth Coleman
December 11, 1931–October 16, 2009

This book is dedicated with appreciation to James R. "Roddy" Rodgers Jr.
Without his help, this book would not be possible.

Contents

ACKNOWLEDGMENTS

The Travelers Rest Historical Society is indebted to the citizens of the community for their generosity in sharing photographs for use in this book. Unless otherwise stated, all photographs were loaned by individuals interested in preserving the history of our town. We especially thank Mann Batson for his guidance and advice. We are grateful to the Sargent Library staff, Loftis Printing Company, Allegra Print and Imaging, Diane Dilworth, Larry McCauley, Dianna Turner, Lynn Duncan, Walt Cottingham, all *Echoes* contributors, and the Travelers Rest mayor and city council.

Members of the Travelers Rest Historical Society committee who aided in the compilation of this book include Marie Williams Batson, Dot Neal Bishop, Ann Styles Burgess, Eric Cunningham, Amy Bruce Doser, Diane Southerlin Drake, Thomas M. Drake, Evelee Bridwell Fender, Nell Anderson Gibson, Randy D. "Country" Hawkins, Frances Holtzclaw Lockaby, James R. "Roddy" Rodgers Jr., and Larry Seigler.

INTRODUCTION

Nestled within the rolling hills of the northwestern corner of South Carolina at the junction of two main roads leading to North Carolina is a small town known for its beautiful mountain scenery and hometown feeling. The little city abounds in historic wealth that has left its mark on generations of people who have lived here as well as on "transplants" who have sought real Southern comfort. Once used as a stopping point for cattle drovers coming from Kentucky, North Carolina, and Tennessee to areas in lower South Carolina and Georgia, the community received the name Travelers Rest. Originally, the name of the town was spelled "Travellers Rest." Then for a number of years, the two versions of the name were used interchangeably until the mid-1940s, when postmaster William F. Griffin officially changed the spelling on the postal cancellation stamp to Travelers Rest.

The town was built on land that was long considered the domain of the Cherokee Indians, and their artifacts can still be found throughout the area. The Cherokees were extremely proficient in cultivating, harvesting thousands of bushels of corn, creating their own alphabet, and trapping deer. It is said that the deer hides were shipped around the world and that some were used in clothing for Napoleon himself. In 1776, a treaty was signed between the governor of South Carolina and the Cherokee chiefs giving Carolinians control of the land. By 1780, many of the Cherokees had left the area.

The town has always been populated with people of daring character and resolve. During the Revolutionary War, a young girl named Dicey Langston helped save the lives of many patriots in the battle for independence. She married one of the early settlers, Thomas Springfield, and they made their home in Travelers Rest. A memorial to her can be seen at the original homestead. Many have claimed that Travelers Rest is home to some of the most hard-working, independent, patriotic people, and that is in no small thanks to the forefathers who founded the town. Family ties were strong, and religion was held to the highest level, which made Travelers Rest a wonderful place to experience true Southern hospitality.

Travelers Rest was once considered a resort location. Many people traveled for days from the Lowcountry via stagecoach to escape the hustle, bustle, and sweltering heat of the lower cities. Homeowners opened their doors and welcomed travelers who were either in search of healing mineral waters near Caesar's Head or just the cool mountain air and scenic views. As the years passed, more travelers became acquainted with the small town that overflowed with a feeling of warmth and spirit. A post office opened, businesses sprang up, the railroad ran through town, and train depots were built as stops between Greenville and River Falls.

Because of Travelers Rest's location along rivers, businesses opened thanks to the abundance of good, pure water. Within a few years, gristmills, cotton gins, lumber mills, and a blacksmith shop were thriving. Manufacturing was introduced into the community, allowing many farmers the opportunity to leave their fields, especially in times of bad crop yields, to supplement waning incomes and help their families survive.

Some of the original homes can still be seen standing, while others are remembered through the pieces of original wood that have been recycled into other uses in homes and businesses. Churches were built, and free schools were introduced, allowing for the continued influx of visitors and settlers. Attracted to the town's location on a main road wending from Greenville to Asheville and Knoxville, new companies opened their doors. Franchise companies have also seen the benefits of Travelers Rest's location, and some have moved in to capitalize on a growing economic force.

Travelers Rest falls within the jurisdictional boundaries of Greenville County, South Carolina, and reaps the benefits of the county's tax dollars. A new revitalization effort through the county is being felt in Travelers Rest. A beautification process on the city's Main Street has been completed. The new Swamp Rabbit Trail challenges avid bikers, walkers, and runners, providing families with the opportunity for a small nature excursion in their own backyard. Businesses that closed as a result of a down economy are now being replaced in a new excitement for the city.

The authors hope that readers will take this book as a guide for their travels to this wonderful little city. Many direct descendants of the original founders of Travelers Rest still live in town. Their histories are strong and colorful, full of emotion and stories. The impact of their ancestors' lives can still be seen.

One

Inns, Postal Service, and Transportation

Commissioned in 1808, the first Travelers Rest post office was in the home of Maj. Thomas Edwards near the present-day location of New Liberty Baptist Church. Years before this event, the little village of Travelers Rest was becoming established. Nestled beneath Paris Mountain in the foothills of the Blue Ridge Mountains, this area—along the trails running through the gaps in the mountains—had become a favorite place of rest and refreshment for drovers bringing animals to markets in Greenville, Augusta, and the towns along the coast. Travelers Rest was a place of respite and solace for the "Lowlanders" who came to the North Carolina Mountains to escape the heat and humidity of coastal South Carolina. In the late 1800s, the new railroad that ran through Travelers Rest and improved roads made travel and commerce easier. Each succeeding postmaster moved the post office south so that, by 1900, it was situated in the center of the bustling little community. This chapter will explore the early places of rest, railway travel, and mail service.

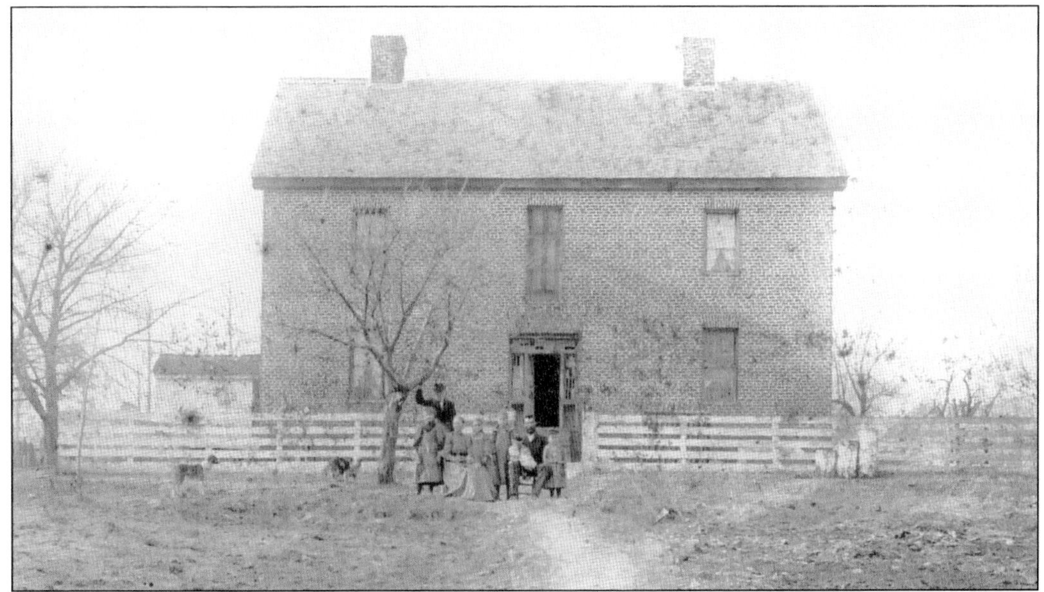

The White Horse Inn was built in the early 1840s by Squire George Washington McCarrell as a home for his wife, Caroline Phillips McCarrell, and their family. This 1896 photograph shows Squire McCarrell (standing by tree) with his daughter Carrie's family: (from left to right) James; Carrie Nesbitt; Mary; Pauline; Carrie's husband, Will Nesbitt, holding Clara; and Mills. Following the War Between the States, the home was used as an inn and was also the designated post office for White Horse, South Carolina, prior to 1886.

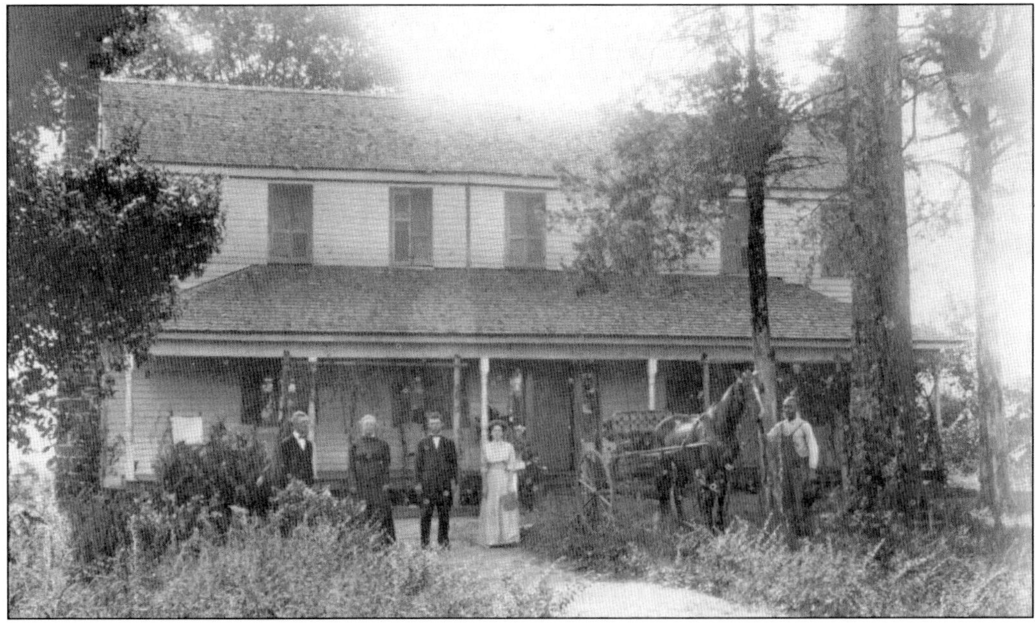

Arriving in Travelers Rest in 1828, Maj. Henry E. Lynch bought land and settled on Highway 25 at Tigerville Road. He built a 14-room house with the third floor made up of a number of small rooms to accommodate travelers. It was a stagecoach stop, the Travelers Rest Post Office, and a drover's stand. The property passed into the hands of Major Lynch's son-in-law, Col. S. S. Crittenden, and it became known as the Crittenden place.

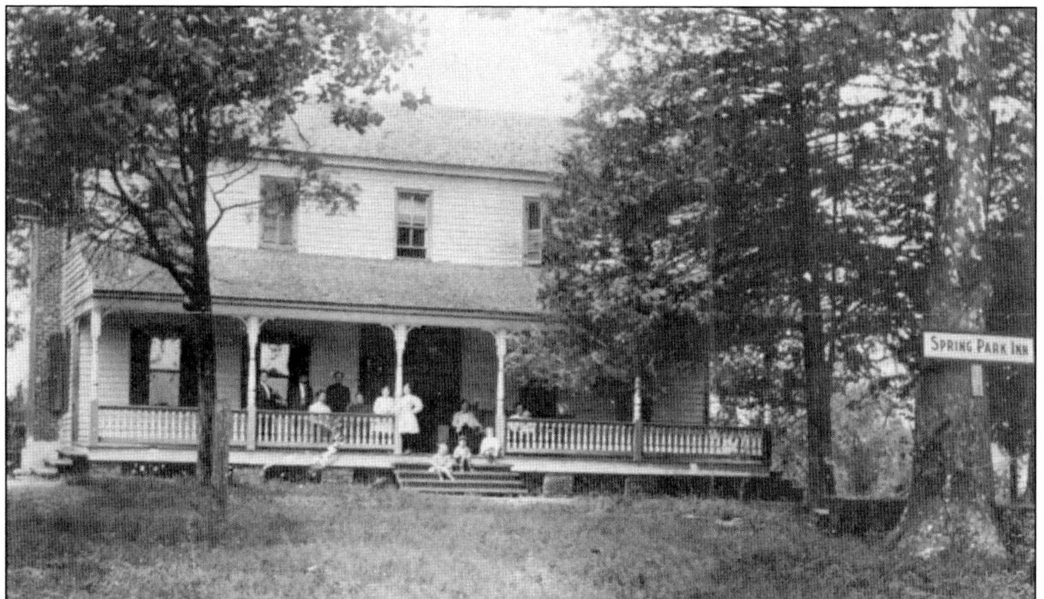

Chevis Montgomery built this large home in 1851 and ran it as an inn before it was purchased in 1873 by Robert Wright Anderson, who continued to operate the inn. In 1898, the Andersons' daughter and son-in-law, Edward Y. and Minnie Lee Hillhouse, acquired the house and named it Spring Park Inn. The "Swamp Rabbit" train brought visitors to the hotel. At the death of Minnie Lee Hillhouse in 1941, her nephew, Robert LeRoy Anderson, inherited the home. The Andersons and their children resided there while renting apartments and single rooms on the upper floor to local teachers. Later this home became a private residence, and now it is the home of Nell Anderson Gibson and her husband, Thomas Gibson.

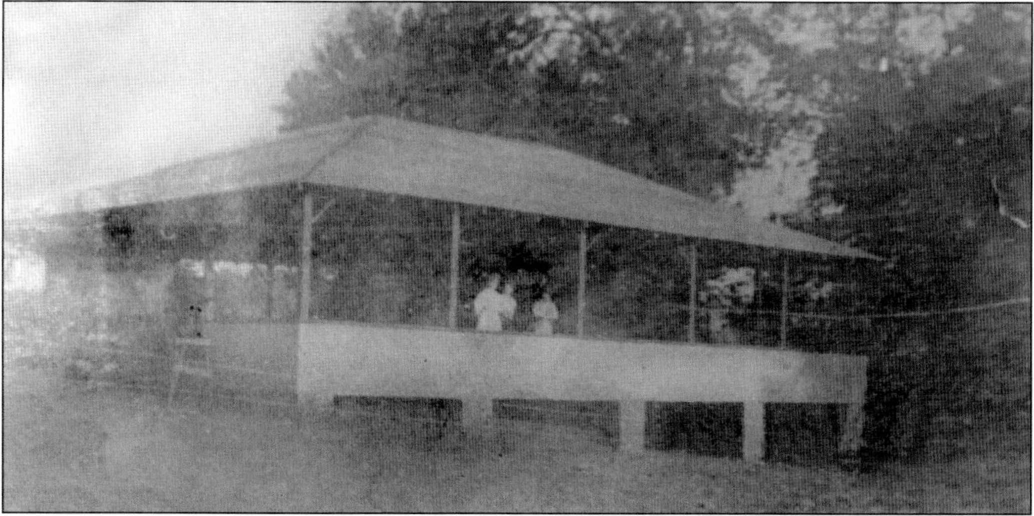

According to Mann Batson in *Early Travels and Accommodations*, the Carolina, Knoxville, and Western Railroad built a pavilion on the property near a large spring behind Spring Park Inn. This enticed passengers to come for outings, and special trains were run on demand. Dances, ball games, picnics, church activities, Fourth of July celebrations, footraces, horseshoes, and mountain hikes all took place at—or began at—the park. It was a tradition at that time for the Greenville County political campaign speaking rounds to begin at the pavilion.

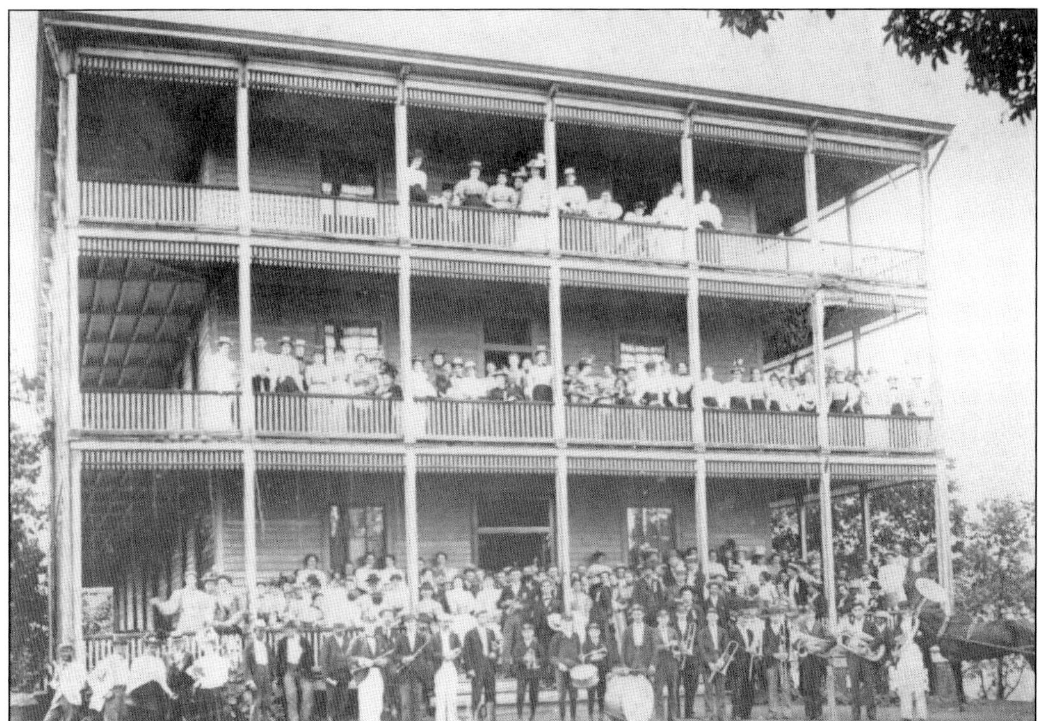

Located on Paris Mountain, the Altamont was a popular resort in the 1890s, but it did not prosper. The hotel, a large three-story wooden structure with piazzas on all sides of each story, was typical of resort hotels of the period. It was reached from Greenville by a coach of four horses driven by John Marchbanks. The colorful trip took over two hours, and Marchbanks blew his bugle on the final mile to announce the number of guests he was bringing. The building burned in 1920.

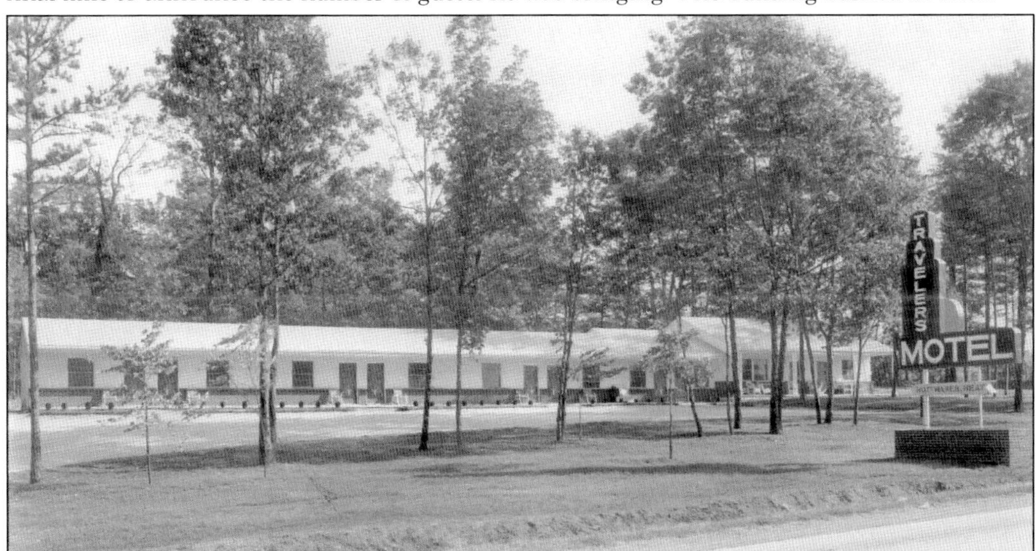

The Travelers Motel was built in 1954 by Al Drake and was operated by the Drake family until 1959. It was located a mile north of Travelers Rest on Highway 25/Poinsett Highway. Several years after the Drakes sold the motel, Poinsett Highway was widened. The original building was demolished, and a new building was constructed.

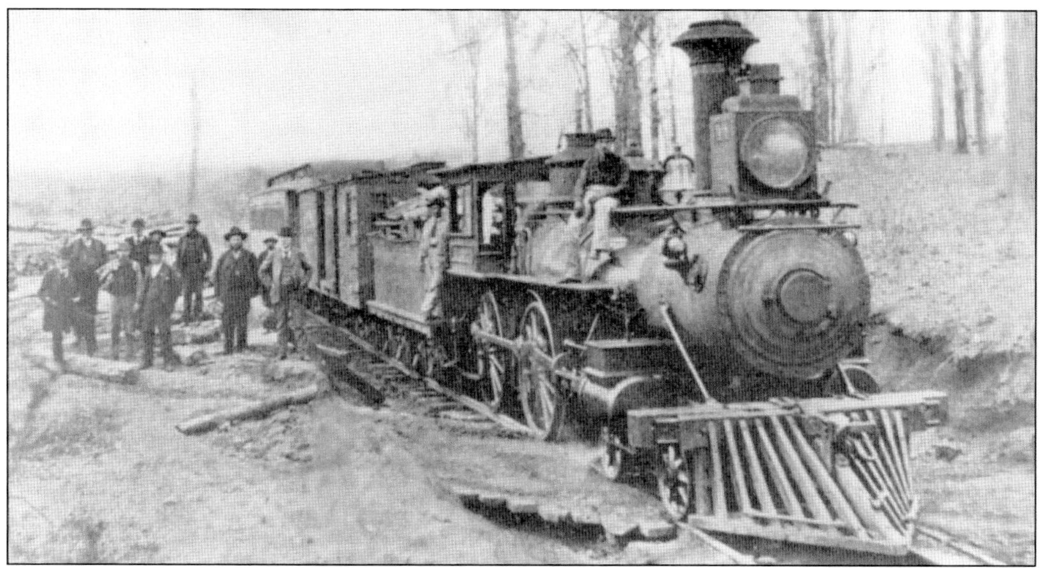

The second volume of *Echoes* features this *c.* 1889 photograph of the *Richard Humbolt* on one of the first trips through Travelers Rest to Marietta. The men pictured beside the train are, from left to right, (first row) William Y. Batson, Harry Hunt, Mack Williams, R. Mays Cleveland, and Captain Byrd; (second row) Joab Langford, Lee Salmon, and unidentified. The man in front on the rail of the locomotive is Jim Henderson.

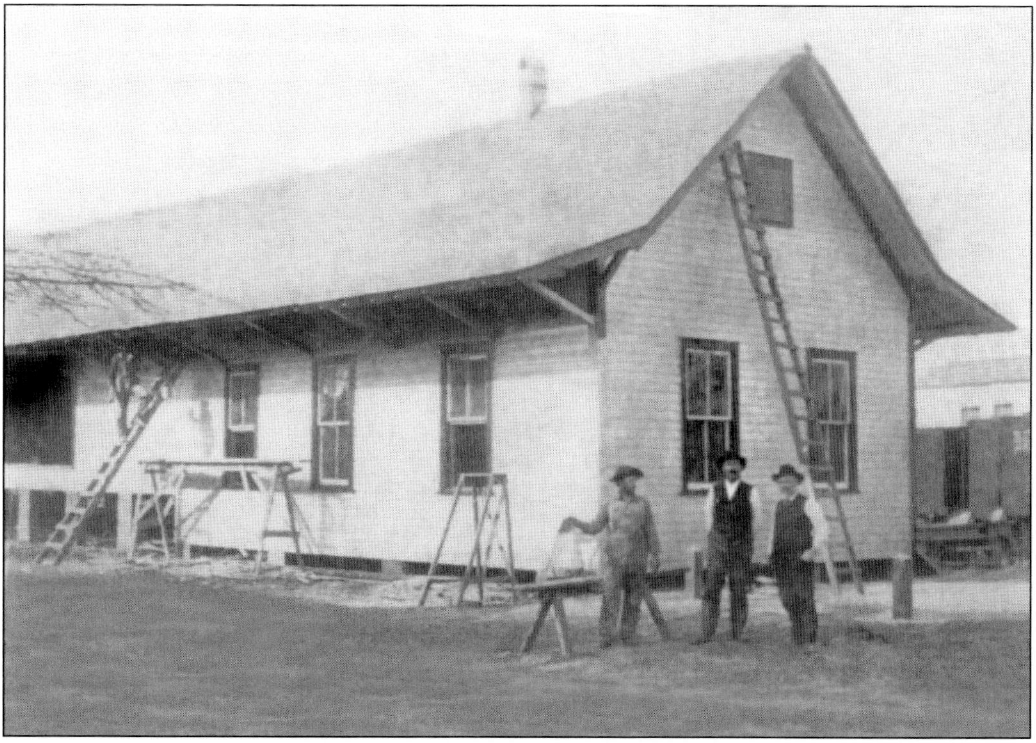

This is a picture of the Travelers Rest depot, the "Upper Station," as it nears completion about 1893. The men seen here are, from left to right, Jim Winn, Jasper Watson, and Dr. B. F. Goodlett. The Upper Station was located in the vicinity of the present-day Sunrift Adventures.

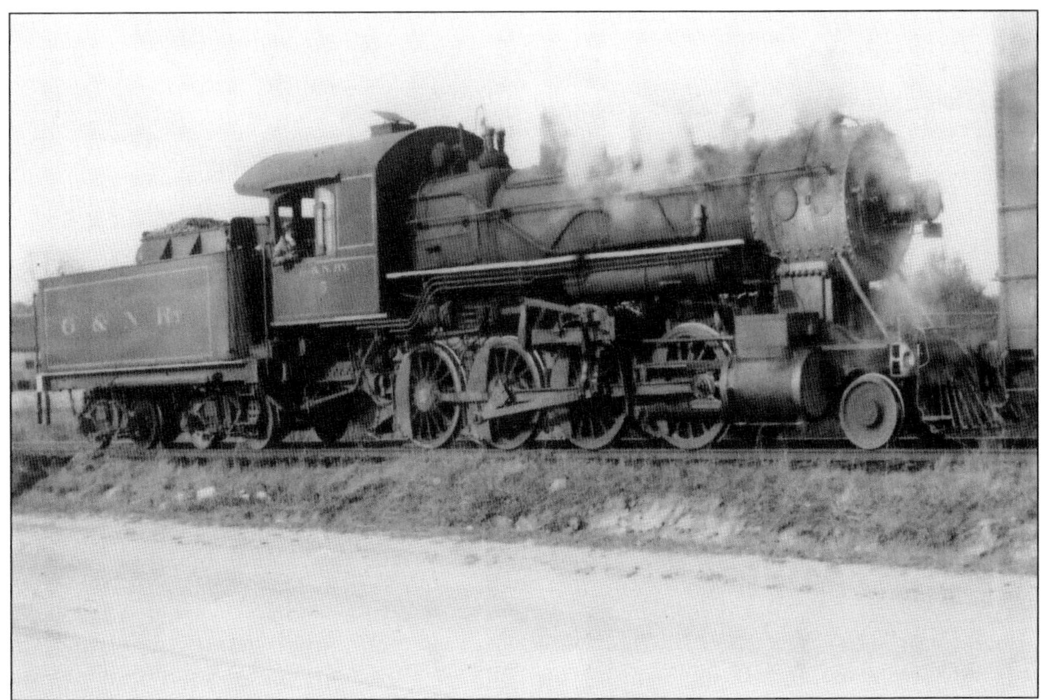

Steam engine No. 5 of the Greenville and Northern Railway was one of the engines nicknamed the "Swamp Rabbit." The Swamp Rabbit was the nickname of the steam engine, but when it was replaced by the diesel engine in the 1940s, the Swamp Rabbit name was no longer used.

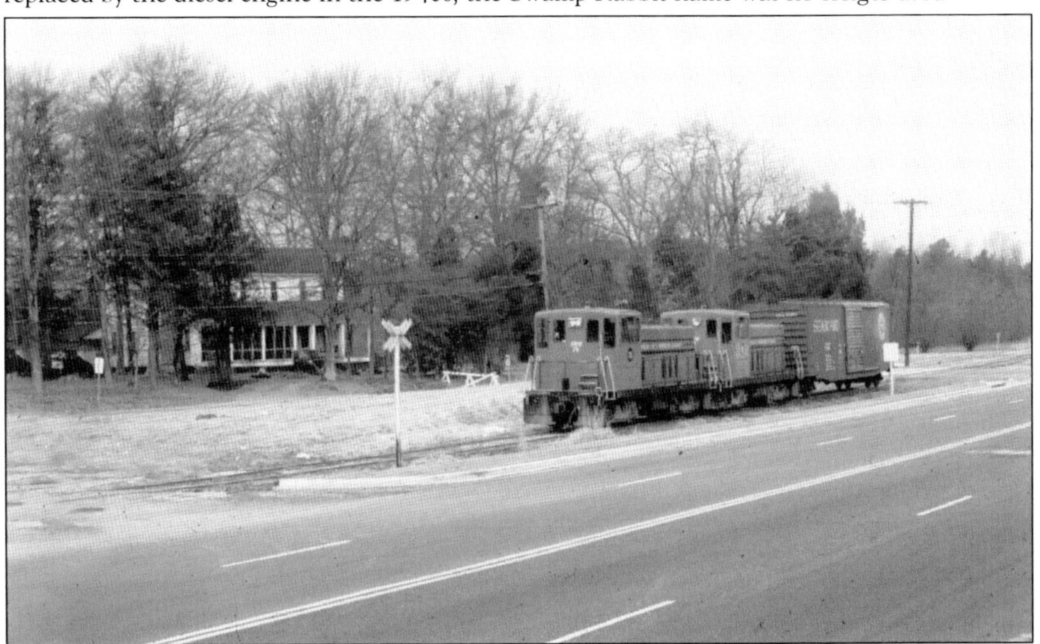

On February 20, 1978, Greenville and Northern Railway No. 75 and the Claremont and Concord Railway No. 9 head south in downtown Travelers Rest. Note the Anderson home on the left. The train is directly in front of the location where the city water park was built in 2009. (Photograph by James D. Sheppard.)

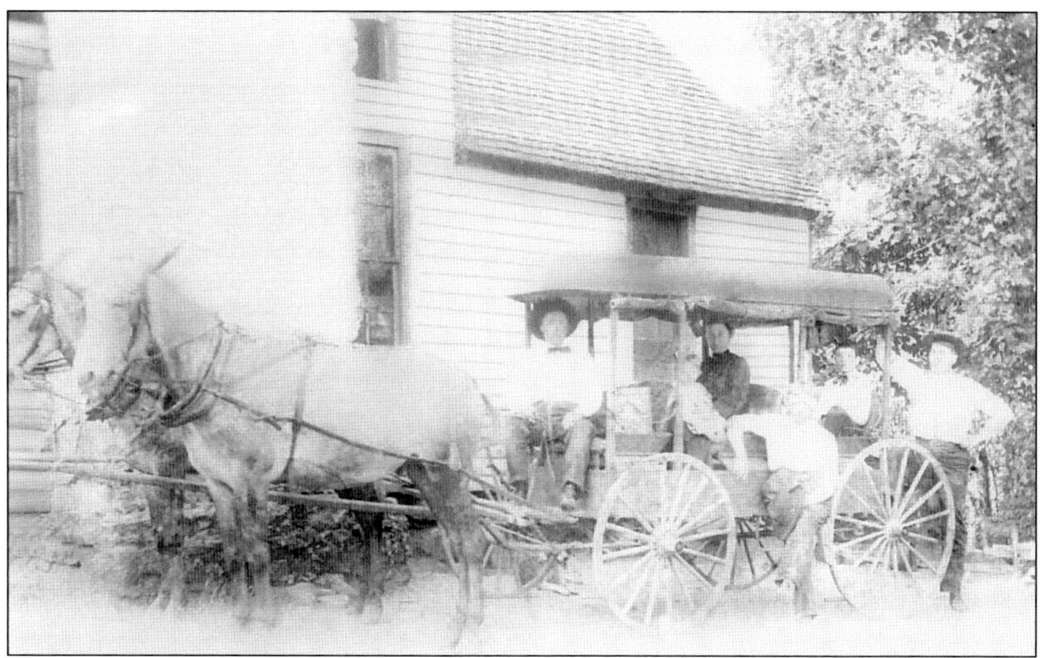

This *c.* 1906 photograph shows the "hack" that was used by Harvey Southerlin to carry mail from Travelers Rest to Brevard, North Carolina. Passengers would often catch a ride with him to North Carolina. They stopped at springs along the road for a drink of water.

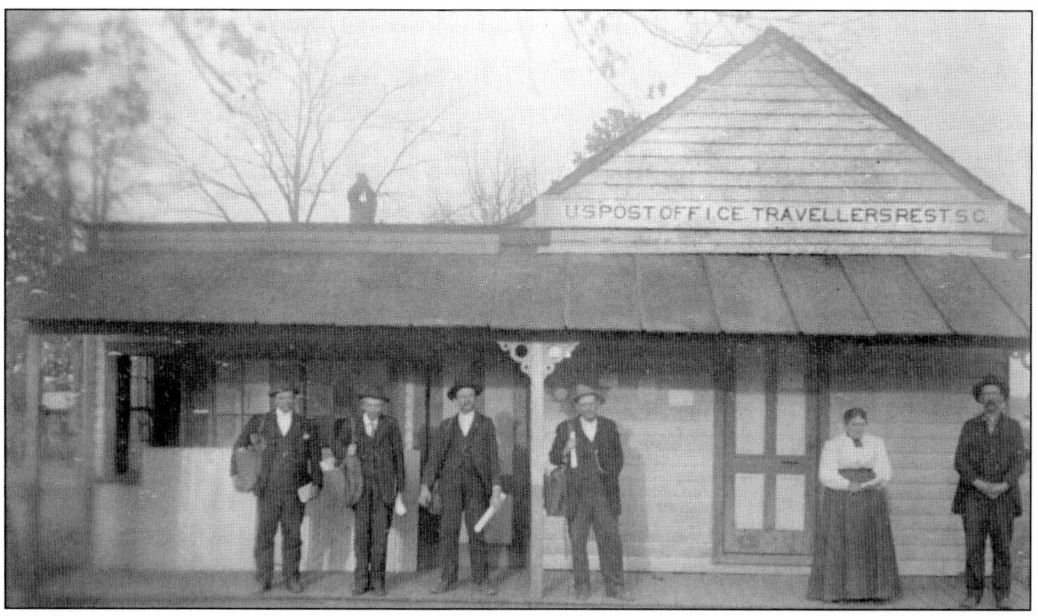

This is a picture of the wooden Travelers Rest post office built by Tom Cunningham. Pictured in this 1910 photograph are, from left to right, W. A. Benson, T. Y. Hellams, T. D. Cooper, H. J. Williams, Theodosia Cooper Watson, and postmaster Jasper E. Watson. This one-story frame building was located at the corner of Geer Highway and McElhaney Road.

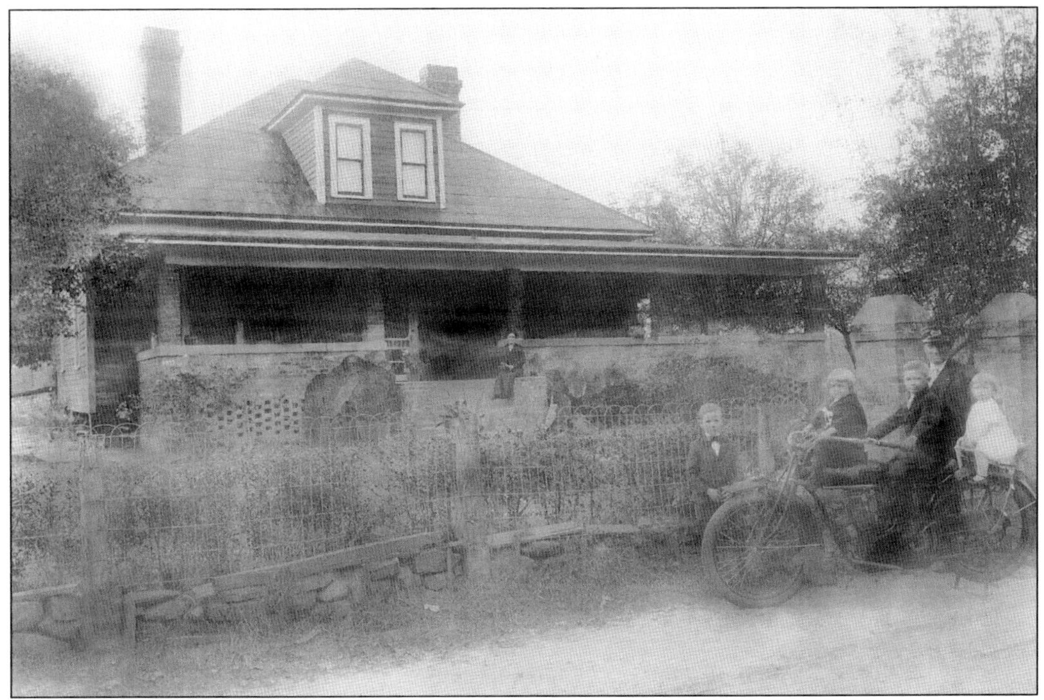

Harvey Southerlin carried the mail on Route 3 from December 1, 1910, until 1932. He delivered the mail on his Indian motorcycle, seen in this *c.* 1914 photograph. Southerlin is standing behind the motorcycle with four of his children. The Southerlin children are, from left to right, Hugh, Beverly, Hobert, and Reba. Harvey's wife, Myrtle, sits on the steps of the house, which was located on McElhaney Road beside the Travelers Rest First Baptist Church.

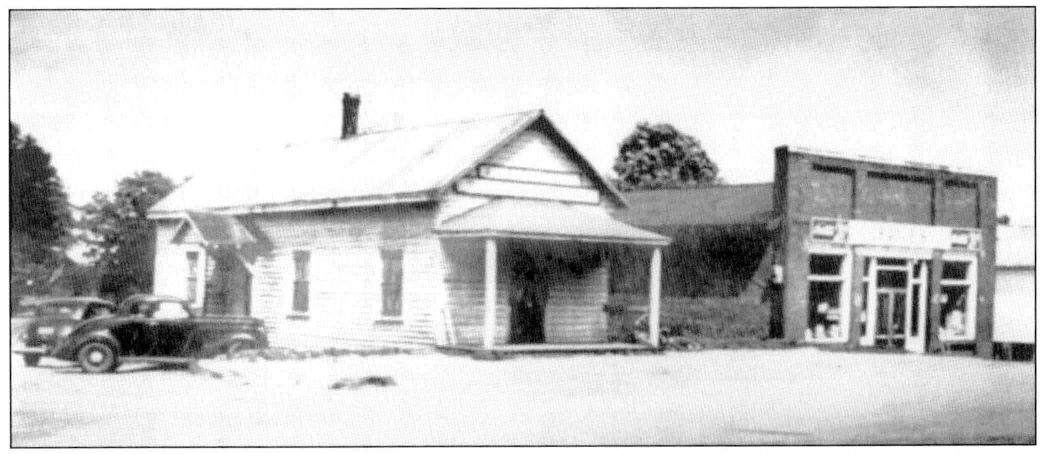

Home to the Travelers Rest post office for many years, this building stood next to League's Grocery Store on the corner of Highway 276 and McElhaney Road (Center Street). It was rolled backward during the construction of the new brick post office in 1944. Later the little building was moved again across Highway 276, where it served as Milt Hunt's appliance repair shop for many years.

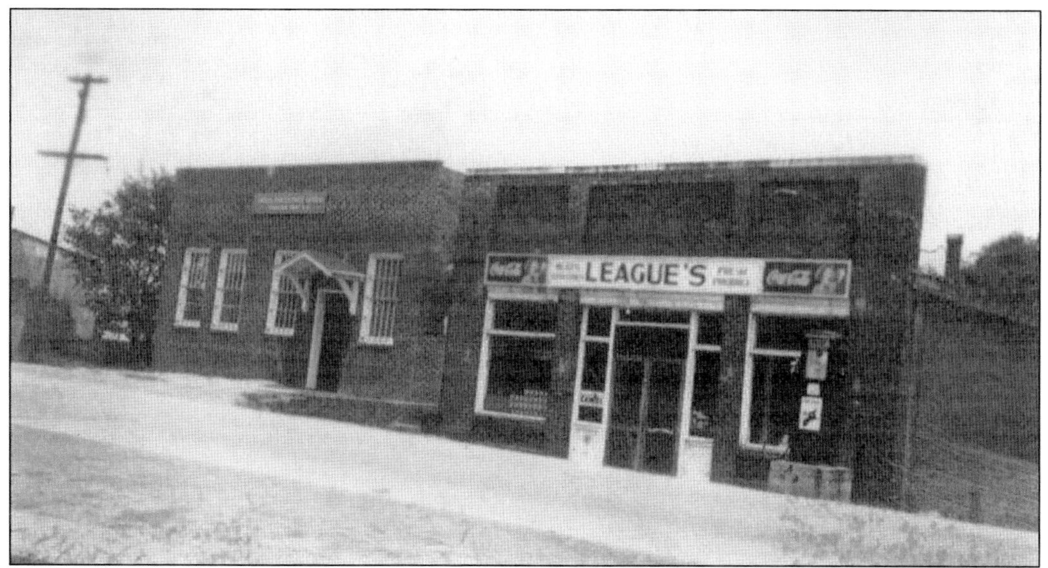

The one-story brick post office was built in 1944 by Gaither Pearson "Mac" McKinney. Located next door was League's Grocery Store, operated by Joe League until his death in 1938. Joe's son Allen assumed operation of the grocery until 1953, when his son (Joe's grandson), Robert "Bobby" Allen League Jr., began operating the store—first as a supermarket and later as a convenience store.

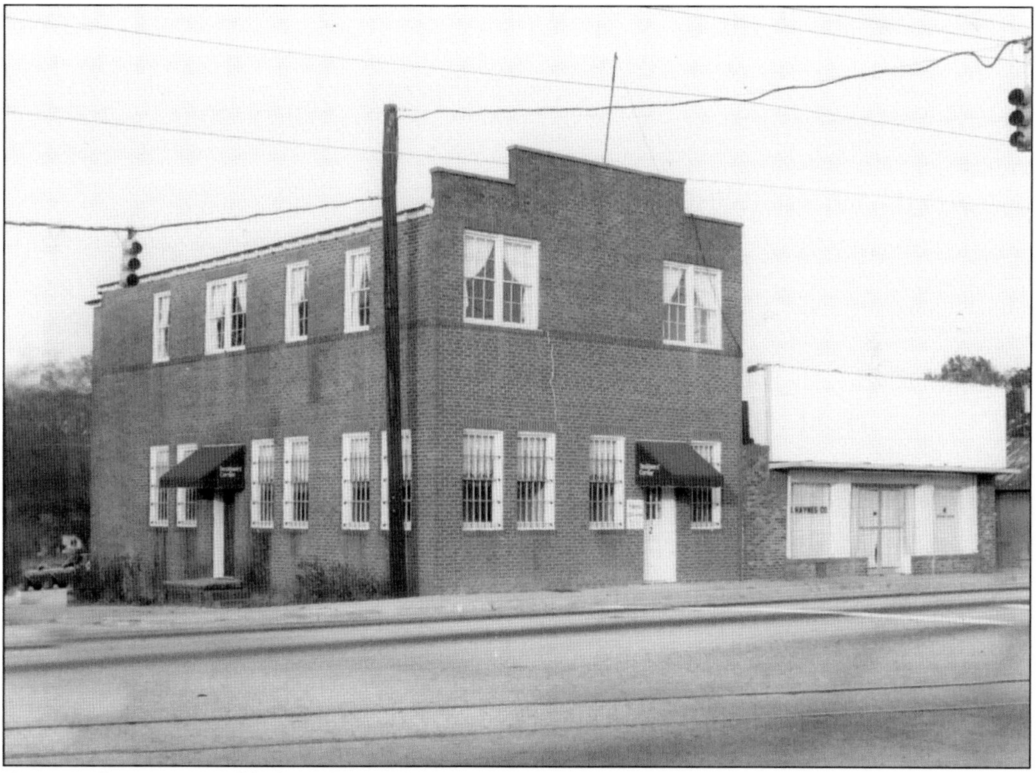

A second story was added to the brick post office, and in 1947, the Cooper Lodge No. 282 was relocated to a room above the old post office. This room remained the meeting place for the Masons and Eastern Star until their new building was completed in 1966.

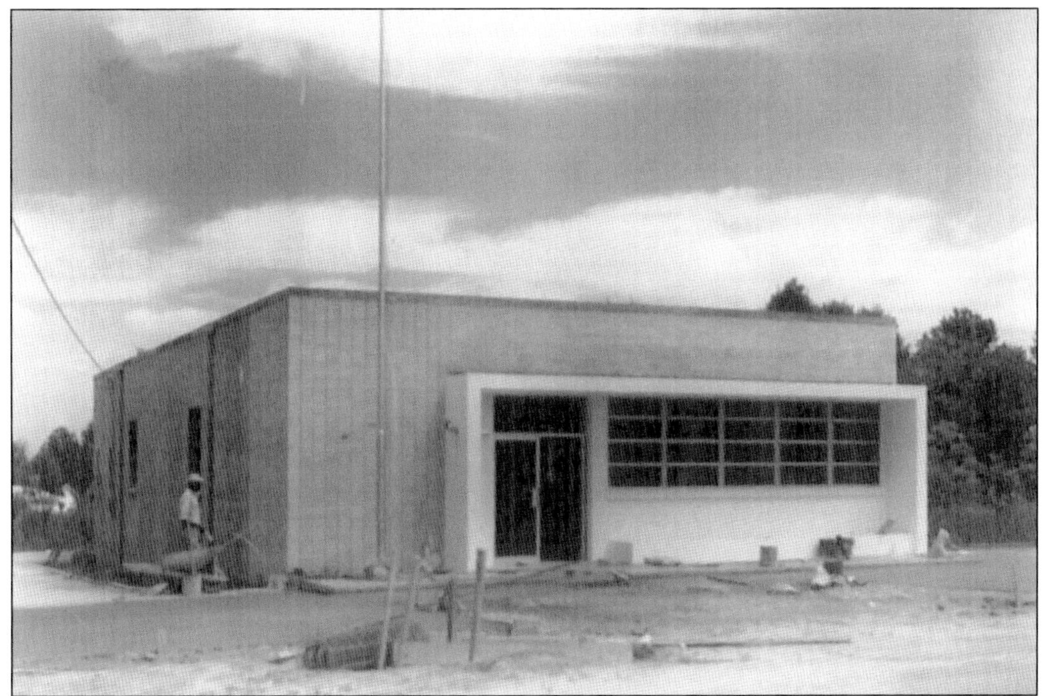

In October 1958, a large, modern post office opened in this location at 26 Main Street adjacent to the new Vernon's Drug Store. The post office remained here until it was moved to 6704 State Park Road in 1968. The Leopard Forest Coffee Company occupied the building from January 17, 2005, until late fall 2010.

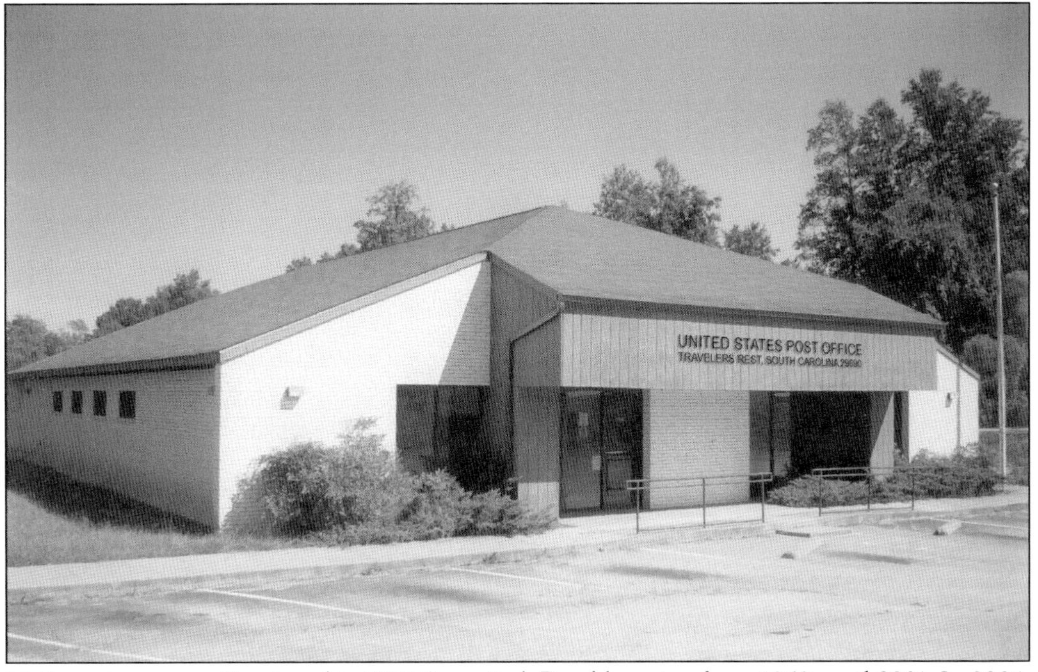

Mail services were offered at this 6704 State Park Road location from 1968 until 2001. In 2004, Cleveland Park Animal Hospital occupied the building and remains there in 2011.

Two

CHURCHES

A church, by most standards, is a place where people sharing the same spiritual beliefs join together on a regular basis for worship and fellowship. A church is almost always synonymous with faith, which is treasured deeply by many Southerners. While religion and churches have progressed with the times, often with a new church being erected on nearly every street corner, the original inhabitants of early American towns did not have that luxury. Travelers Rest, much like many other settlements in the original 13 colonies, usually had only one church located nearby. This meant that services were not held as often as they are now. The buildings were usually one-room log cabins, sparsely decorated with no comfort or pretension. A community's church building was normally the first thing to be erected after its homesteads.

Early frontier pastors were uneducated and underpaid for the most part. Many traveled a circuit of different churches, preaching at odd hours and using their own personal resources in order to teach the word of God. Through the years, churches have become more than just places for Sunday service, and the Bible has remained the main component of most family libraries.

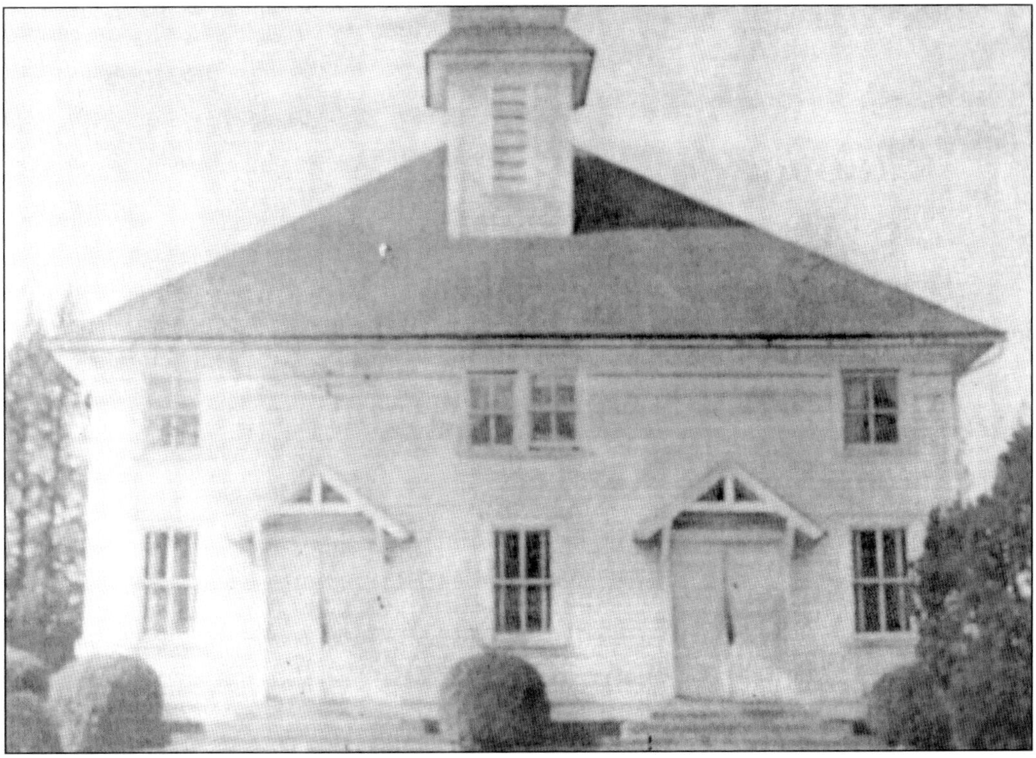

In his *History of Reedy River Baptist Church*, Mann Batson states that Reedy River Baptist is the oldest church in the area. It was established prior to 1789 as the Head of Enoree Baptist Church. In 1820, John Salmon gave 2 acres "lying on the waters of Reedy River near where the old meeting house now stands for the full and proper use and benefit of the said church." The building pictured above was built in 1910. Pictured below is the church building on Homecoming Day in September 2004. Reedy River Baptist Church is known as the "mother" of many of the area's early Baptist churches, including Shoals Creek, Tyger, Rock Springs, Double Springs, Clear Springs, Ebenezer, Berea, Mount Sinai, Enoree, Forestville, and First Baptist of Travelers Rest.

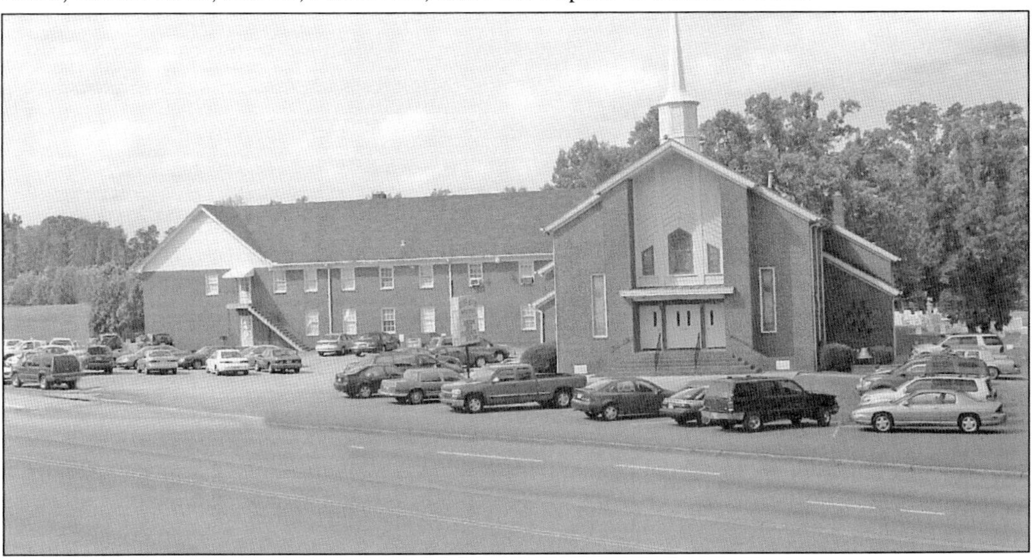

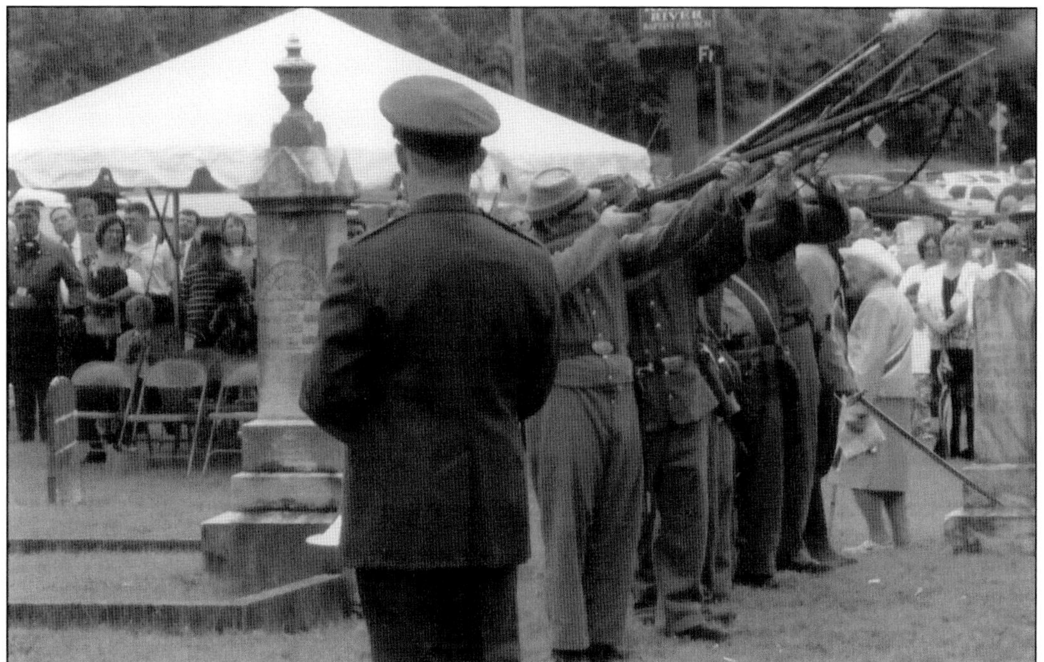

The long history of Reedy River Baptist Church is commemorated and appreciated in many ways. This image was taken in May 2009 during a 220th anniversary celebration. The church held a special service honoring the members of Reedy River who have served their country in military service. During this ceremony, 30 new Confederate Crosses of Honor joined 8 existing Iron Crosses that mark the graves of Confederate soldiers. Among the graves in the cemetery are those of early white settlers, slaves, and free people of color as well as veterans of many wars.

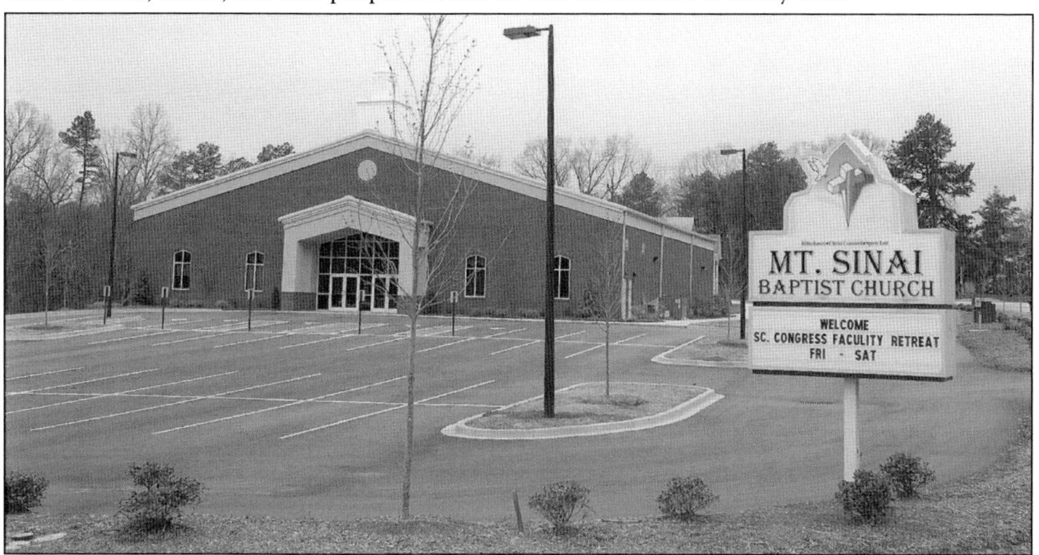

Eli Moore organized the Mount Sinai Baptist Church in 1869, and a log house was erected on donated land for the first church building. Baptisms were performed in a creek across the road. Through the years, several church buildings have been constructed: one in the early 1900s, another in 1935, and in 1962, the fourth one had indoor toilets, a baptismal pool, and central heat. A new multipurpose sanctuary located at 1101 Roe Ford Road opened in April 2009.

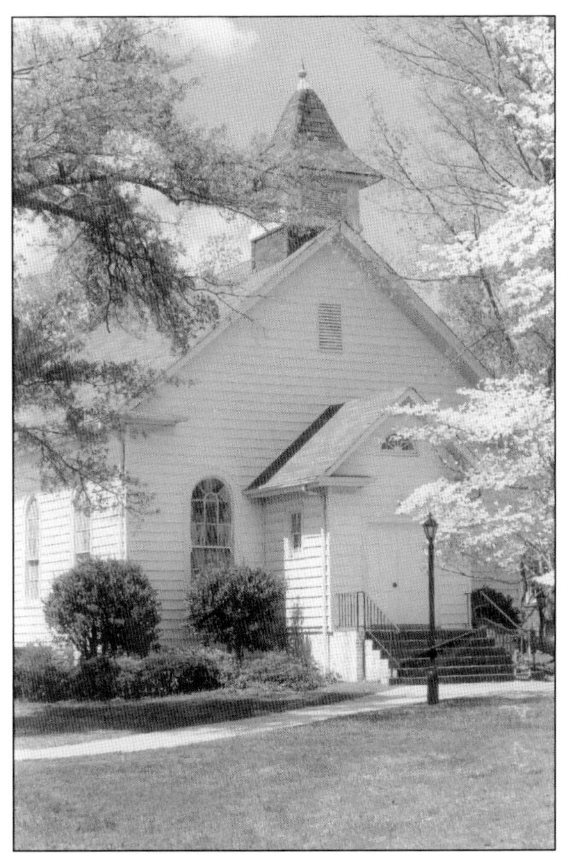

Frances Lockaby states in *Travelers Rest United Methodist Church: 1893–1993* that Travelers Rest United Methodist Church was organized in November 1893 with nine charter members. Built on property donated by Robert Wright Anderson in 1894, the one-room building (seen in the photograph at left and second from left below), lighted by oil lamps and heated by a woodstove, also served as home to new churches of other denominations. Several additions were made to this building. In 1964, the education building was completed, and a new sanctuary was built in 1987. The Family Life Center (far left below), with a gym, kitchen, and parlor, was built in 2002, along with a playground, ball field, and picnic shelter.

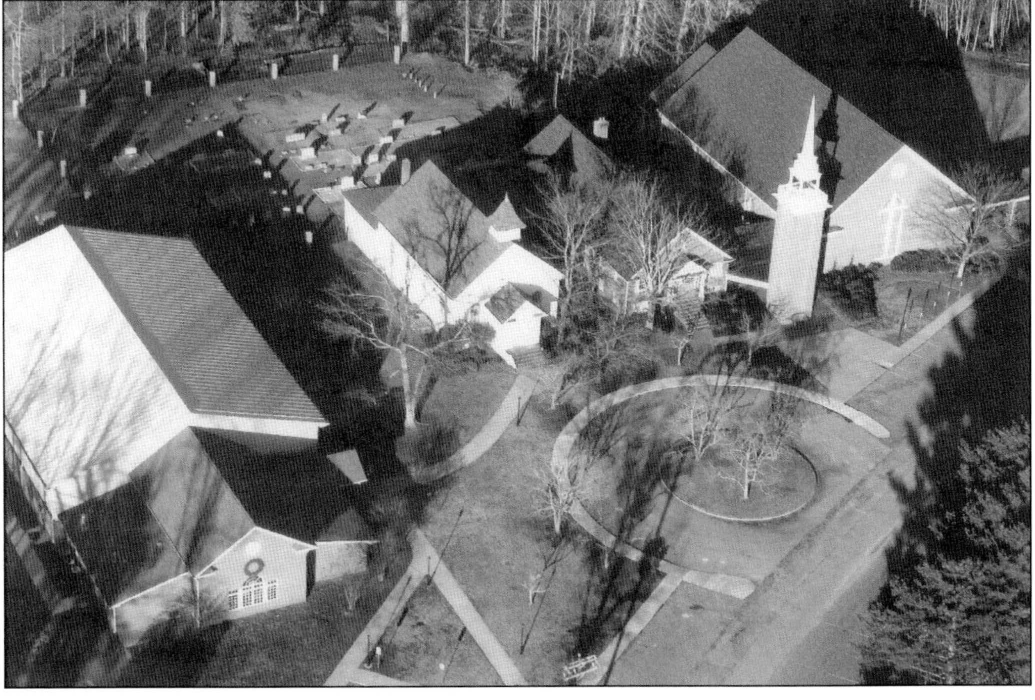

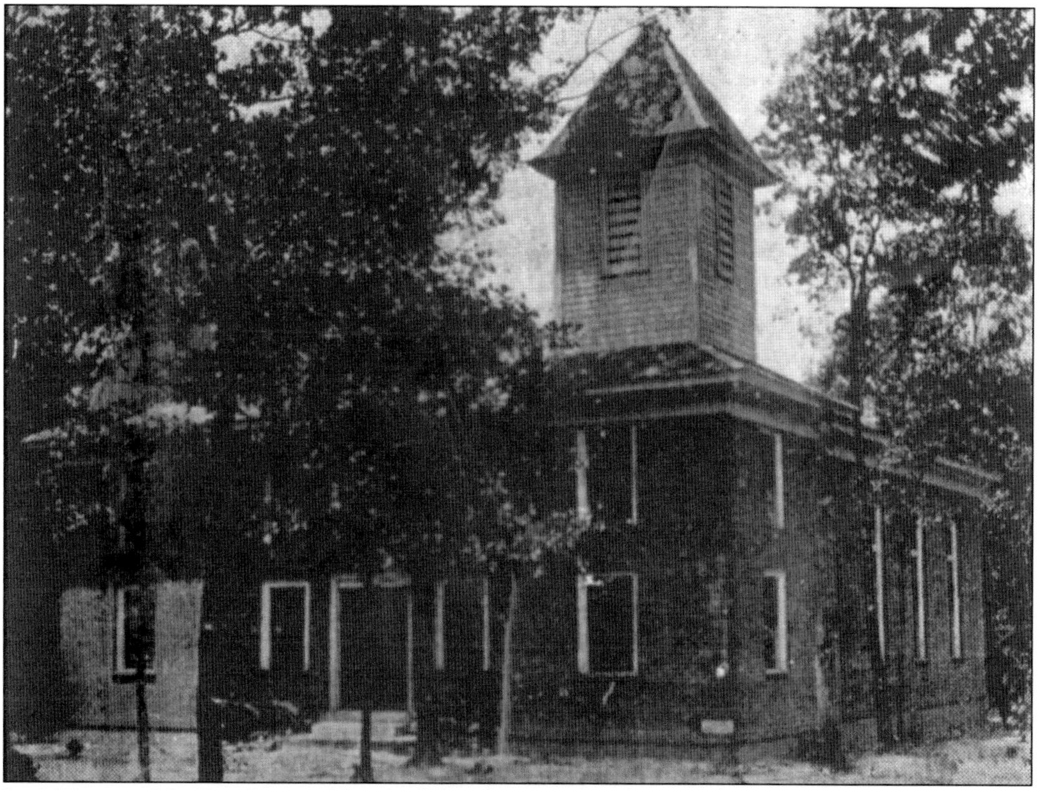

In *A History of the First Baptist Church of Travelers Rest, South Carolina*, Rev. J. N. Watson described the organization of Travelers Rest First Baptist Church. In the spring of 1913, some 37 members from Reedy River, Enoree, and Ebenezer joined together to organize the Travelers Rest Baptist Church. The Methodists shared their building for all preaching services until the new church could be built. In August 1913, the church voted to accept two lots originally owned by J. D. Cooper on McElhaney Road at a cost of $275, and in November 1913, the first service was held in the brick building pictured above. In 1951, the present auditorium was built, and educational space, a gymnasium, kitchen, and dining areas have been added.

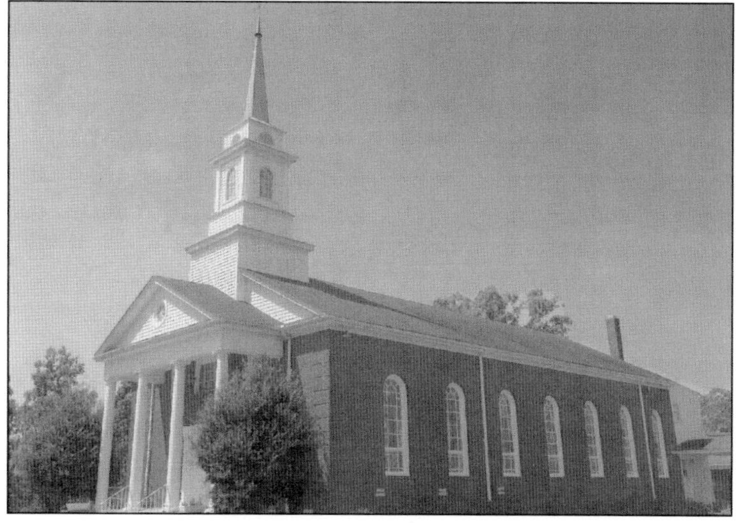

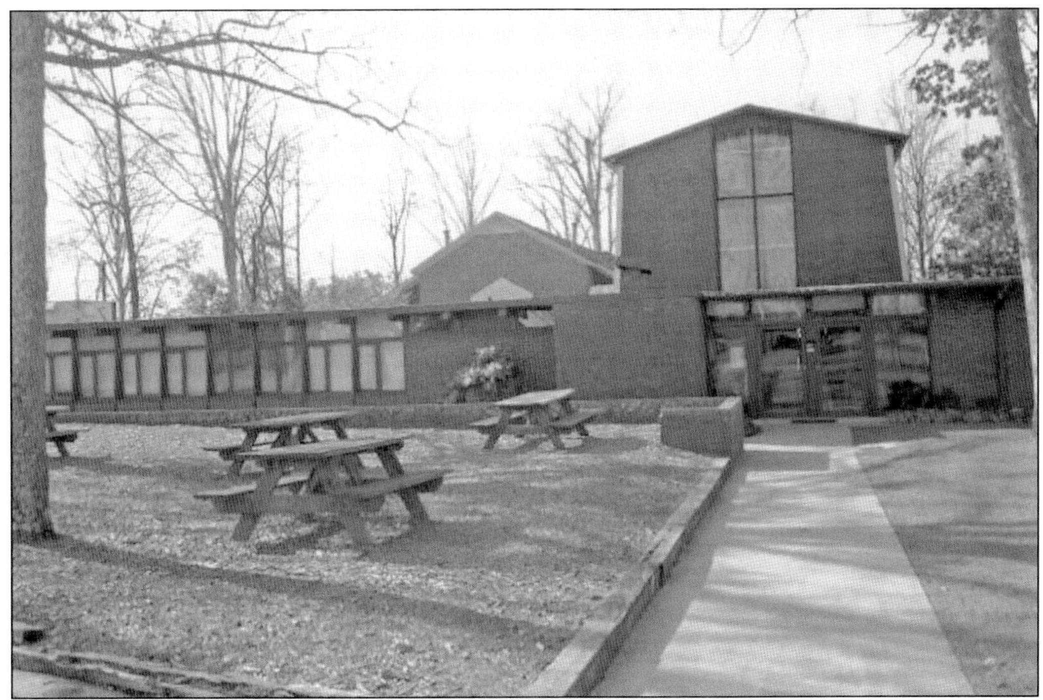

Trinity Presbyterian was organized in 1933 as part of the Union Church at Renfrew Village (see page 91), where Presbyterian, Baptist, and Methodist congregations alternated services. Trinity built a new sanctuary (above) on Howard Street (now Wilhelm Winter Street) in 1959, and another new sanctuary was built in 1991 (seen behind the original building above). In 2009, the original sanctuary and educational buildings were razed, and a large new gym, educational building, and McKinney Hall were constructed (below).

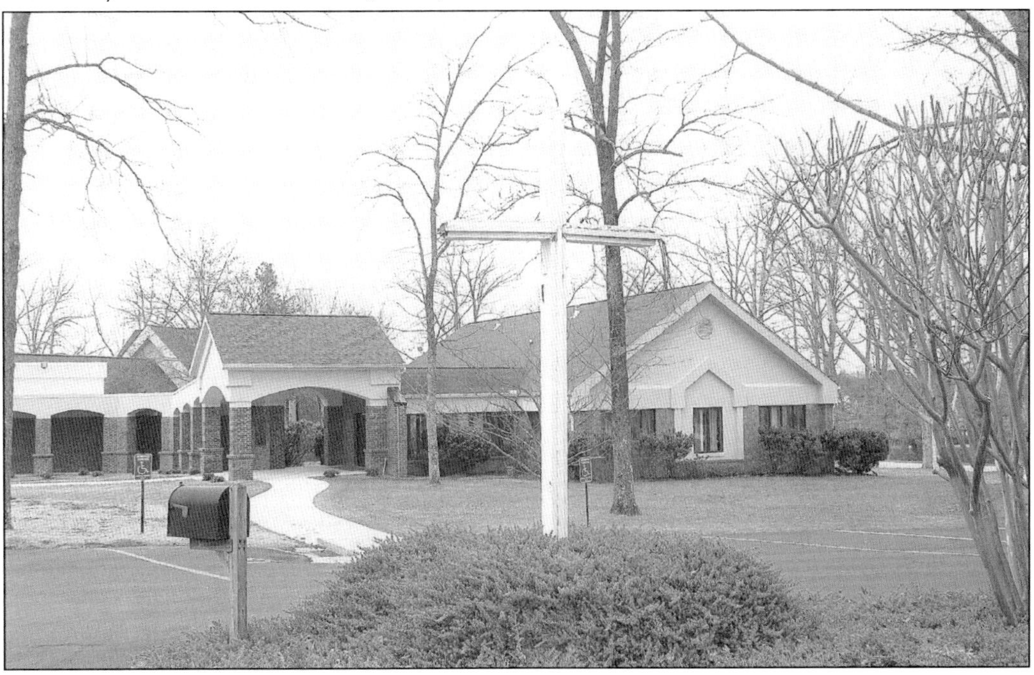

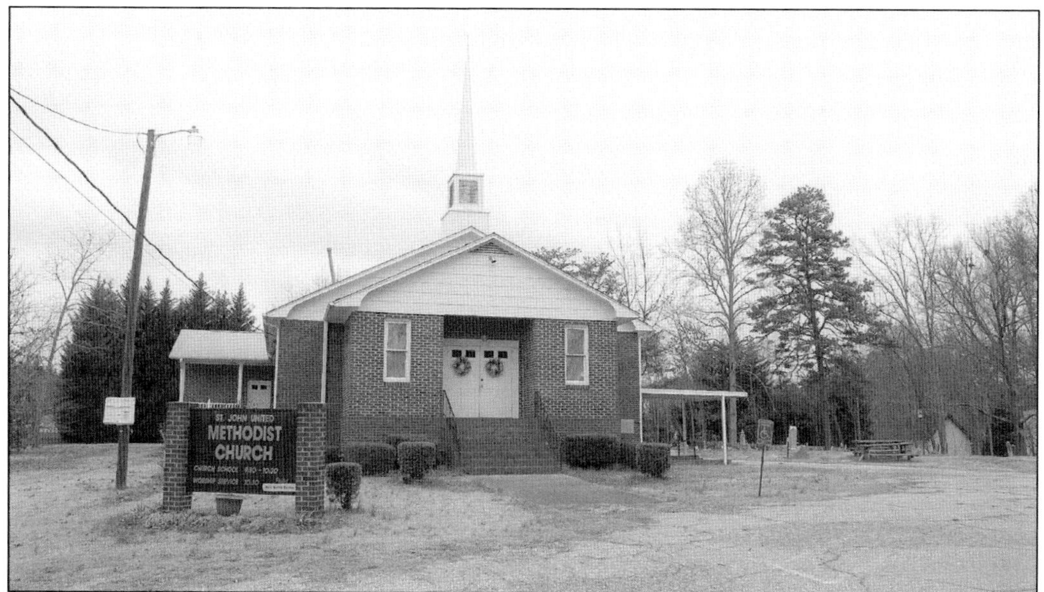

St. John United Methodist Church is located at 2120 Roe Ford Road. It began in the 1860s when a group of African American Christians met together for fellowship, Bible study, and prayer. Families would pitch tents and worship for a week. Eventually the group voted to request the Methodist conference to establish a church in the area. Fr. James Roseman was the first pastor. In 2010, St. John united with St. Luke and Mount Carmel Methodist Churches to become North Greenville United Methodist Church, located in the Enoree community.

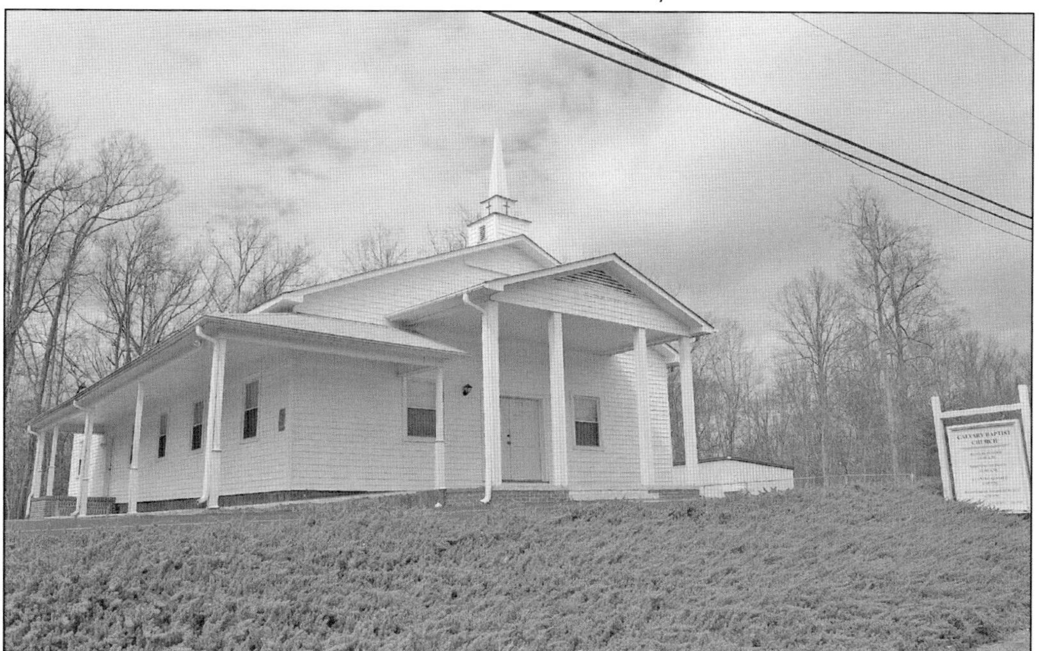

Calvary Baptist Church, located on Cox Street, was established in August 1970. The congregation met for quite a while in the basement of the church before the sanctuary was built. In 2005, a new fellowship hall was constructed. The pastors who have served this church are over the years are Paul R. Ballenger, Jimmy Johnson, Clyde Jones, and Michael H. Sargent.

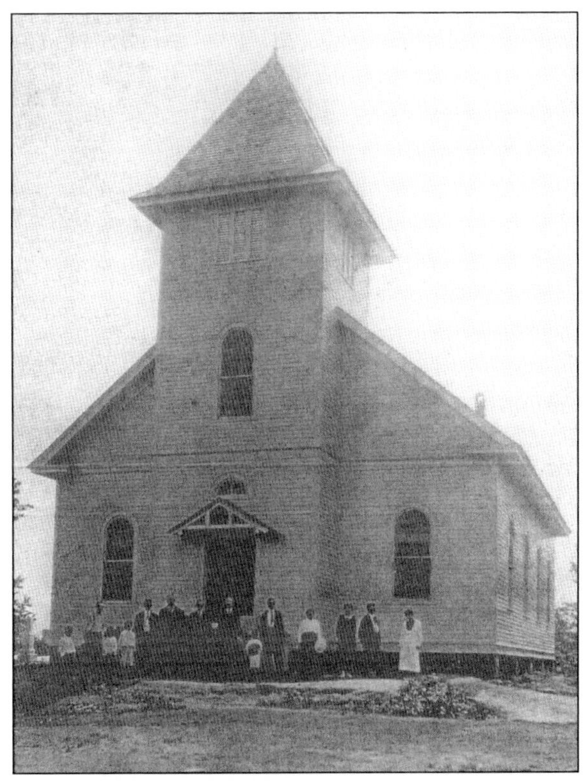

Ebenezer Baptist Church was organized in 1835. The first building was made of logs and had no chimney or floor, and it was used as a schoolhouse and a church. According to Mildred Goodlett in *Travelers Rest at Mountain's Foot*, there are reports of one of the first pastors, Samuel McWhorter, preaching barefooted on a dirt floor. The records of the church from 1835 to 1900 were destroyed by fire. Several buildings have served as home to the congregation. The older building pictured at left was built in 1917, and the current Ebenezer Baptist Church is seen below.

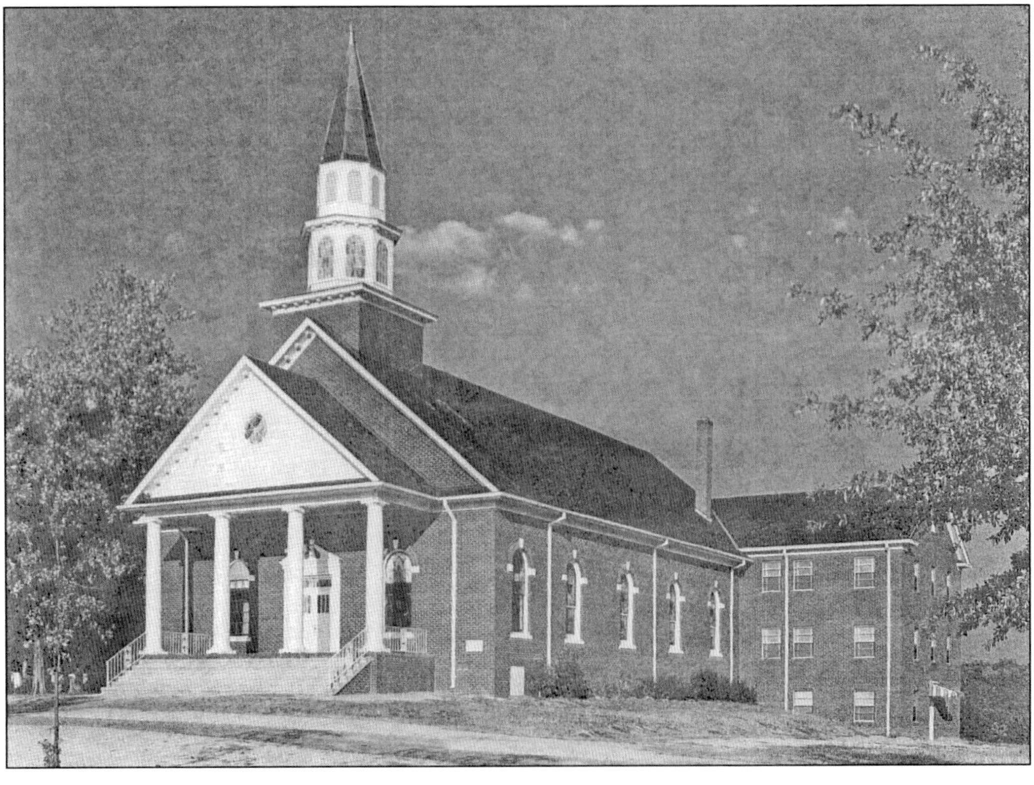

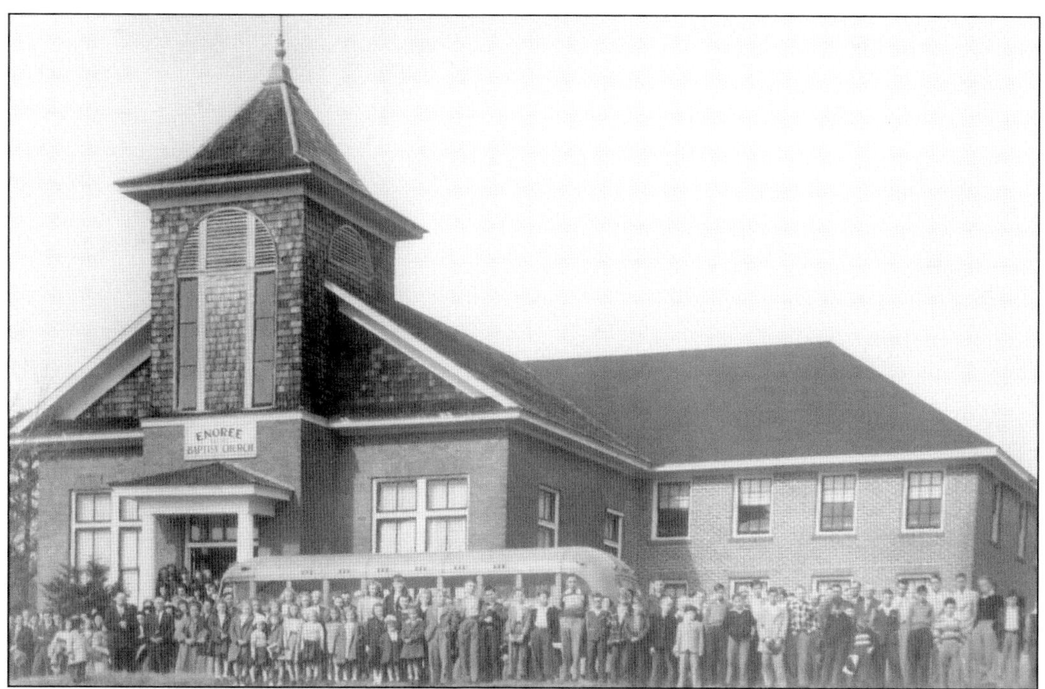

Organized in 1851 with 17 charter members, the first Enoree Baptist Church building was a log structure. A "Sabbath School" was established in 1861, and baptisms were held in an outdoor concrete pool on Robertson property across the road from the church. A new brick building (above) with Sunday school rooms was completed in 1917. The church bus and congregation are pictured in front of the church building in 1949. The existing sanctuary (below) was built in 1954. An educational wing and gym were constructed in 1969, and an education/fellowship building was added in 1999. A walk through the cemetery reveals much of Travelers Rest's history.

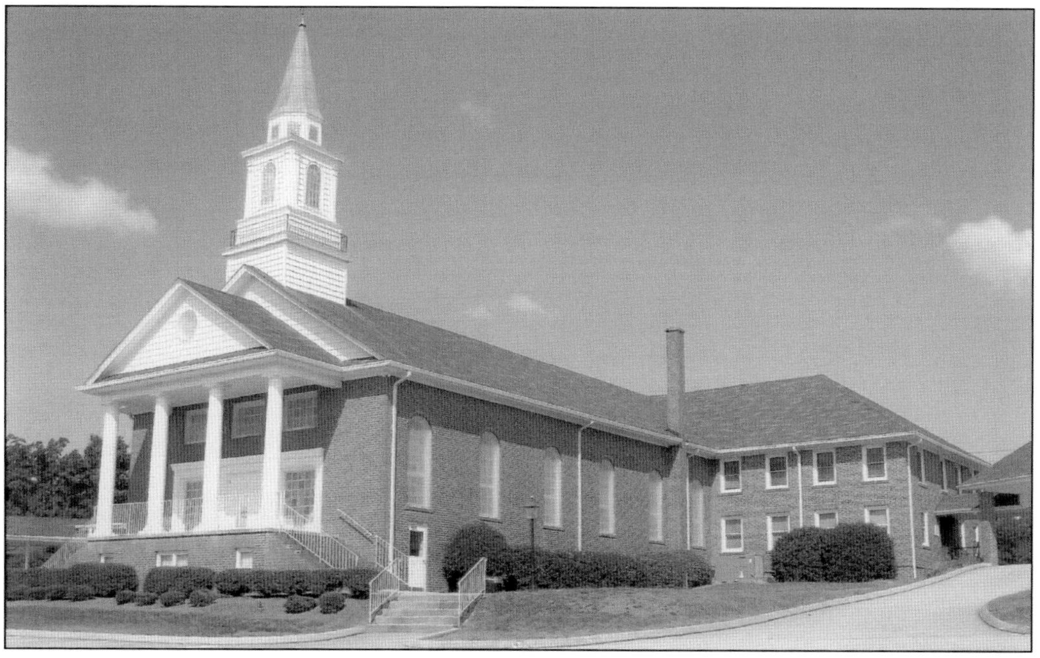

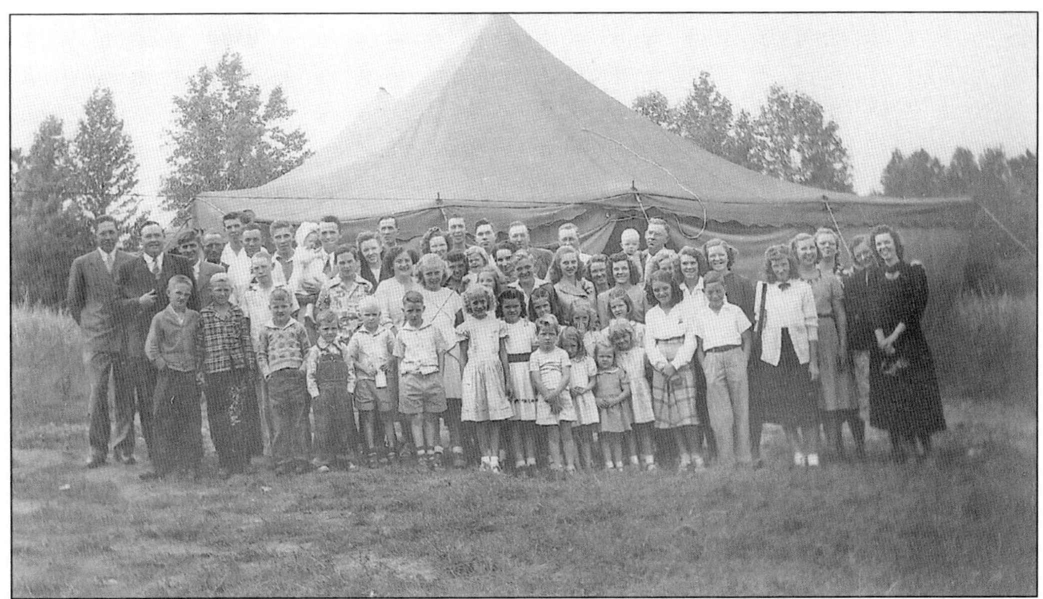

The Little Texas Assembly of God Church met in a tent in the pasture across State Park Road from Groce's Fishing Lake until a building was constructed on State Park Road in 1948. The wood used in the construction of the building was cut from land that belonged to Bill Powell. Among the many families of the Little Texas community pictured here in about 1947 are the Batson, Bayne, Kelly, Turner, Nix, Powell, and Rice families.

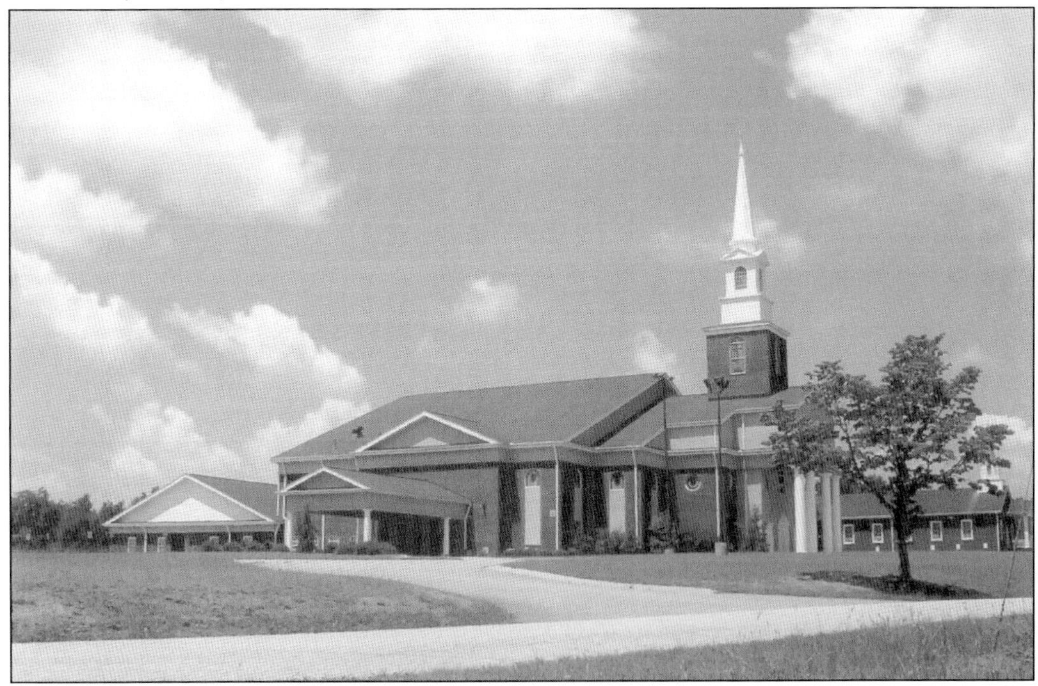

Located in the Little Texas community, Clearview Baptist Church was organized in December 1953 with 46 charter members. The Little Texas schoolhouse served as the first church building until the new sanctuary opened in August 1954 with 145 members. An educational building was completed in 1964, and a new sanctuary was finished in 2000.

Three

HOMES

A house is a structure that serves to protect its inhabitants from the elements brought forth by Mother Nature. A home is more than just the physical structure; it is the sense of comfort and the heartwarming feeling instilled within by the people who inhabit it. When a new home was constructed, a neighborhood came together and was built from the bottom up. Few of Travelers Rest's notable houses have survived. The surviving homes serve as reminders for the generations to come of the sacrifices that were made, as modern amenities were not needed—just a good, sturdy structure to protect a family. Many intricacies of the original homes in Travelers Rest can still be seen today in the boutiques, inns, lodges, and mortuaries they have become. Each home tells its own story, and some of those stories can be seen here.

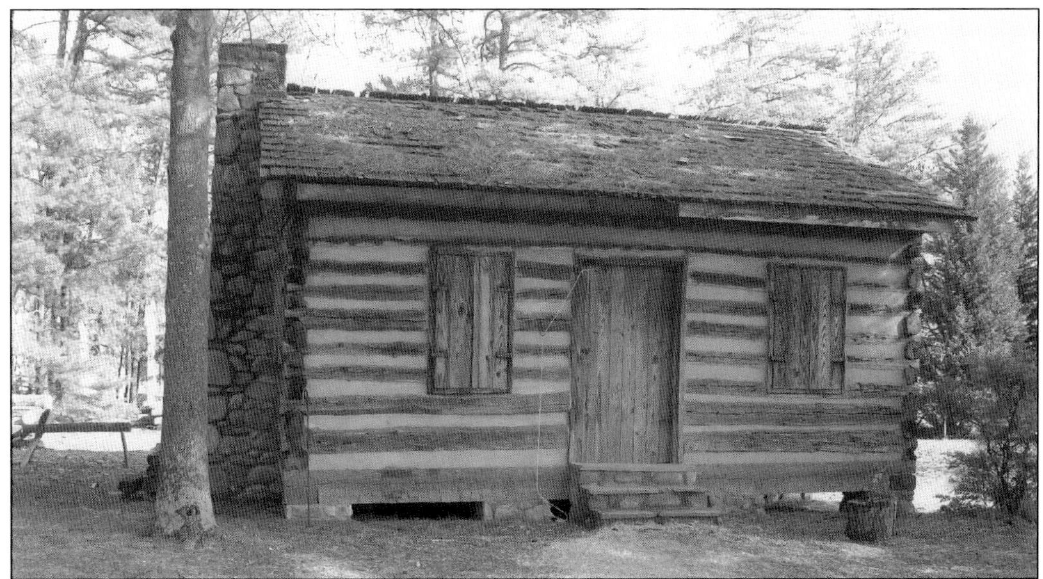

On land originally owned by Cherokee Indians and acquired by Isaac Green as a land grant from the King of England, Andrew Jackson Green built this log cabin around 1851 with timber harvested from the acreage. The cabin was the birthplace of his children—Luther, Wilbert, and Annice. In 1986, the cabin was donated by Joanne Greene Turner to the Greenville Historical Society and moved to the Roper Mountain Science Center.

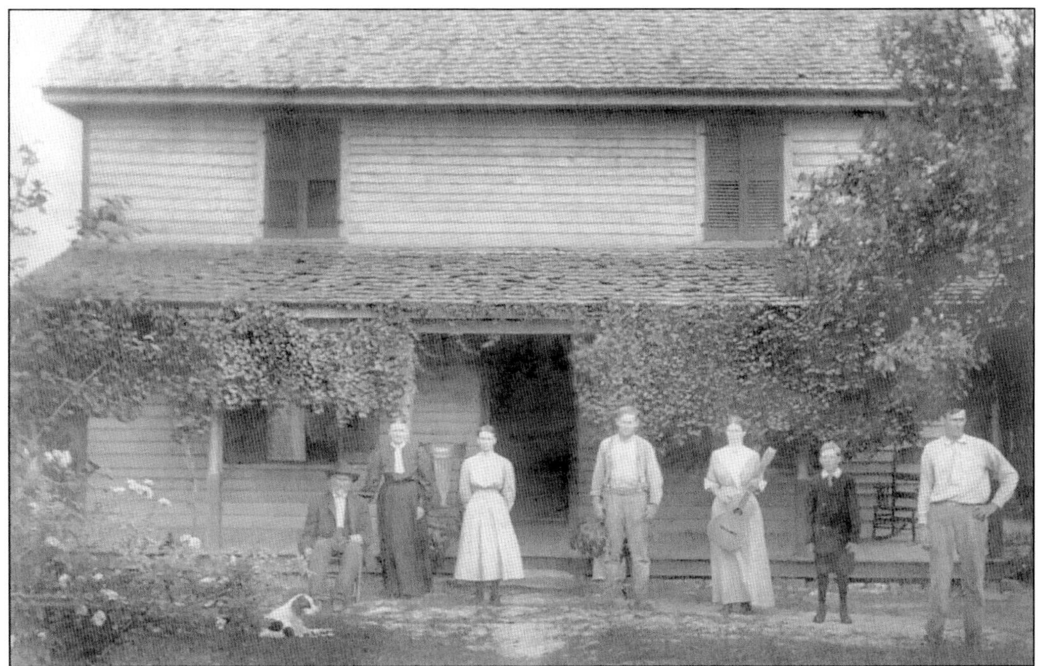

This c. 1910 photograph shows the Luther Edward Greene family in front of their home, Greenedale Farms, located on Old White Horse Road. Shown from left to right are Luther Edward, son of Andrew Jackson Greene; Josephine Elizabeth Hawkins Greene, his wife; and their children, Kate, Robert, Mealon, Walter Edward, and Joseph Benjamin "Joe." The house seen here has been occupied by members of the Greene family for at least 100 years.

The present-day Watson Crossing subdivision is located on the site of the home of John James and Elizabeth Cunningham Watson. They were the parents of 14 children. John was second lieutenant in the 16th Regiment of the South Carolina Infantry in the War Between the States, a justice of the peace, and at the time of his death in 1905, a representative of Greenville County in the South Carolina Legislature. (Drawing by Roddy Rodgers.)

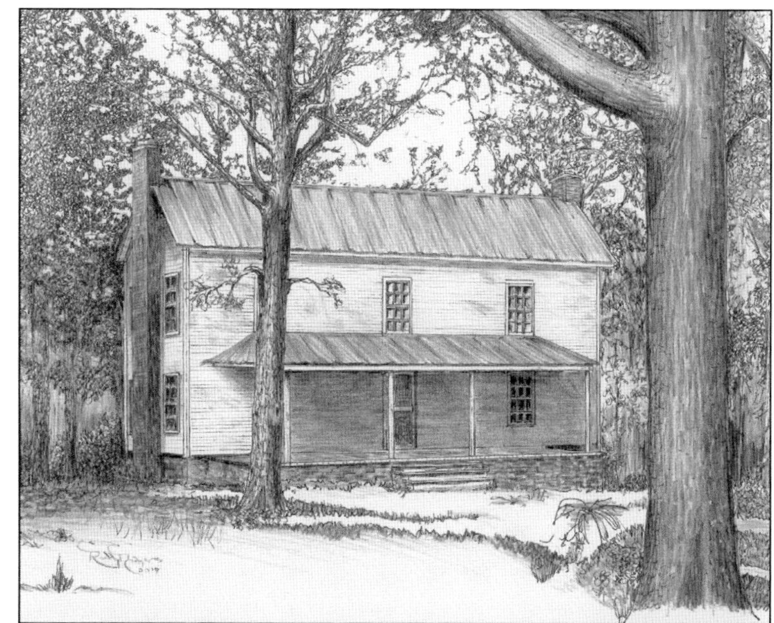

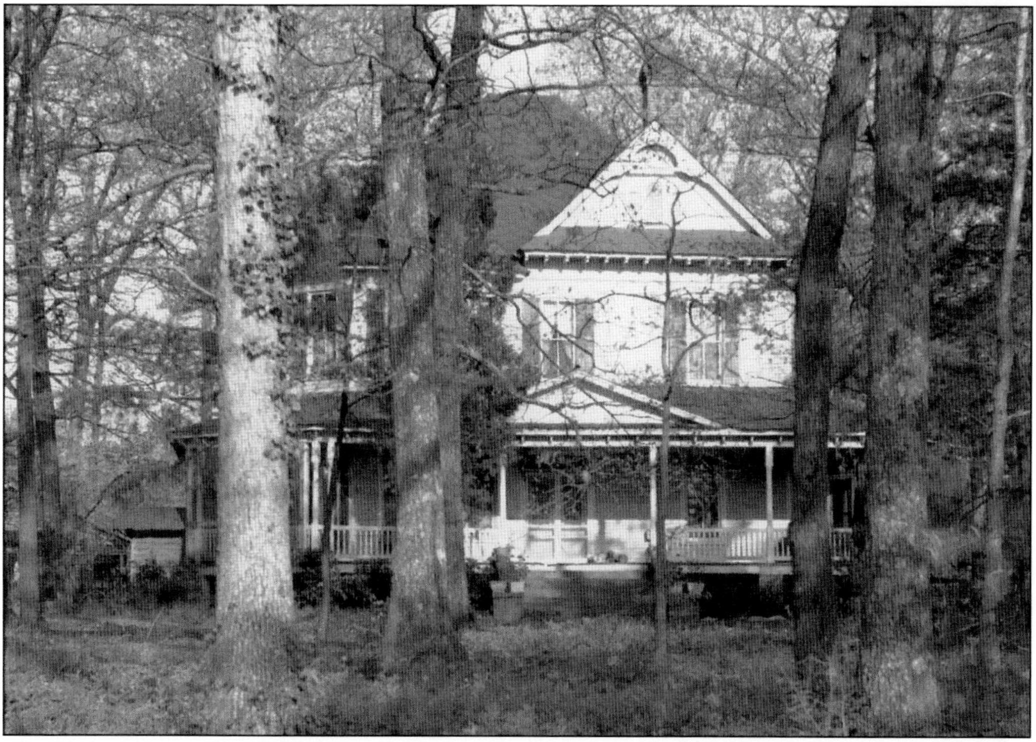

The Roe House, a Victorian house built in 1893, stood on the land where the current Travelers Rest post office is located on South Main Street. Volume 10 of *Echoes* states that there were fireplaces in every room of the house, and Nora Neves Roe kept the yard swept clean with brush brooms made from dogwood limbs. The road that is now South Main Street was built in 1928. Between this area and the current Highway 25 were farm buildings, including a large barn that housed over 20 mules and horses, a combine shed, a mill house, and an outhouse.

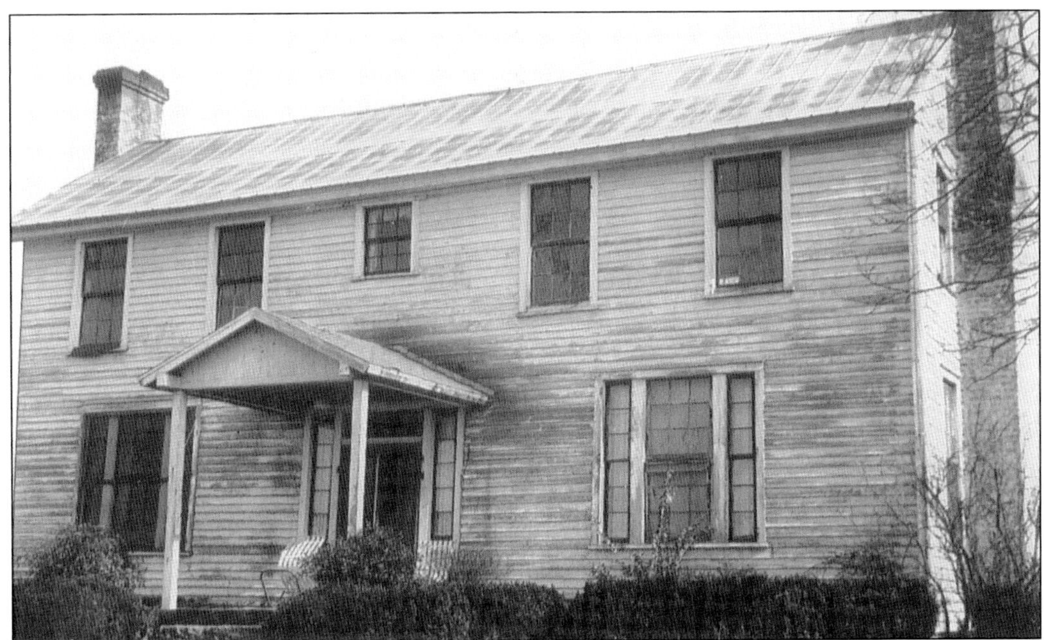

The original structure (above) built at this location, 751 Old Buncombe Road, was first the home of Dr. J. P. Hillhouse, who came to Travelers Rest to practice medicine in 1848, according to Mann Batson in A *History of the Upper Part of Greenville County, South Carolina*. Following the Hillhouse family, the Stephen Marchbanks family lived in the house and operated the nearby gristmill. Later a son, Samuel Stephen Marchbanks, also lived in the house and operated the mill. The house then became the home of Frances Marion Edwards and his family. Disassembled and rebuilt in 1955, the B. J. Edwards family used much of the original materials when building the house pictured below.

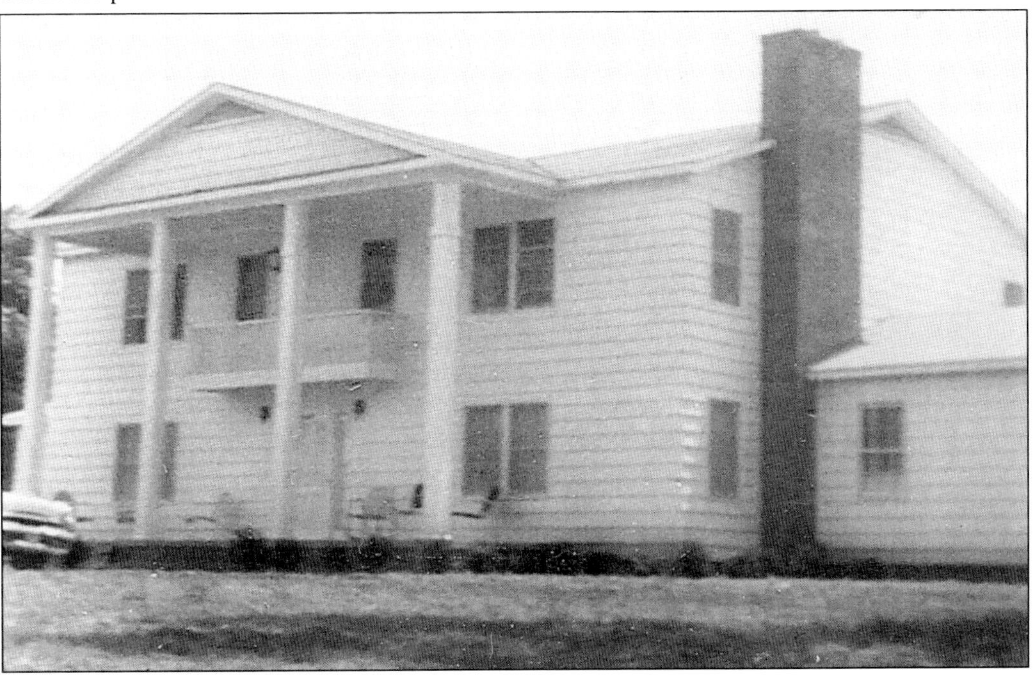

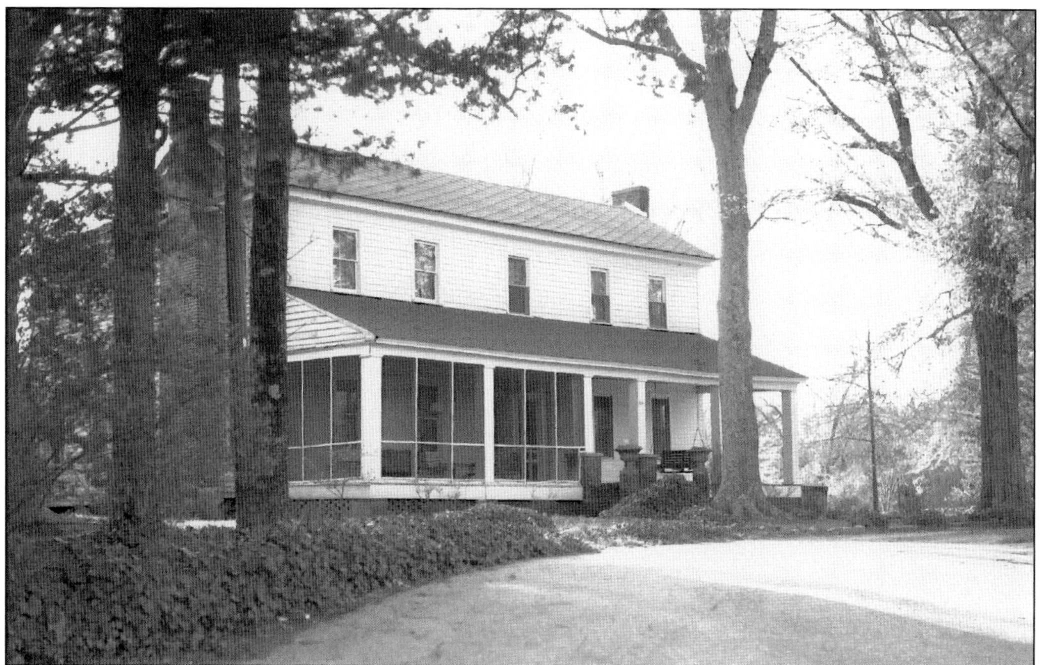

This large white home on Old Buncombe Road near the center of Travelers Rest has long been a symbol of the village, now a thriving town. Situated beside the Swamp Rabbit Trail, it has been a private residence known as the Anderson/Gibson home.

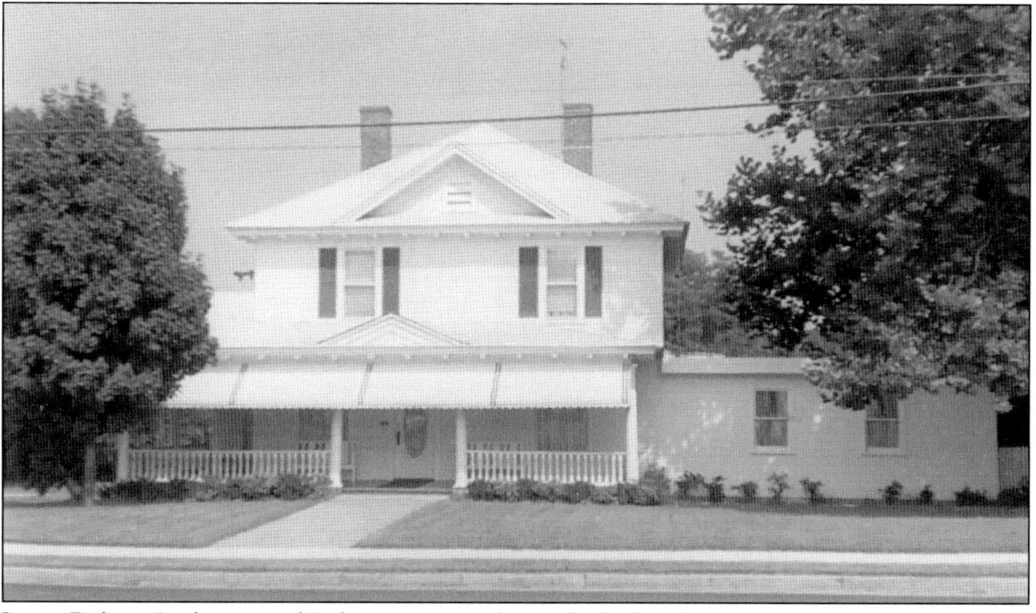

James Robert Anderson and Lula Watson Anderson built their home around 1911 on the corner of what was then Buncombe and Little Texas Roads. They were the parents of Mary Nell and Robert Leroy Anderson. James operated a livery stable and was a cotton buyer, fertilizer dealer, and Travelers Rest postmaster. This house, located at 319 South Main Street, has been used as Odell Mortuary, Howze Mortuary, Piedmont Auction House, and at present in 2011, it is the home of All About Me.

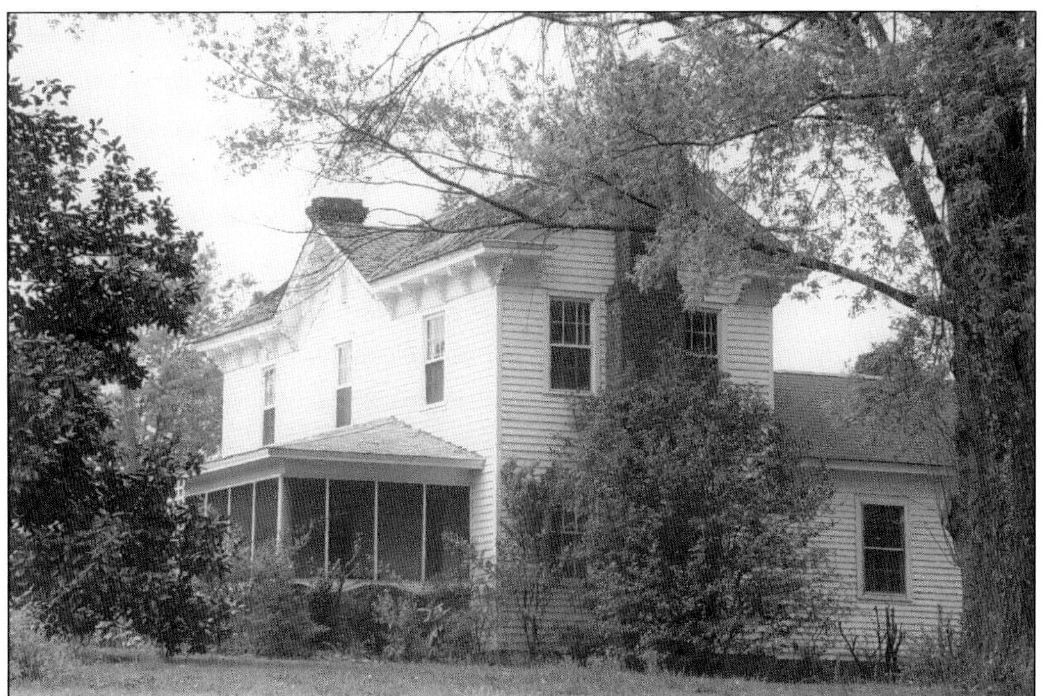

This Travelers Rest landmark was located at the intersection of Geer Highway and Buncombe Road. It was the home of Dr. B. F. Goodlett. In 1883, he married Fannie Estelle Anderson. Shortly after their marriage, they moved into this house and lived there the remainder of their lives. At their death, it became the home of their son Claud Goodlett and his wife, Mildred. The house was destroyed in 1996.

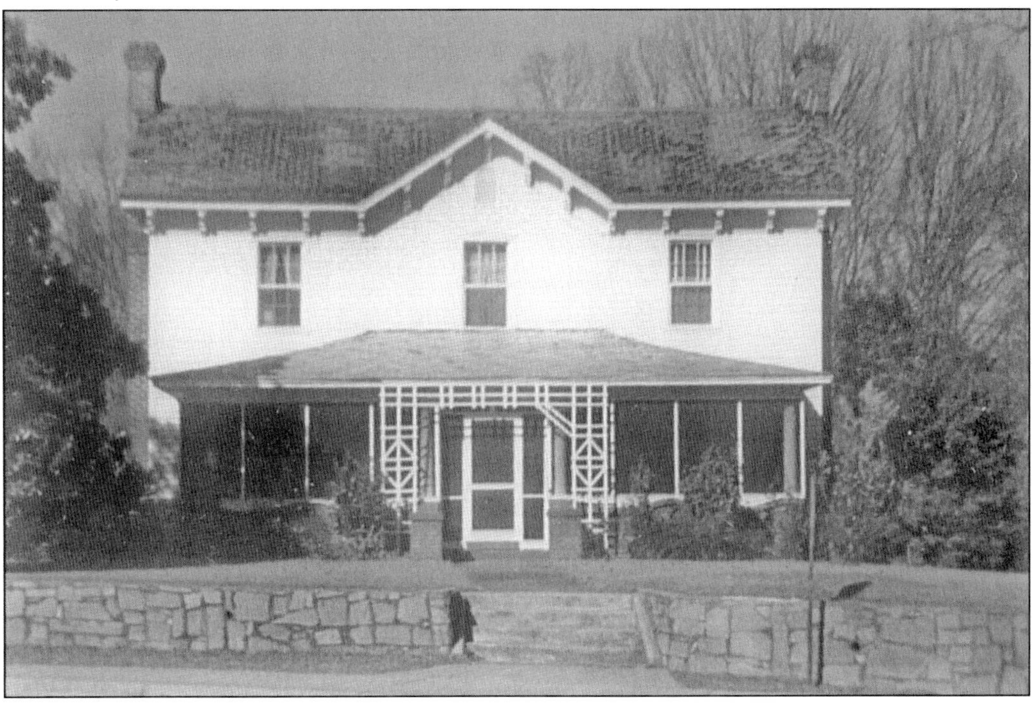

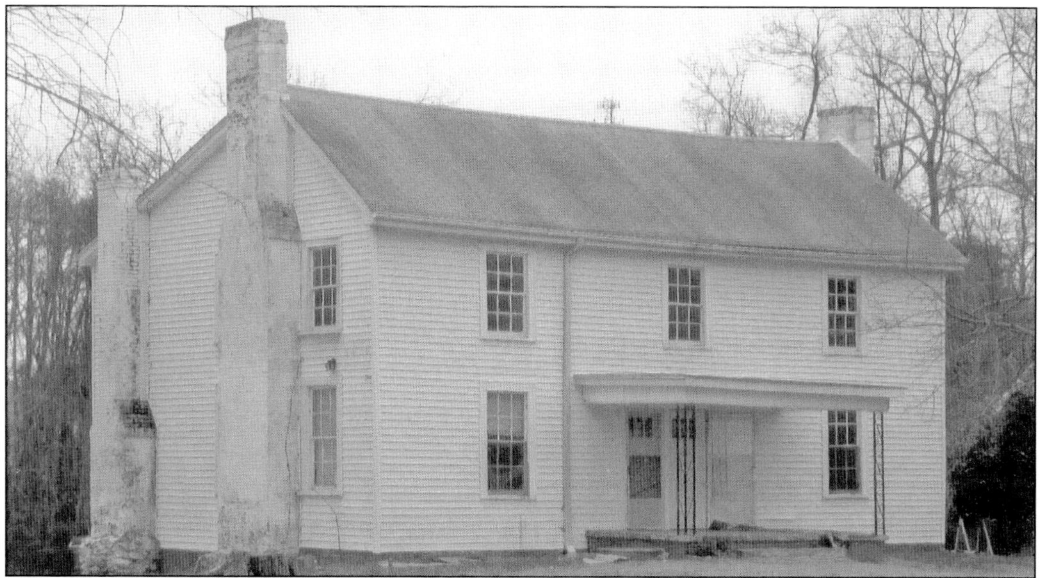

The John P. O'Gara Love home was built around 1850. John P. O'Gara Love was born in Donegal, Ireland, in 1818 and died in 1896 in Travelers Rest. He was a farmer when he enlisted on April 14, 1861, in Greenville, South Carolina. John served as a private with the 4th Regiment of South Carolina Volunteers in the War Between the States. He married Elizabeth Miller, granddaughter of Dicey Langston Springfield. This home, located on Poinsett Highway, was formerly used as the offices of the Travelers Rest Family Practice, the Stilwell Mortuary, and as a private residence for many years.

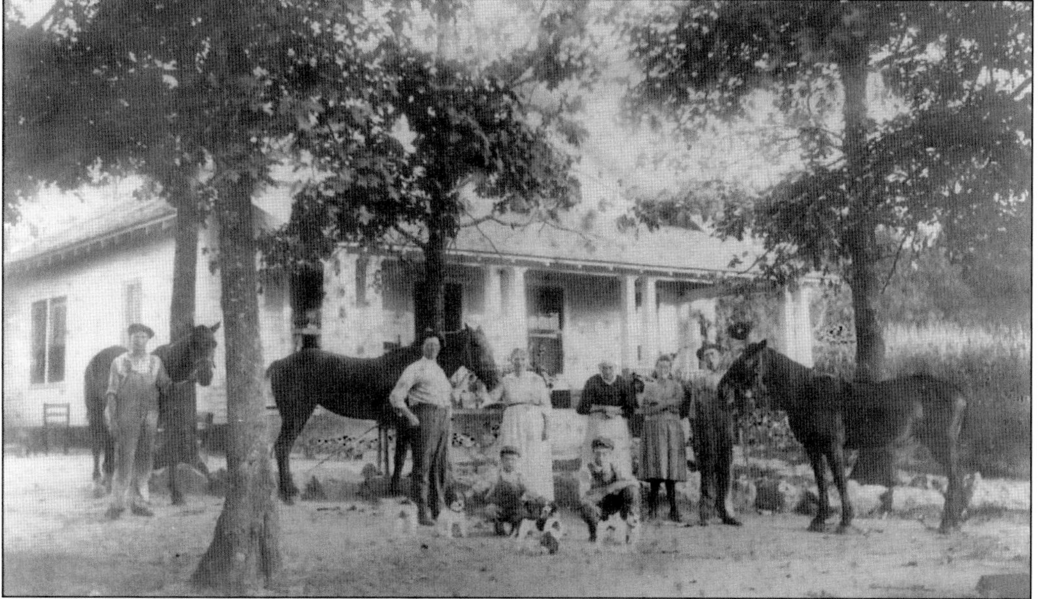

The original home of David Burns was located in the area of a present-day Walmart. In 1921, this house completely burned. The Travelers Rest Community came together and rebuilt the house in 14 days at a cost of $1,500. Burns was a well-known area citizen—he was a member of Reedy River Baptist Church, a magistrate judge of Bates Township, a mule and horse trader, and the Worshipful Master of Cooper Masonic Lodge for many years.

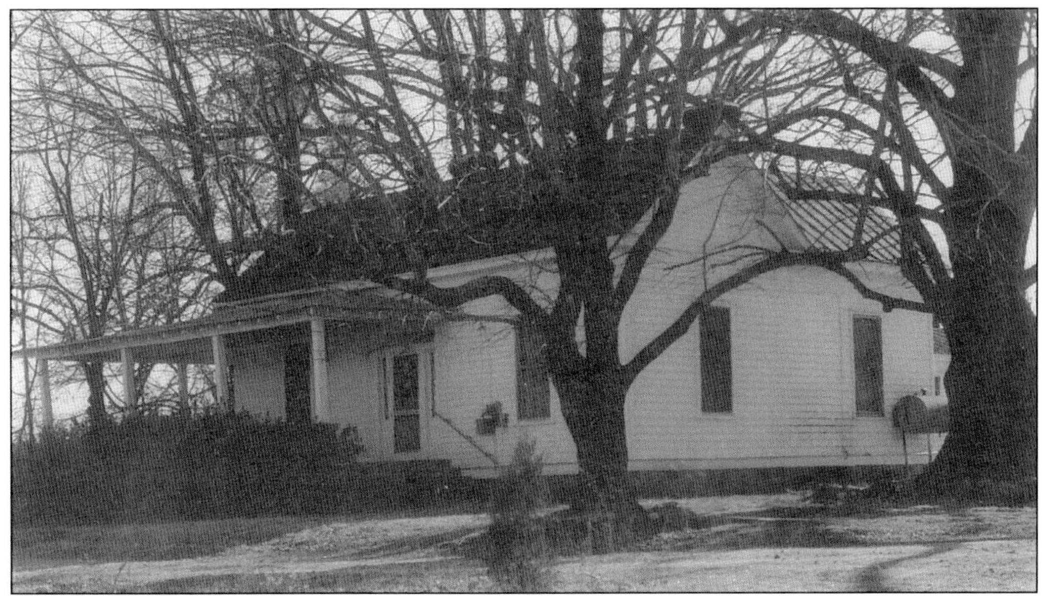

The Travelers Rest High School, built in 2007, stands on ground that was once the backyard of this old home place located on Geer Highway. Jasper Watson built the house in the late 1890s, and later, his daughter, Pawnee; her husband, Wade League; and their family lived here. Many of the trees that surrounded the house have been preserved. One of the large trees on the hill is an American basswood tree that was certified as a Champion Tree in 2004.

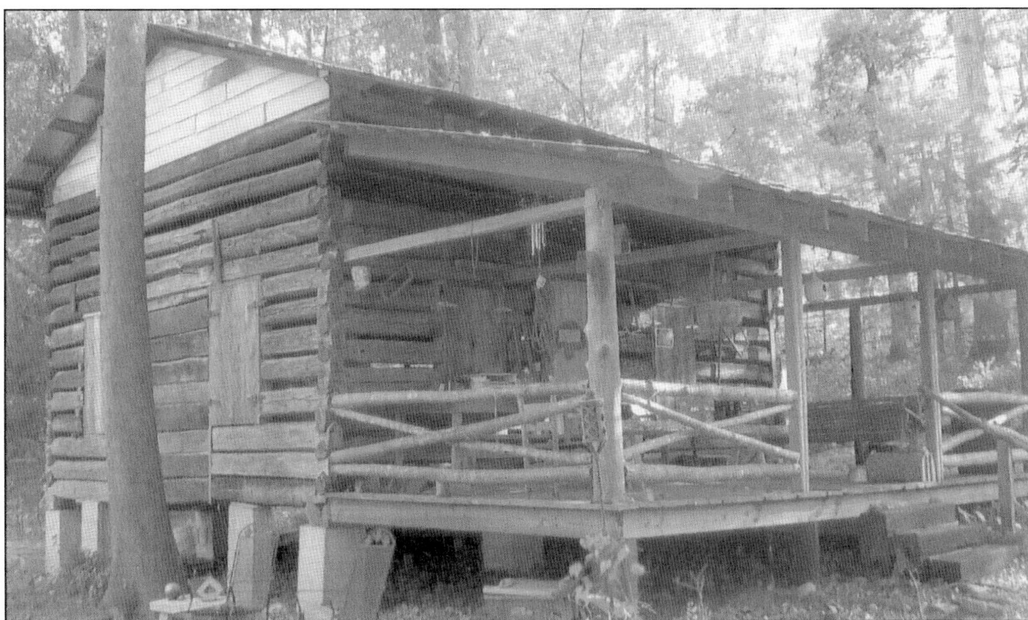

One of the oldest structures in the area, this log cabin originally stood in the area near the upper entrance to Travelers Rest High School. It was the birthplace of Terrell Watson in 1886, Pawnee Watson League in 1887, Tave Batson in 1897, and Sally Batson Pitts in 1898. For many years, it was covered with white clapboard. Columbus Washington and Minerva Rainey Campbell lived in the house until his death, and later, Edward and Sally League lived here. Mann Batson moved the structure to Batson Lane around 1960 and returned the house to its original state.

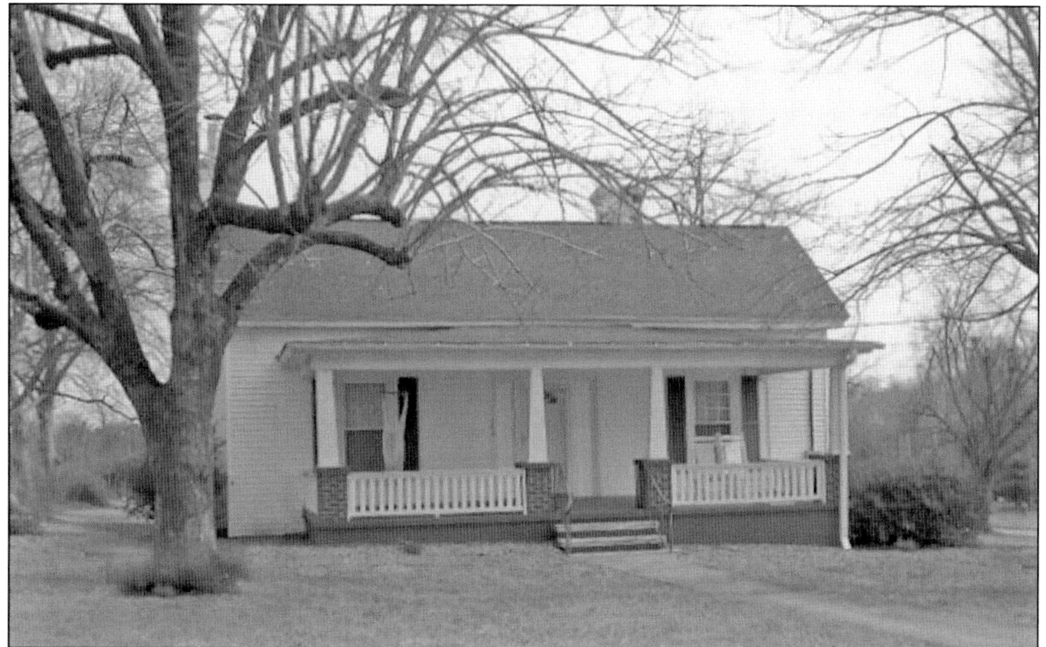

This home, located on North Main Street, was the birthplace of Dr. John Laney Plyler, former president of Furman University. It is distinguished by being the only house in the vicinity with marble steps. It was purchased in 1921 by Arthur and Flora Henderson. Employed by Renfrew Bleachery, Arthur Henderson served many years as a school trustee. In 2009, this home was converted into a gift shop, Kramer's Korner.

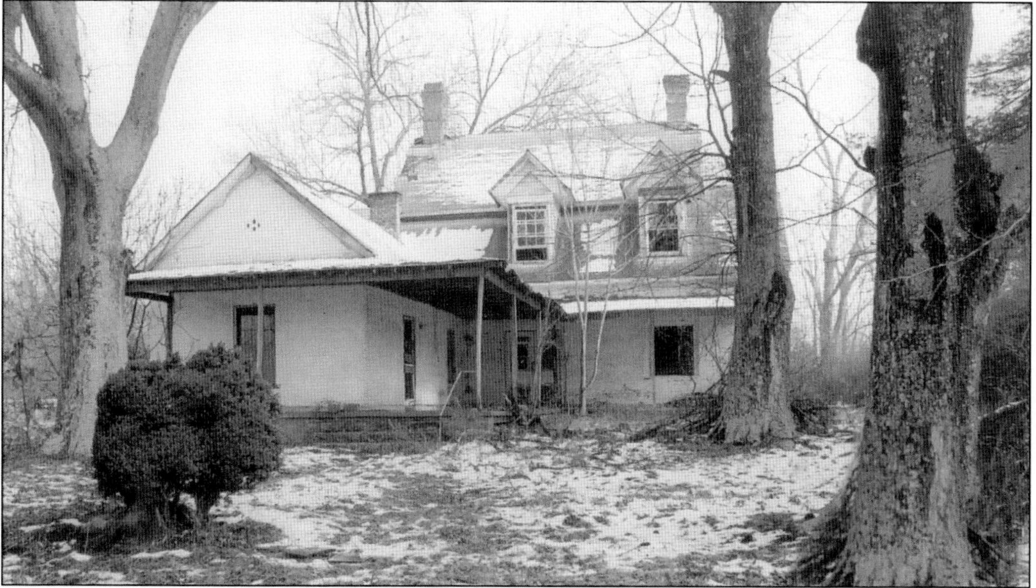

Built in the 1870s, this house was located directly across Geer Highway from the new Travelers Rest High School. The first resident was Moses "Mose" Fowler, whose daughter Cassandra married J. D. Cooper. The Arthur Williams family lived in this house for a time. Later, Prof. Arthur W. Lee and his family lived in the big, rambling house for many years. Professor Lee taught singing schools for more than 50 years. The house was demolished in 2008.

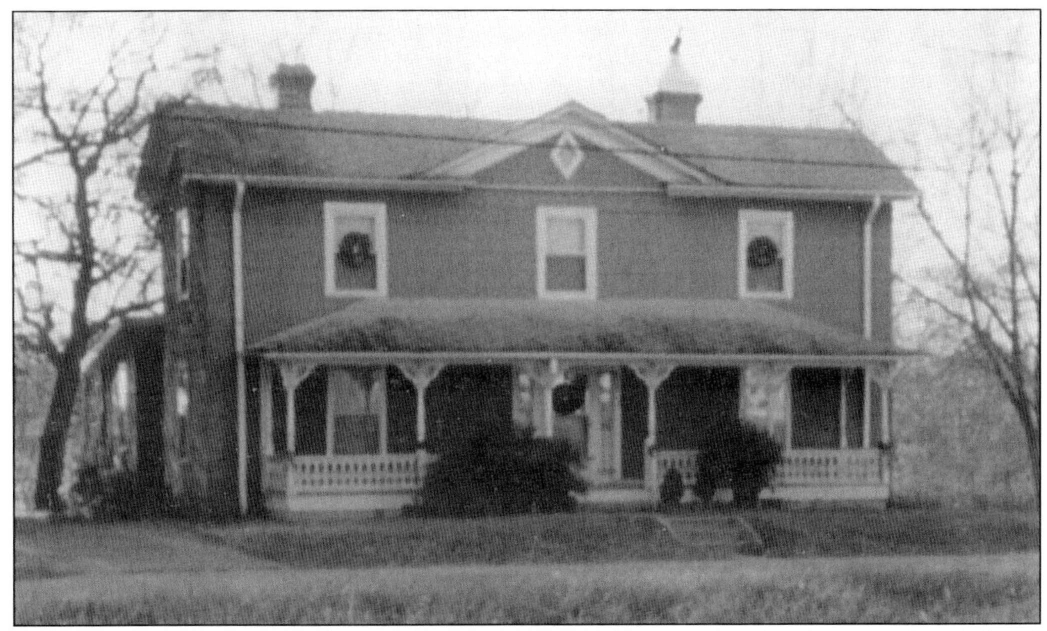

This house stood on Geer Highway (North Main Street) between the Travelers Rest High School, built in 2007, and the Tankersley Dirt Moving office. George Nicoll had the house built, and at one time, he operated a gristmill and a garage on the adjoining property. It became the home of Sidney and Jennie Coleman Burns and later became the home of Lillian Burns McKinney. It burned in 2006.

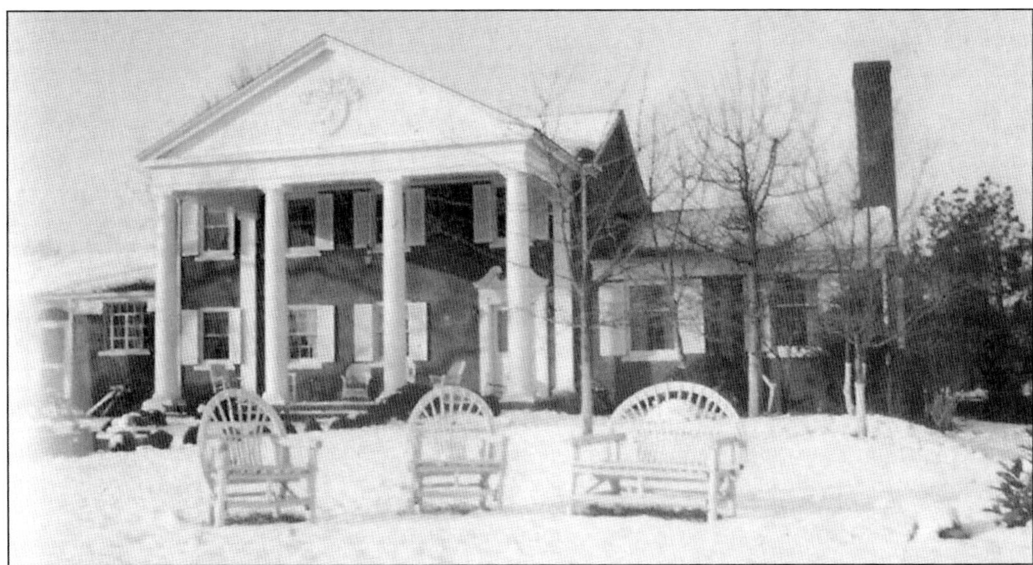

This Williamsburg-style brick home located on Highway 276 was constructed in 1939. It was designed by Henry Gaines, cousin of Mary Coleman Scruggs Thomason Becknell. Gaines also designed Green Valley Country Club, the Coleman Hospital in Travelers Rest, and Dr. T. E. Coleman's home on Highway 25 North. Henry Gaines was a renowned architect from Biltmore Forest, North Carolina, who is best remembered for his Virginia Tidewater facades. Now owned by Paul and Sandra Scruggs Scarpa, this home was one of the last in the area to have been "hand-tooled," in that little, if any, electrical equipment was employed in its construction.

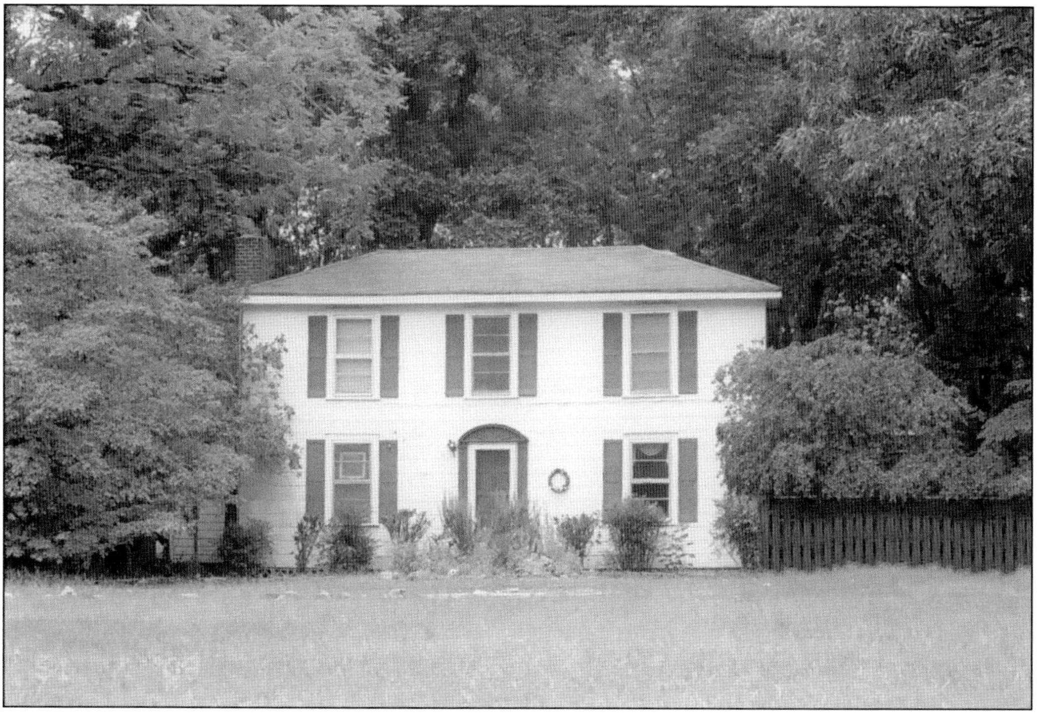

The two-story house built by Dero Cooper still stands on McElhaney Road. Historians estimate that the house was built before 1890 on land owned by James D. Cooper, father of Dero Cooper.

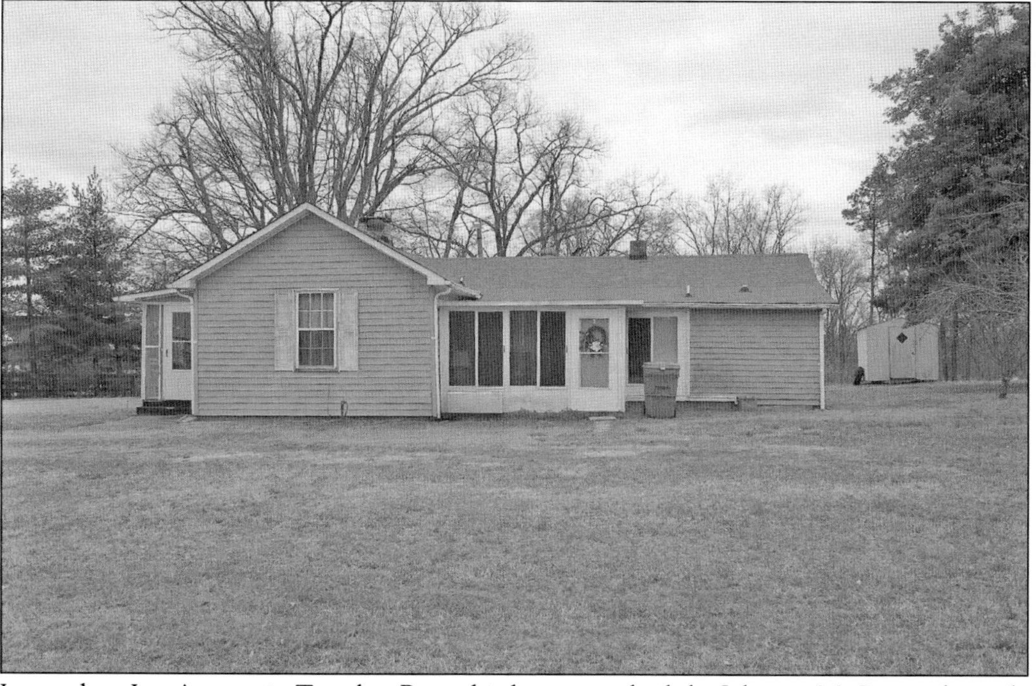

Located on Ina Avenue in Travelers Rest, this house was built by Johnson McCoy in the early 1900s and has been constantly occupied by the McCoy family for over 100 years. The McCoy home has one of the most spectacular views in the entire area of the Blue Ridge Mountains.

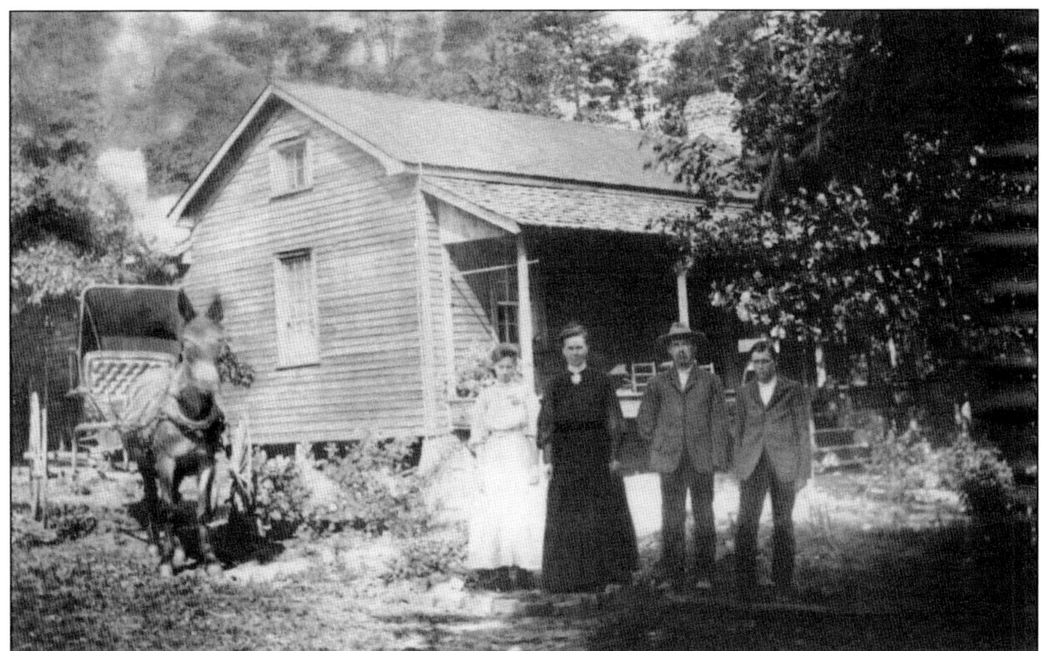

This 1908 photograph of the home place of Emma Lockaby and family is in the Belvue community of Travelers Rest. The house still stands on Belvue School Road. Pictured from left to right are Pauline Pruitt Bridges, Emma Lockaby Bridges, Aaron Virgil Bridges, and John W. Lockaby. The buggy is pulled by a mule named Tobe. Lewis Tyler Lockaby was born in this house in 1925.

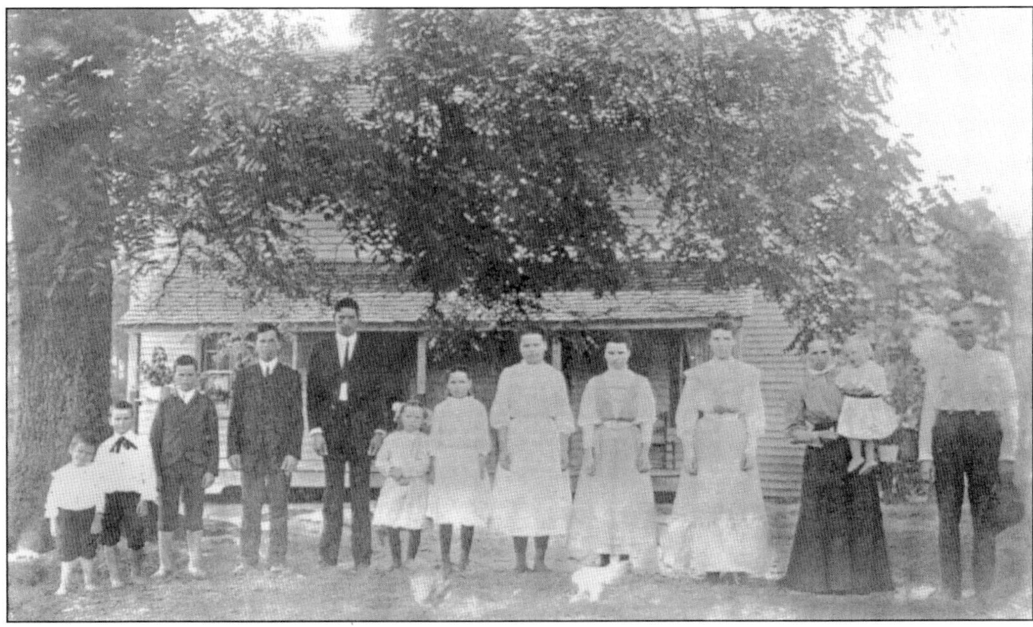

The Zion Perry Batson family home is located off old White Horse Road in the Ebenezer community. The family members seen in this 1908 photograph are, from left to right, Pride, Porter, Avery, Dayton, Calvert, Flauzy, Esther, Della, Mittie, Lorene, Lyda (holding Leland), and Zion Perry. Confederate veteran Aquilla Batson was Zion Perry Batson's father. The home and outbuilding were remodeled by the Freeland family, who still reside on the property.

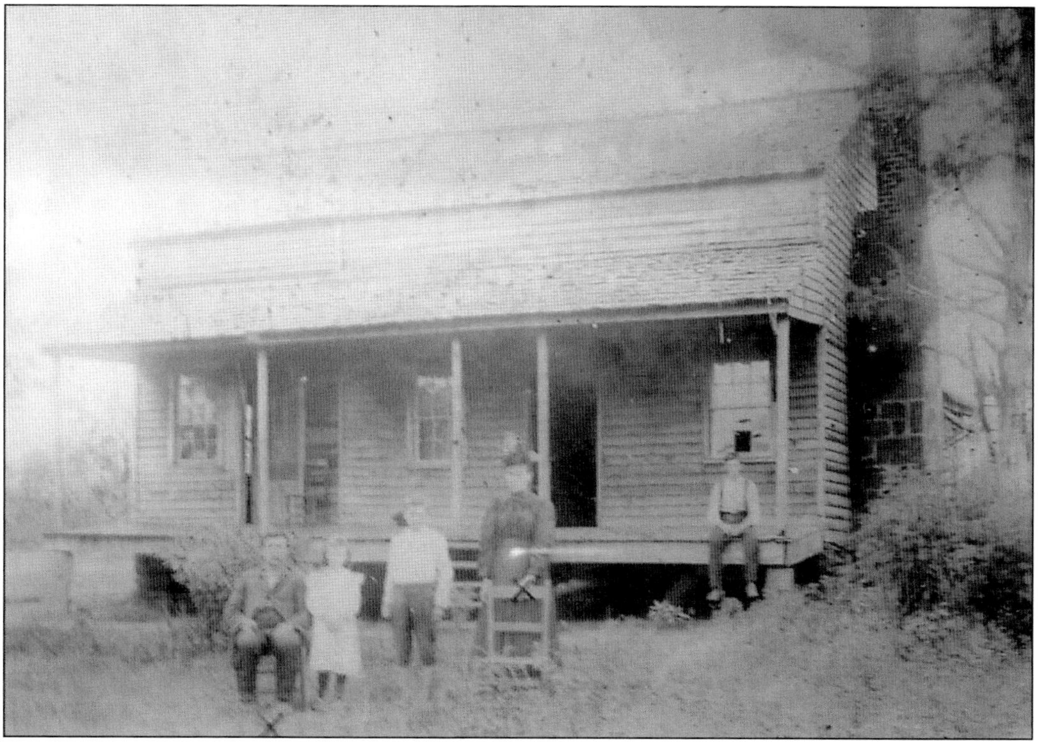

Located on Tigerville Road, the Hart home was constructed in the early 1830s. Pictured in the photograph above are, from left to right, Alexander Hart, Effie Hart, Charlie Hart, Emma McCauley Hart, and Walter McCauley. The home has been continuously occupied by the Hart family since the 1830s. The photograph below shows the home as it looks today after extensive remodeling.

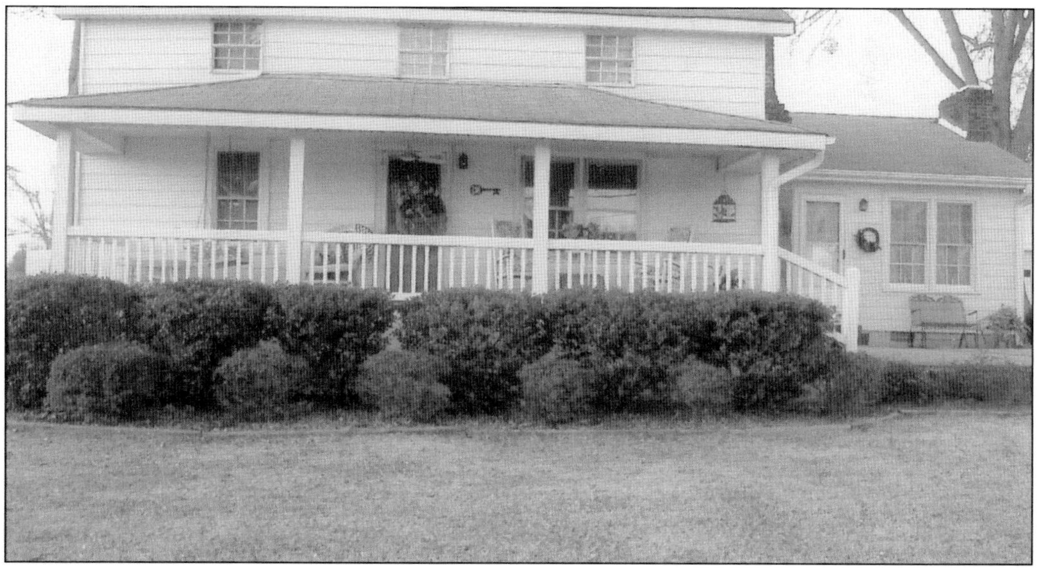

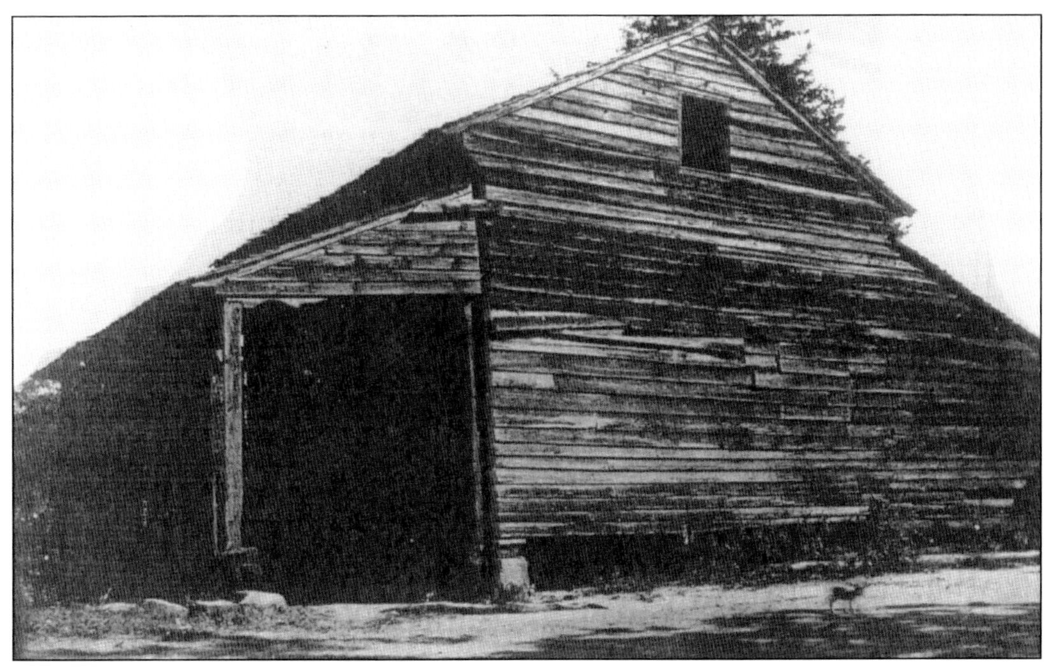

Originally located on Tigerville Road, the home of Dicey Langston and Thomas Springfield no longer stands. The structure used as the barn is pictured above. The drawing below is an artist's rendition of the Springfield home using all available printed information. Langston died in her home on May 23, 1837. (Drawing by Roddy Rodgers.)

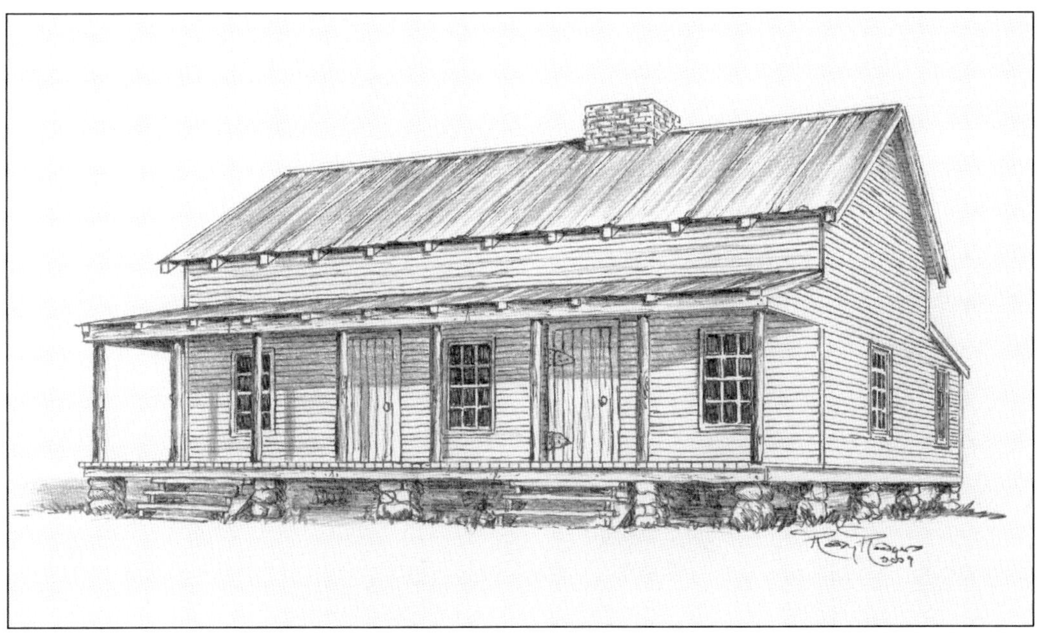

Four

Schools

As early as the days of Daniel in the Bible, schools were created, as humans have always been learners by sheer nature. Schools allow for the opportunity of social interaction among peers of various backgrounds while learning the basics. The first free schools within South Carolina were created in Orangeburg in 1798. Nothing more became of any effort to create free schools until 1811, when South Carolina governor Henry Middleton pushed for the establishment of free schools, one where elementary education was imparted to all pupils free of charge. At the inception of free schools, state legislatures would set aside $300 of the state's annual budget for each school. Schools were not allowed to be established until the inhabitants of the neighborhood built a schoolhouse that would hold anywhere from 30 to 40 students at a time. Throughout the years, and with the growing population, Travelers Rest schools have become solid educational leaders for the state. Take a look at the first school from the 1880s, and study the history of each new school's inception and growth through the World Wars, Great Depression, fires, segregation, and the 21st century's technology. As with anything, the creation of schools and their building, development, and cultivation is a learning process with a strong curve.

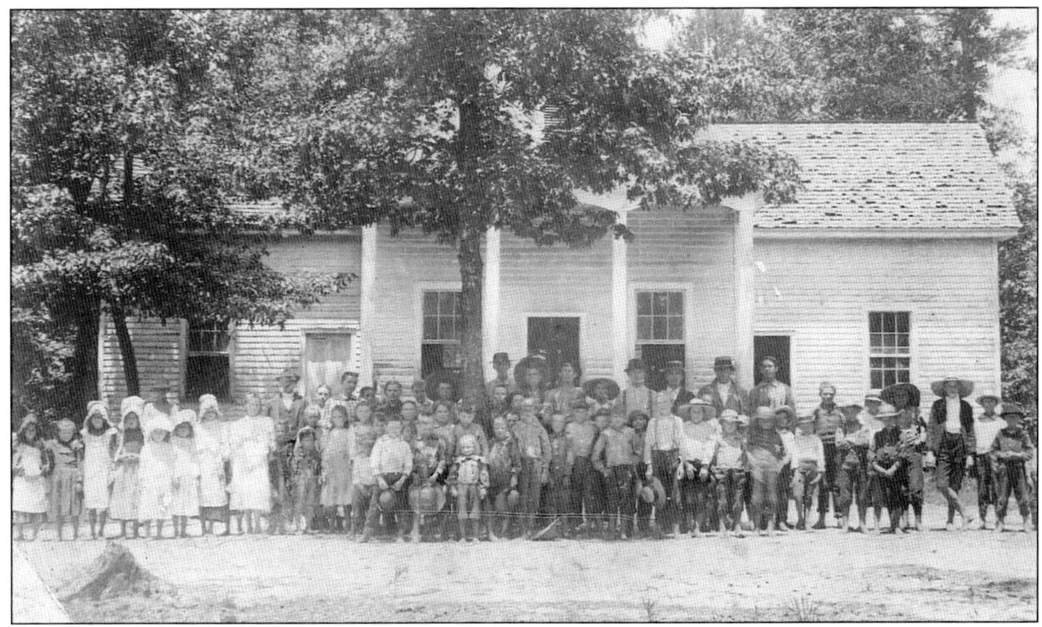

The student body of Travelers Rest School posed in front of the schoolhouse that was built in the 1880s. It was located near the old Peterson Lumber Company on Poinsett Highway and consisted of three rooms containing partitions, which could be moved when a larger meeting area was needed.

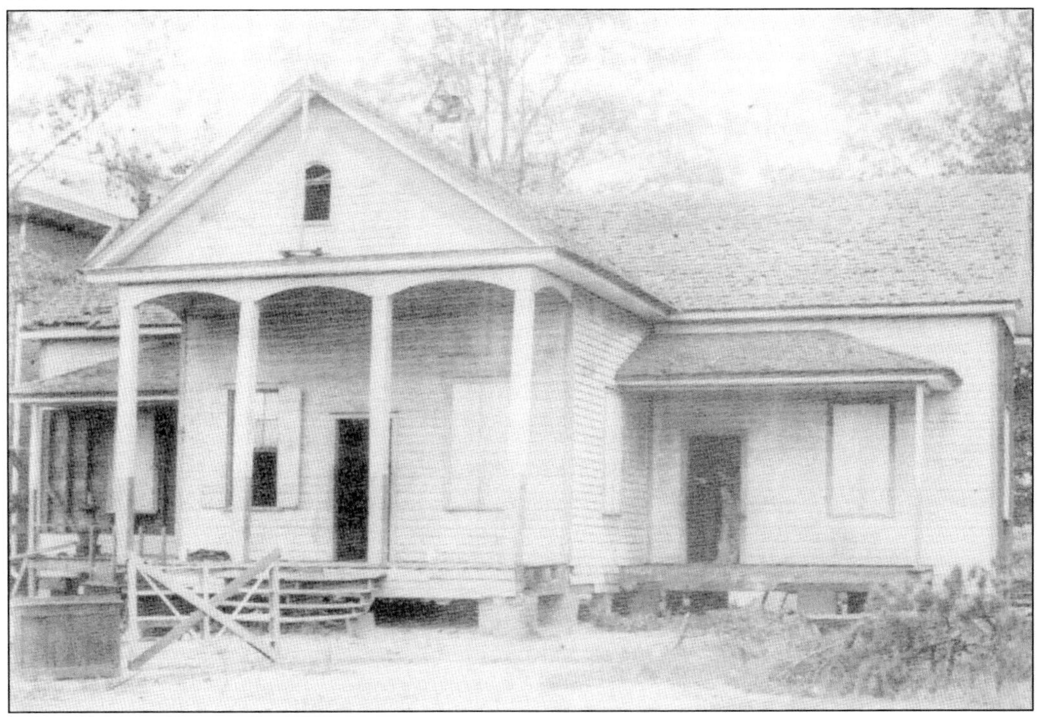

The 1880s Travelers Rest School building was replaced in 1914 by a new, large brick structure on adjoining property near 403 North Poinsett Highway. Note the brick building under construction at left.

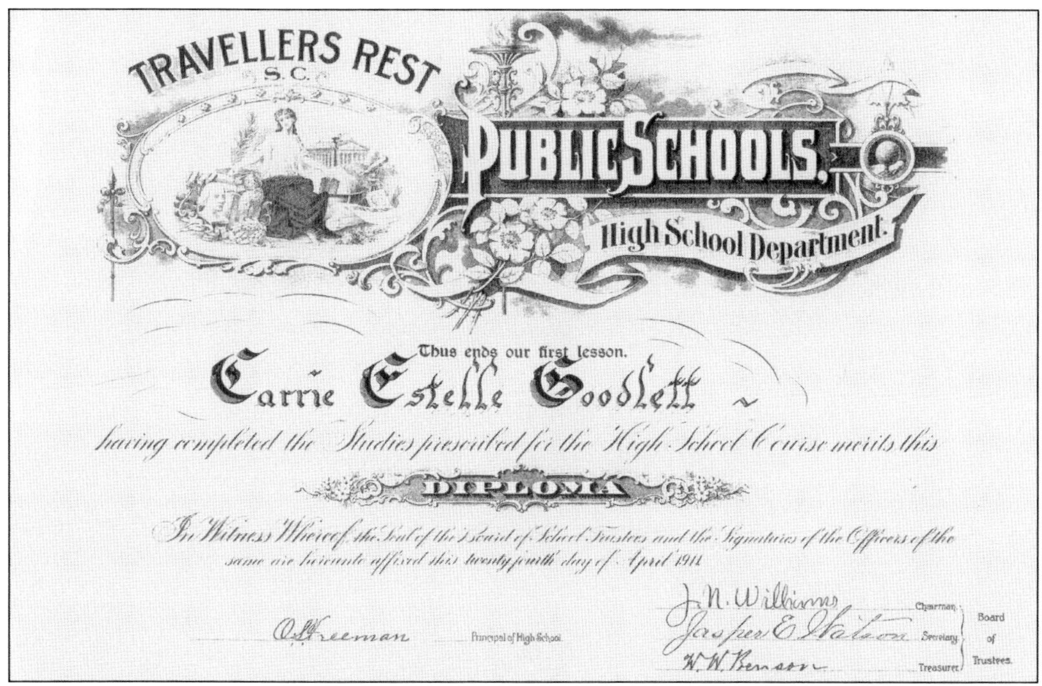
TRAVELLERS REST
S.C.
PUBLIC SCHOOLS,
High School Department.

Thus ends our first lesson.

Carrie Estelle Goodlett

having completed the Studies prescribed for the High School Course merits this

DIPLOMA

In Witness Whereof, the Seal of the Board of School Trustees and the Signatures of the Officers of the same are hereunto affixed this twenty fourth day of April 1911

J. N. Williams Chairman
Jasper E. Watson Secretary
W. W. Benson Treasurer
Board of Trustees

O. L. Freeman Principal of High School

There were five members of the first graduating class of Travelers Rest High School in 1911: Roy Hunt, Lula Coleman Talley, Pearl Hunt Runion, Clifton Talley, and Carrie Goodlett. (Note the spelling of the school and town on this diploma.) In 1961, Pearl Hunt Runion and Clifton Talley were deceased, but the surviving three members (below) met for a 50-year class reunion. They are, from left to right, Lula Coleman Talley, Roy Hunt, and Carrie Goodlett Holtzclaw.

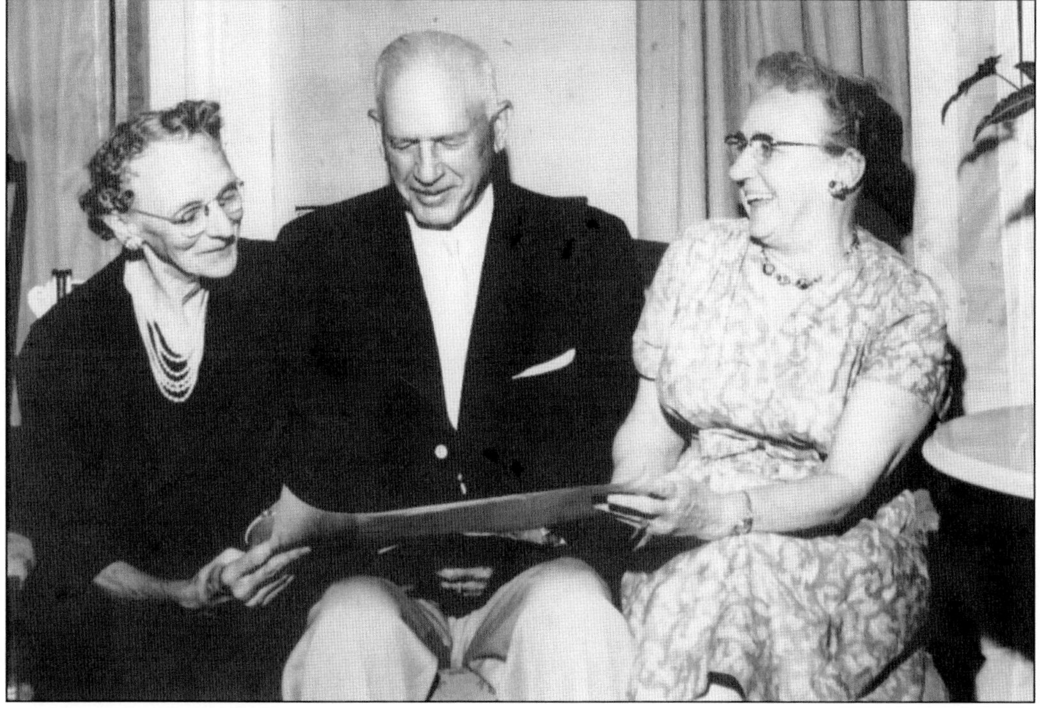

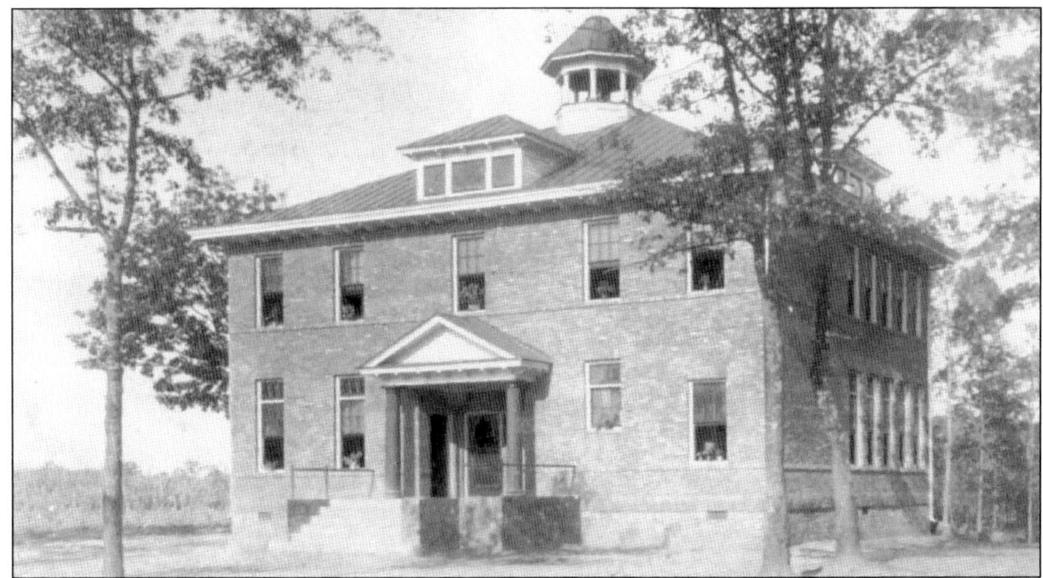

This Travelers Rest High School was constructed in 1914 adjacent to the site of the wooden school building. The third volume of *Echoes* explains that school was on a "lay-by" schedule. Classes began in early August, and then students were released for six weeks in the fall to help pick cotton. When school was in session, students brought lunches from home, and as there was no indoor plumbing, students had to use an outhouse and get drinking water from a well. This building burned on February 12, 1930, and "341 students and teachers marched out unharmed."

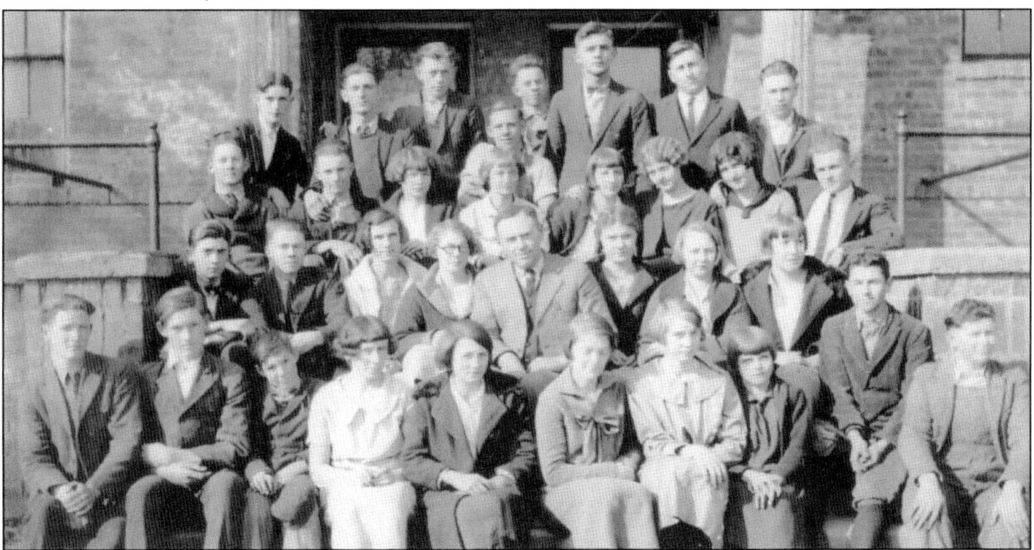

Taken during the 1924–1925 school year, this photograph was shot in front of the brick school, built in 1914. From left to right are (first row) Hugh Southerlin, Julius O'Shields, Lynn Smith, Mae Keeler, Mary Howard, Marian Neves, Corrine Hart, Cecile Clark, Clyde Foster (raised), and Ed Smith; (second row) unidentified, Boyd Evins, Gladys Hart, Belle Keeler, principal Walter Davis, Myrtle Tate, Martha Edwards, and Camille McAlister; (third row) Hobert Southerlin, Oscar Glenn, Mamie Lee McKinney Gilreath, Fannie Coleman, Carrie Coleman, Eva Batson, Azalee Cooper, and Truman Stepp; (fourth row) Ralph Coker, Ralph Robertson, Hiram Morrison, Douglas Coleman (front), Irving Edwards, Paul Hunt, Homer Styles, and Fred Bowers.

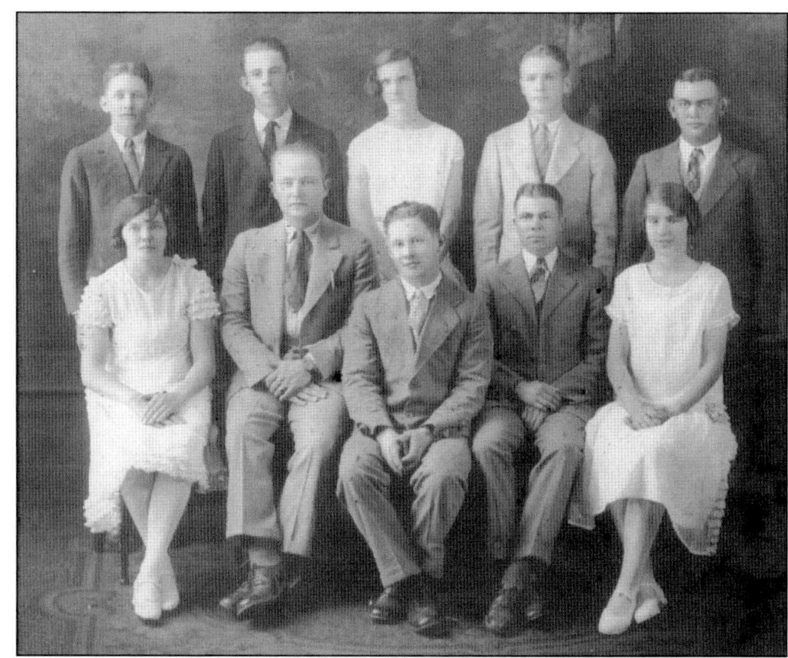

Members of the Travelers Rest High School graduating class of 1926 are, from left to right, (first row) Clara McCarrell, principal A. White Hawkins, Hobart Southerlin, Boyd Evins, and Mildred League; (second row) James Norman Bates, Irvin Edwards, Gladys Hart, Charles Neves, and unidentified.

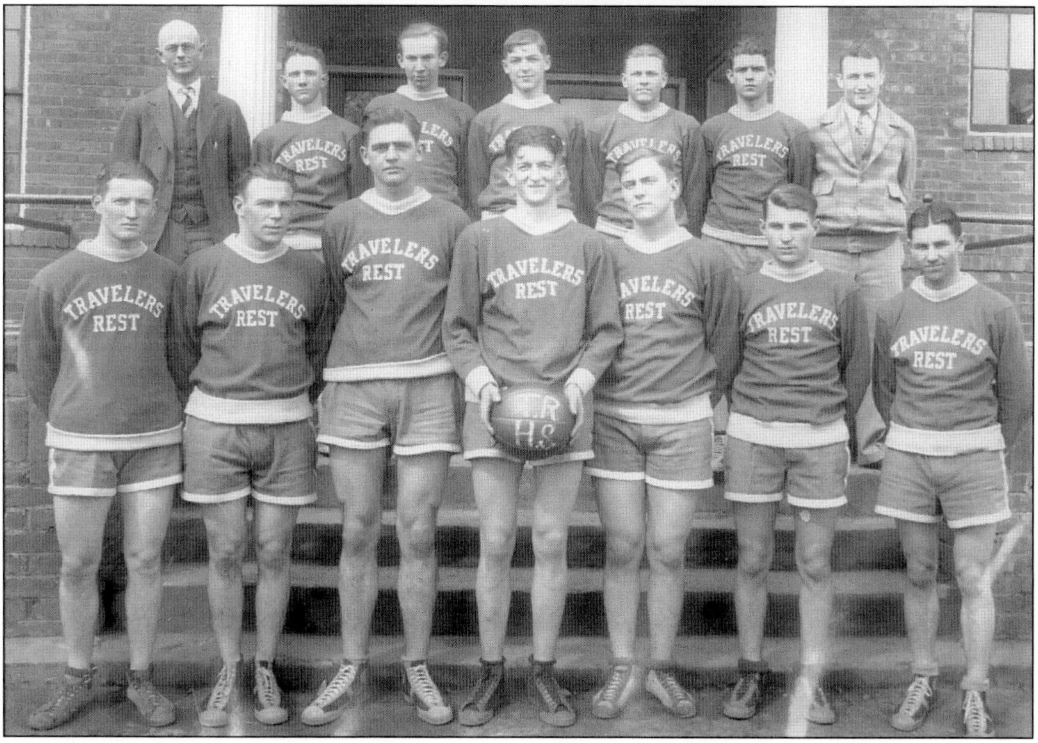

The Travelers Rest boys' basketball team was the 1927 South Carolina Class B champion. Shown here are, from left to right, (first row) Hugh Southerlin, Blane Morgan, Paul Hunt, team captain Claude Hawkins, Sloan Styles, Allen League, and Clyde Foster; (second row) coach B. B. Knight, Roy Glenn, Ansel Poole, Norwood League, Lester McCauley, Charley Hawkins, and assistant coach Otis "Blackie" Carter.

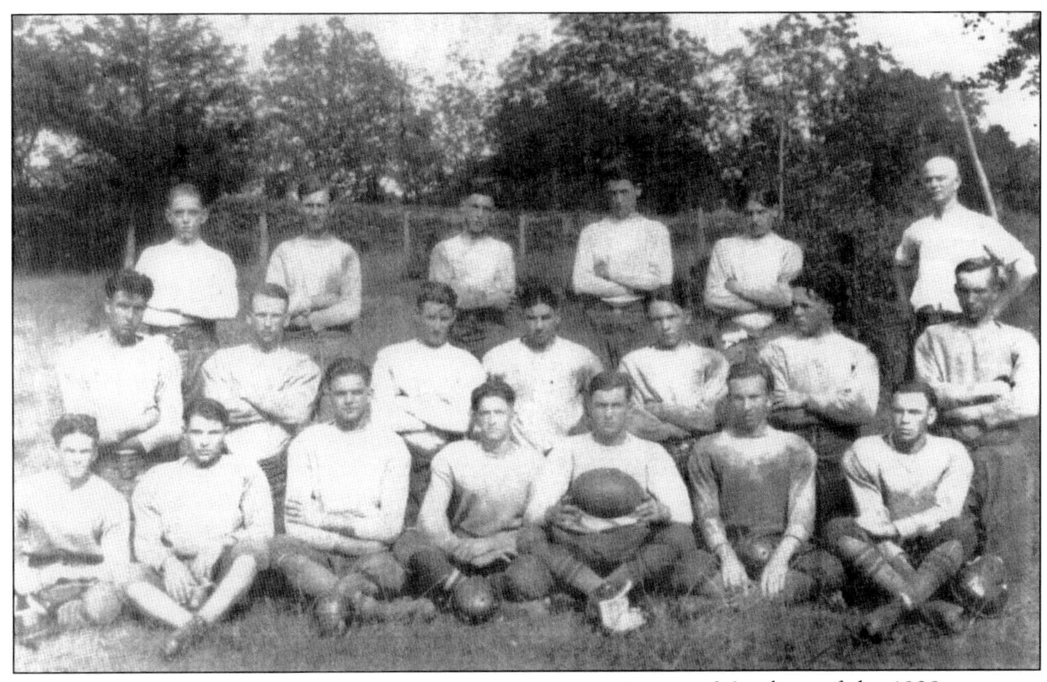

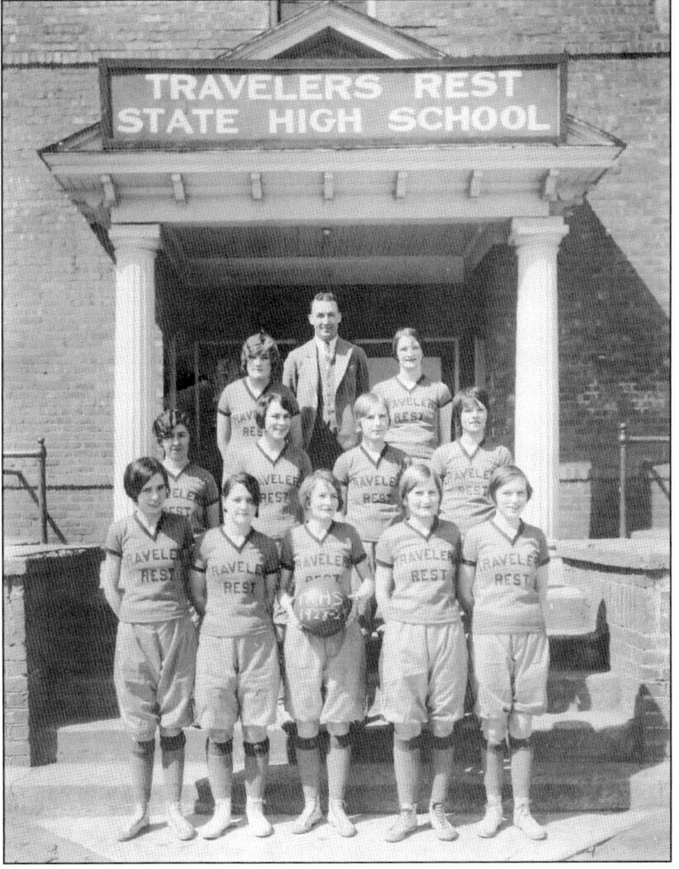

Members of the 1928 Travelers Rest High School football team are, from left to right, (first row) Walter Coleman, Allen League, Paul Hunt, Claude Hawkins, unidentified, Andy Poole, and Blane Morgan; (second row) Doc Mayfield, Hex Moody, Hugh Southerlin, Clyde Foster, Gus Cunningham, unidentified, and Alton Batson; (third row) Elwyn Neves, unidentified, Norwood League, Lloyd Simpson, Ed Duncan, and J. B. Knight.

Posing in front of the high school building is the 1928 Travelers Rest High School girls' basketball team with coach Carter. Pauline Bridwell League is among the players pictured.

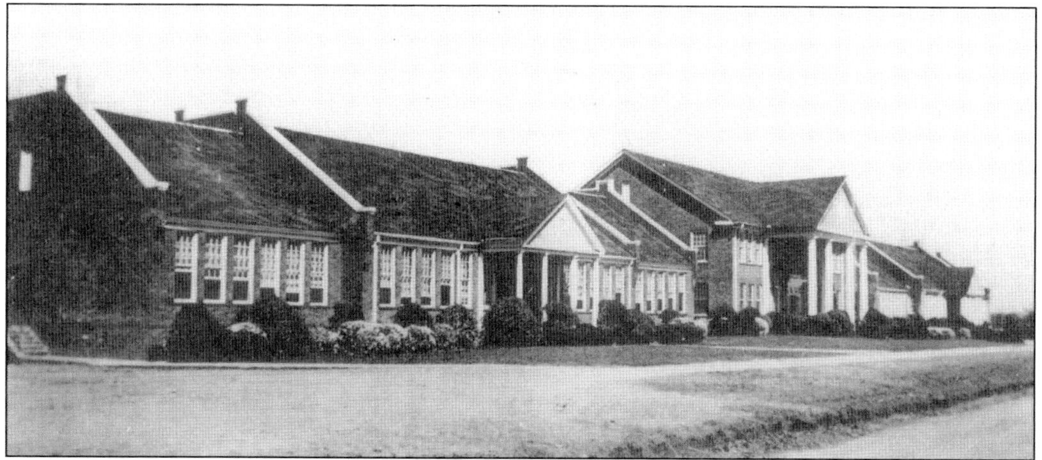

The new Travelers Rest School was partially completed in time for the beginning of the school's fall session in 1930. C. P. Rice was superintendent, and Sloan Westmoreland was the principal. The cannery, potato house, football field, and tennis courts were added in the 1930s, shortly after the school was built. Additional elementary classrooms were added in 1954. This campus was used for both elementary and high school from 1931 until 1956. It became Travelers Rest Elementary in 1956 when a separate high school was constructed. All buildings on the campus were demolished in 1992 because of structural damage.

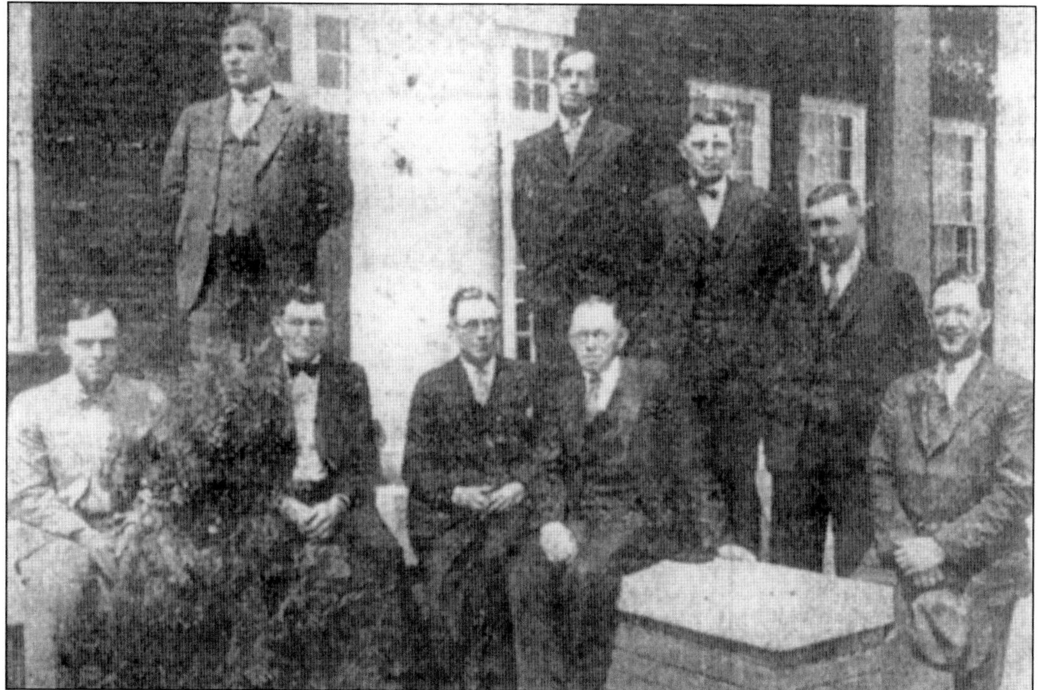

In 1930, the schools of the surrounding areas consolidated with Travelers Rest High School and Elementary School. These men were appointed as trustees from the communities they represented. From left to right are (seated) Hezzie Poole (Belvue), W. C. Stepp (Little Texas), J. Elmer Clark (Union), and Oscar Jordan (Ebenezer); (standing) C. P. Rice, (superintendent), H. L. Batson (Reedy River), Joe League and Arthur Henderson (Travelers Rest), and Chester L. Eddy (Renfrew Bleachery).

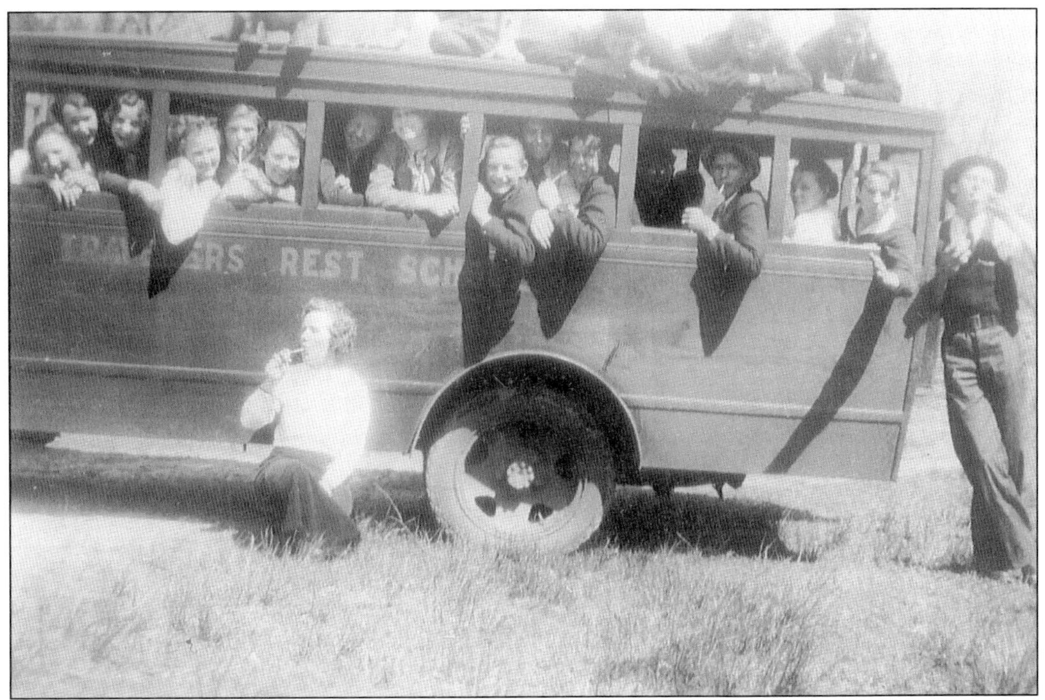

In about 1930, Travelers Rest students and teacher Ruth Gilreath (kneeling in front) enjoy clowning with lollipops while posing in, and even on top of, the school bus.

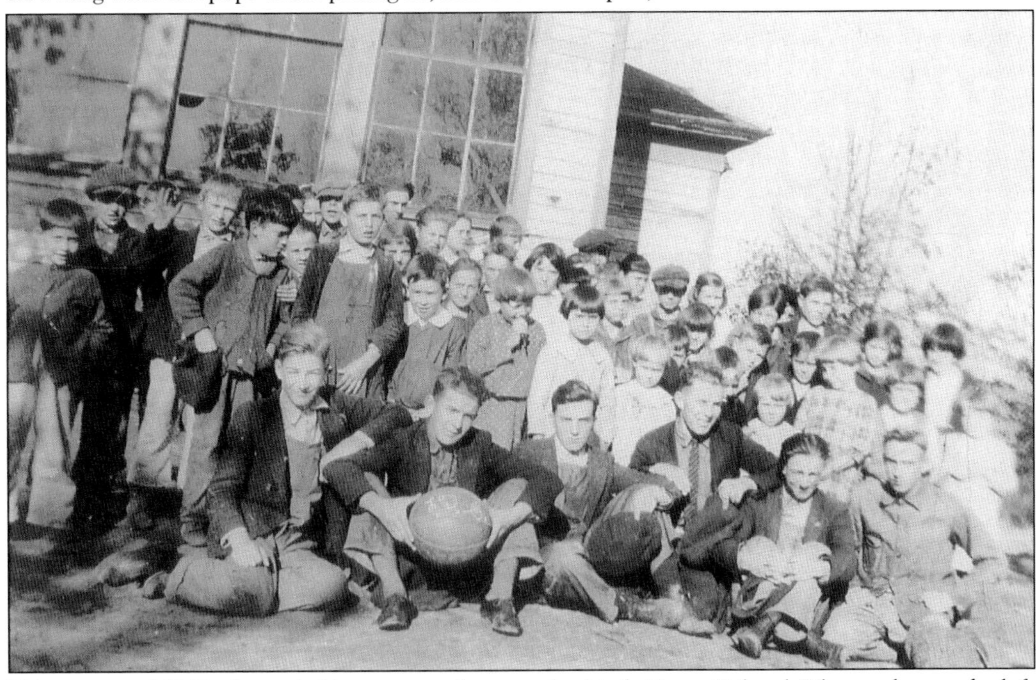

Taken around 1920, these children are students at the Little Texas School. The student at far left in the first row is J. Clyde Hawkins, and the student at far right of the same row is Alton Batson. This building was located on Little Texas Road, later named State Park Road. The structure burned in 2008.

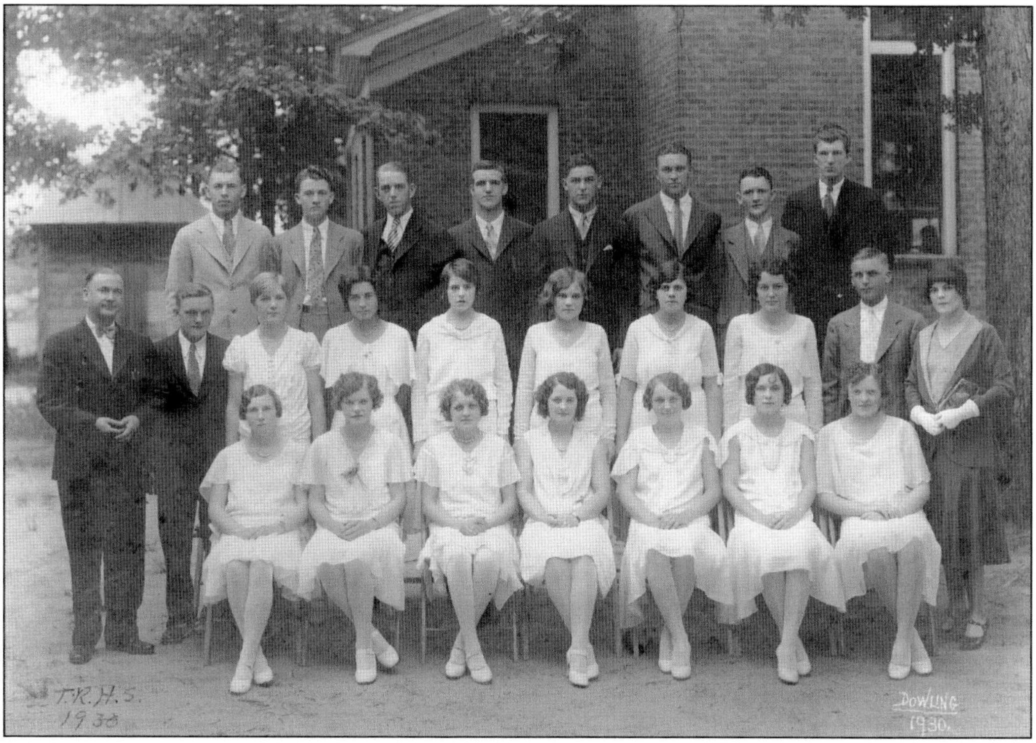

The 23 members of the 1930 graduating class of Travelers Rest High School are, from left to right, (first row) Susan Keeler, Julia Smith, Frances Southerlin, Annie Grace Allen, Azalee Coleman, Hazel McAlister, and Mildred Coleman; (second row) superintendent E. C. Shockley, James Clark, Daisy Neves, Maggie Howard, Nathalie Forest, Elizabeth Chiles, Clarice Sutherlin, Ladelle Simpson, Ansel Duncan, and teacher Lucille Bramlett; (third row) Vance McCarrell, James Watson, Elwyn Neves, Hugh Hawkins, Norwood League, Roy Burns, J. H. Glenn, and Rex Hawkins.

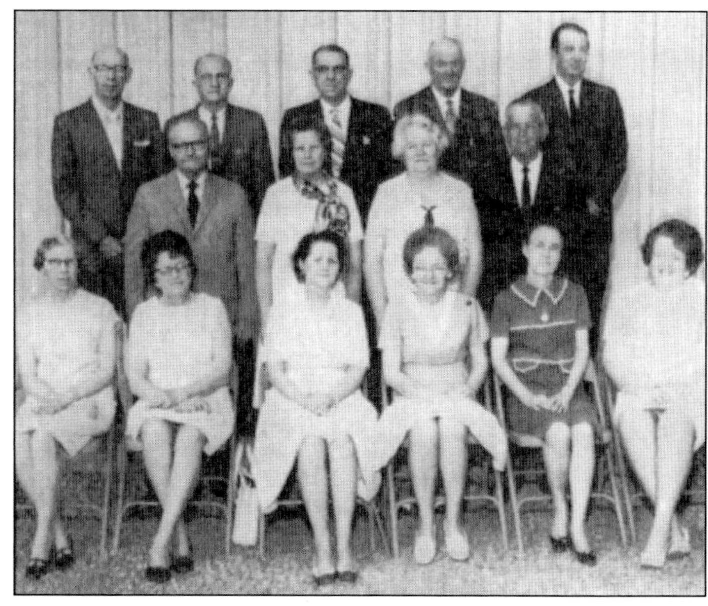

Shown in a photograph printed in the May 28, 1970, *Greenville News* are the former students who attended the class's 40-year reunion. They are, from left to right, (first row) Susan Keeler, Frances Southerlin Fortune, Annie Grace Allen Morgan, Azalee Coleman Duncan, Hazel McAlister Trammell, and Mildred Coleman Jarrard; (second row) James W. Clark, Nathalie Forrest, Ladelle Simpson Hawkins, and Ansel Duncan; (third row) Vance McCarrell, James Watson, Elwyn G. Neves, Roy Burns, and Rex Hawkins.

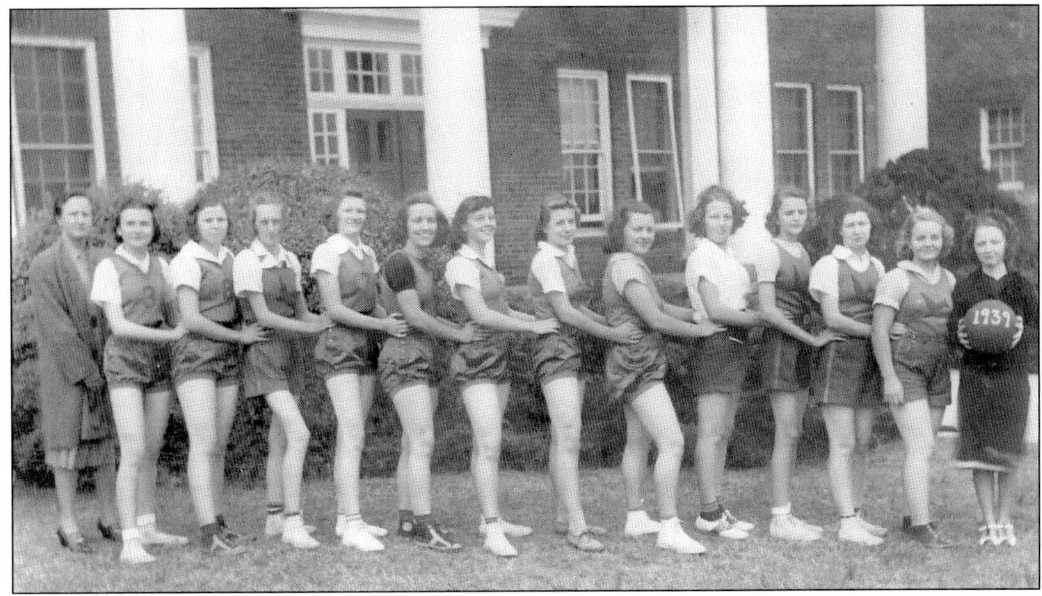

Coach Ethel Burnett (far left) stands with her 1938–1939 Travelers Rest girls' basketball team. The team members are, from left to right, Burnett, Earline Smith, Louise League, Minnie Lee Holtzclaw, Tansey Ridley, Margaret Wood, Helen England, Gaynell Bridwell, V. Bayne, Gladys McDaniel, Mary Jo Coleman, Louise Batson, Juanita Runion, and manager Vivian Moore.

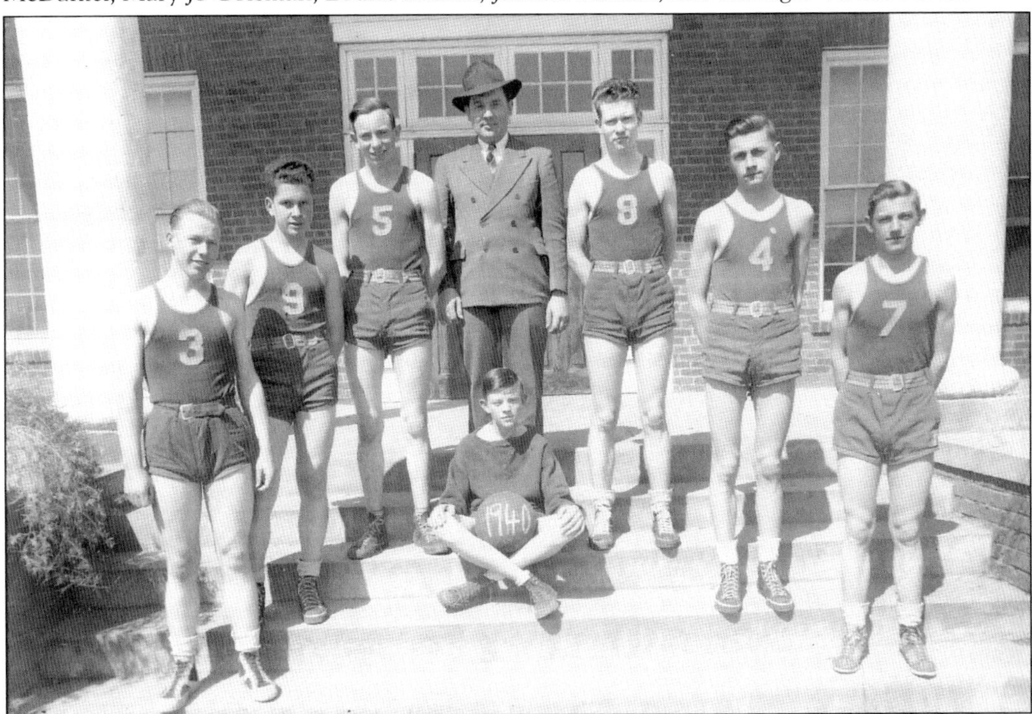

The 1939–1940 Travelers Rest boys' basketball team poses with coach Edwin Lake. The team members shown here are, from left to right, Clarence Glenn, Charles Bridges, Boyce Grier, Lake, Roy Lockaby, Norwood Bridwell, and Douglas DeBrabet. The team's unidentified manager sits in the center.

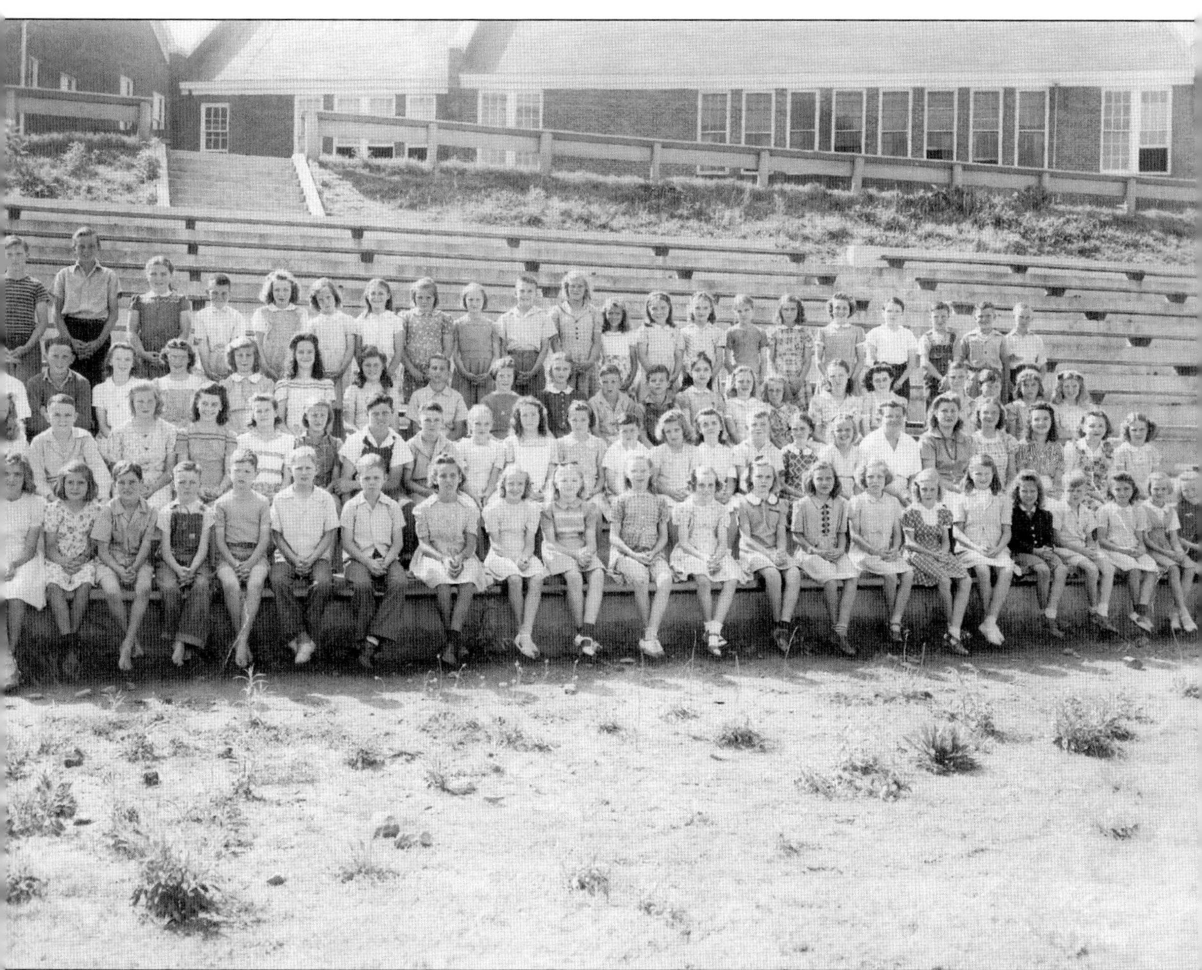

Elementary school students pictured in this 1942 photograph are, from left to right, (first row) Dora Jane Murphy, Ann Murphy, two unidentified, Mac Styles, unidentified, Randall Poole, Mary Phillips, Evelee Bridwell, Nell Anderson, Frances McAlister, JoAnn Coleman, Loise Barker, Jimmie Ruth Thomas, Jean McDowell, Annie Mae McCauley, Irene Hart, unidentified, John Griffin, Mary Bishop, Josh Edens, and Peggy Taylor; (second row) unidentified, Billy Joe Greene, unidentified, Joyce Nix, Margaret Lockaby, Kathleen Burns, unidentified, Joe Ed League, Jane Turner, unidentified, Martha Ann Hodges, unidentified, Bobby Jean Ivey, unidentified, Wilson Goodlett, four unidentified, Mary Thomas, unidentified, Evelyn Hunt, and Lucile Goldsmith; (third row) Metz Robertson, Carol Huff, Bobby Jean Hughey, Doris Pace, four unidentified, Blanche Linderman, Jane Edwards, Harry Johnson, unidentified, Elizabeth Getaz, Sarah Styles, Frankie Evans, unidentified, Carolyn Timmons, Billy Coleman, Fred McClure, Doris Ann Ivey, and Kathleen Styles; (fourth row) Jerry Bishop, unidentified, Evelyn Montgomery, unidentified, Dorothy Bridges, three unidentified, Betty Jo Burns, Caroll Smith, unidentified, Betty Clair Bledsoe, Peggy McDowell, Joyce McAlister, unidentified, Margie Robertson, Sara Ellen Hendrix, two unidentified, Billy Drake, and unidentified.

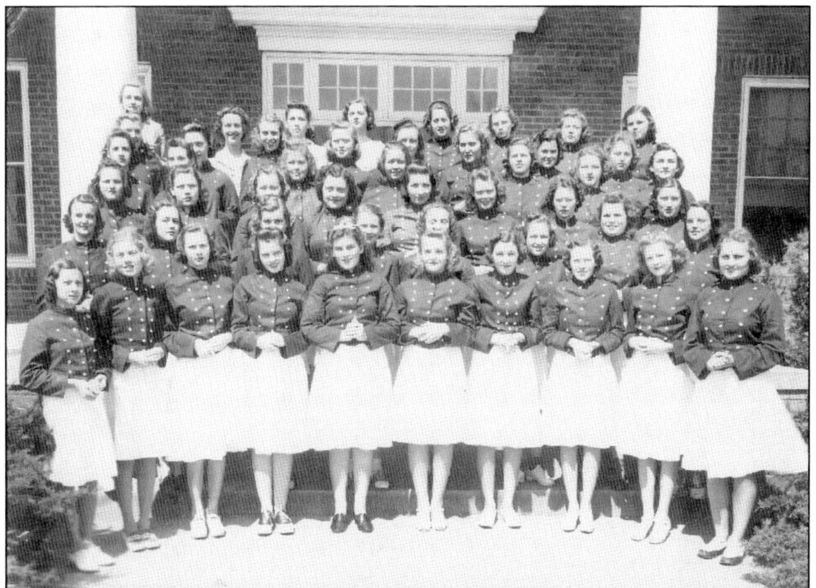

Pictured among members of the 1940 Travelers Rest High School girls' glee club are Ruby Vest Neves (first row, third from right), Kathryn Bridwell (first row, fourth from right), and Mildred Bridwell Burns (second row, third from right).

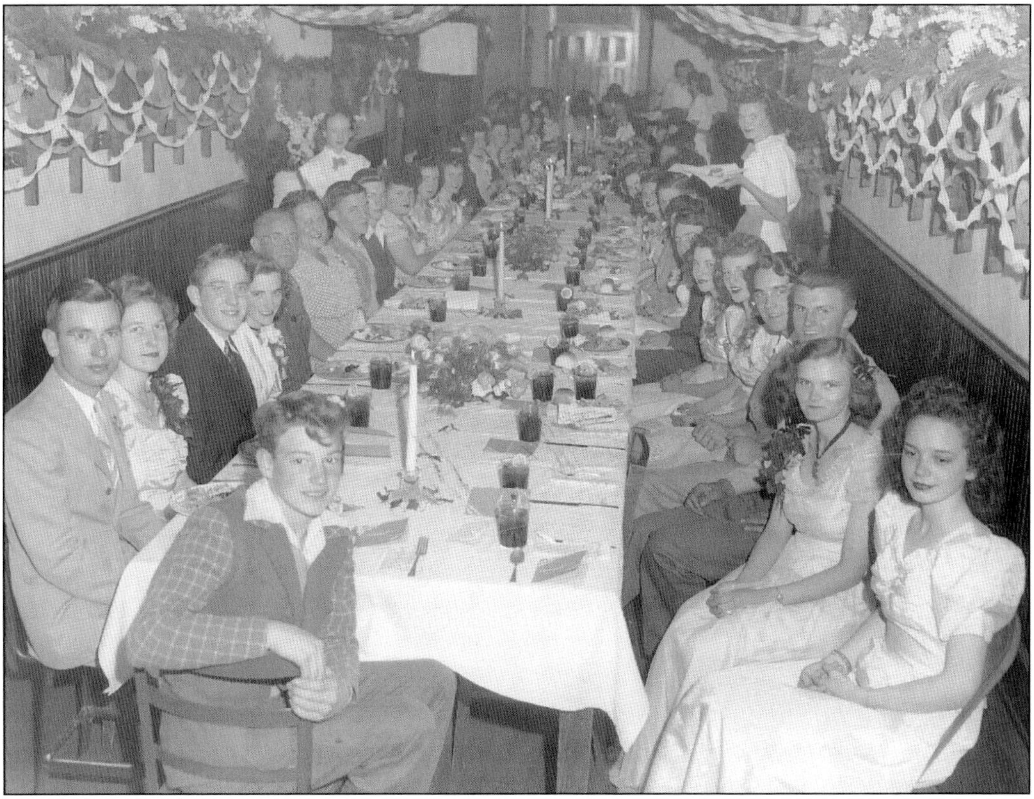

The 1946 junior/senior banquet was held in the decorated hall of Travelers Rest High School. The servers were the home economics students. Some of the students identified here are, clockwise from left to right, Billy Drake (front center), Gene Sprouse (far left), Birdie Phillips (second from left), Bobby League (seventh from left), Evelee Bridwell (standing at left), Charles "Wick" Hart (third from right), and Wavelene Williams (far right).

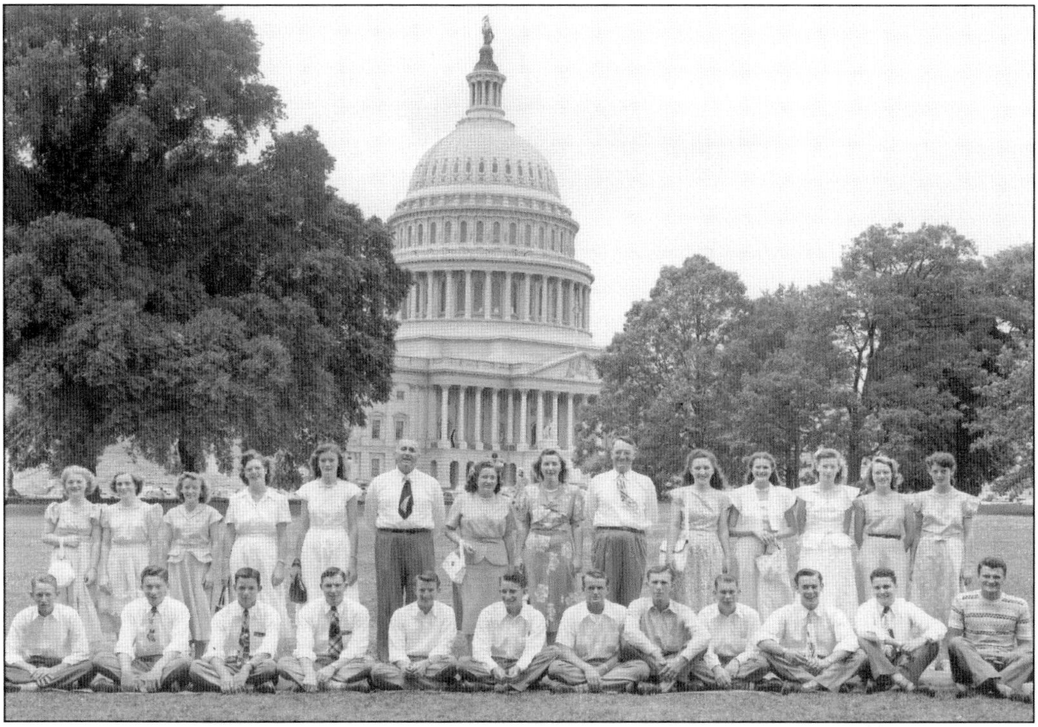

It was a custom of high school graduating classes to visit the nation's capitol at the end of the school year. The class of 1949 is pictured here with their faculty chaperones. This was also the first year that 12 years of school were required in order to graduate in the state of South Carolina. Shown here are, from left to right, (first row) Joseph Bishop, Fred McClure, Thomas Gibson, Jack Greene, Jimmy Crosby, Charles Martin, Calvin Langley, Bobby Bishop, Paul Taylor, Billy Joe Butler, Frank McDonald, and Charles "Wick" Hart; (second row) Nell Anderson, JoAnn Coleman, Evelee Bridwell, Doris Brown, Genevieve Phillips, H. P. Mayfield, Mildred Bridwell Burns, Lewis Batson, John Neal, Mary Childress, Margaret Lockaby, Bobbie Jean Hughey, Frances McAlister, and Josephine Hannon.

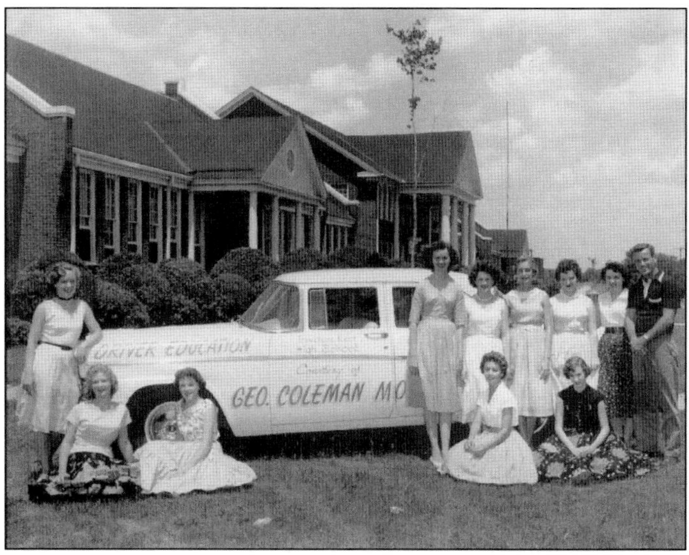

This mid-1950s driver's education class posed around the Ford donated by George Coleman Motors in front of the school on Center Street. Seen in the picture are, from left to right, (first row) Ruby Donna Lee Erwin, Barbara Dean, Sylvia "Dibble" Barrett, and Barbara Ballenger; (second row) Ruby Childs, Anna Louise Phillips, Mary Rochester, Mary Louise Willis, Frances Hines, Doris Williams, and coach Dean "Chico" Bolin.

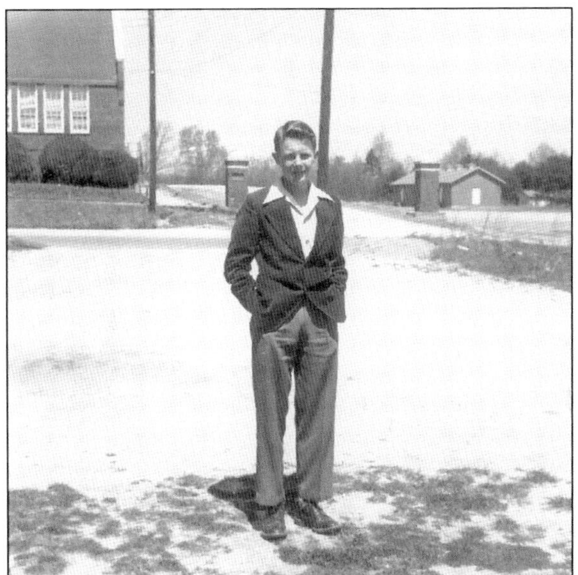

John Griffin stands in his front yard across the street from the school, with the potato house shown in the back right portion of the photograph. Farmers in the Travelers Rest area stored their sweet potatoes in this facility until they were cured and ready for market or personal use. The Sargent Library now occupies the area where the potato house stood.

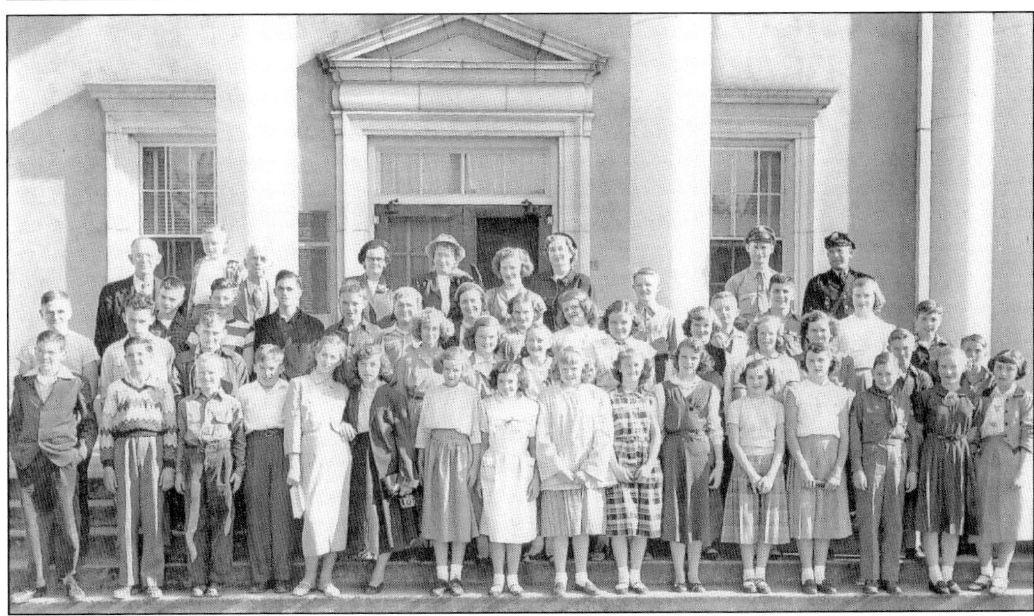

The 1952 seventh grade class traveled to the state capital in order to learn more about South Carolina history and government. Pictured here on the steps of the Educational Office Building in Columbia, South Carolina, are, from left to right, (first row) Donnan Waldrop, Jimmy Cantrell, Charles Bridgeman, T. J. Styles, Mary Meece, Marilyn Moore, Barbara Ballenger, Elizabeth Bishop, Lillian Robertson, Mildred Hawkins, Joyce Clayton, Carolyn Cantrell, Rachel Garrett, Arnold Arrowood, Ida Mae Waters, and Joann Bishop; (second row) Walter Lightle, Melburn Mills, Buddy ?, Mary Louise Willis, Frances Hines, Annie Jean Tankersley, Norma Jean Walters, Frankie Hart, Joanne Greene, Eugenia Moore, Marvin Walters, and Lloyd Smith; (third row) Wendall Batson, Ralph Lathan, Reece Randolph, William Yates, Fred Holden, Pauline Cornell, Shirley Randolph, Carolyn Edens, Tom Drake, Stanley Crosby, Franklin Murphy, Ann Styles, and Larry Hodgens; (fourth row) unidentified, Johnny Moody, unidentified, Texie Drake, Ethel Greene, Mary Ellen Thacker, Flora Styles, and two bus drivers.

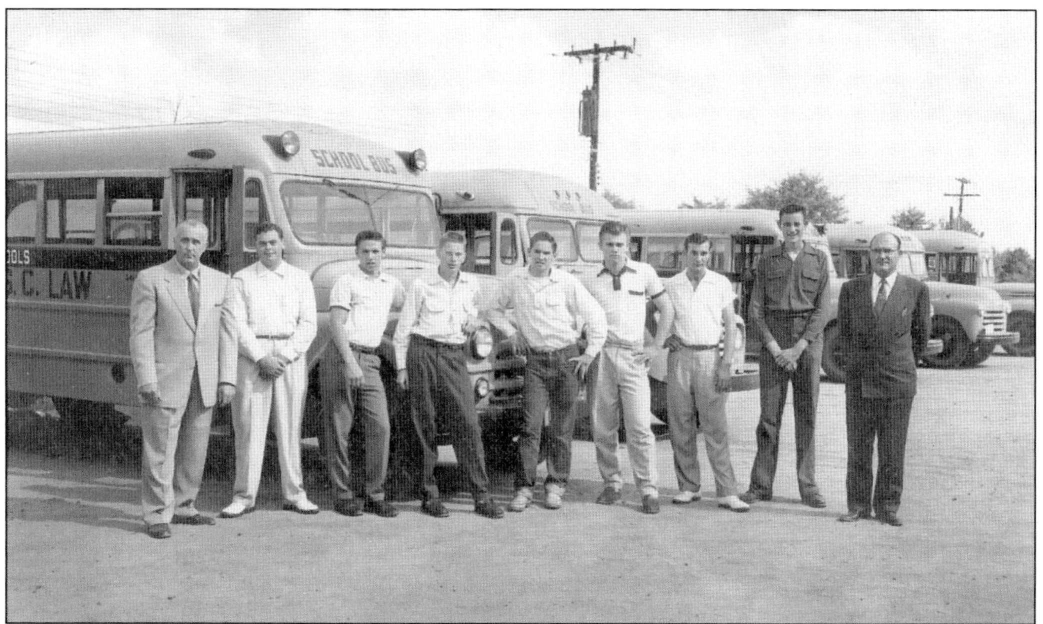

Hal Mayfield (far left) and C. F. Williams (far right) stand with the 1955 school bus drivers. From left to right, the student drivers seen here are Sid McJunkin, Charles Ivey, Allen Robertson, Gary Coster, Metz Looper, Dewayne Batson, and David Nix.

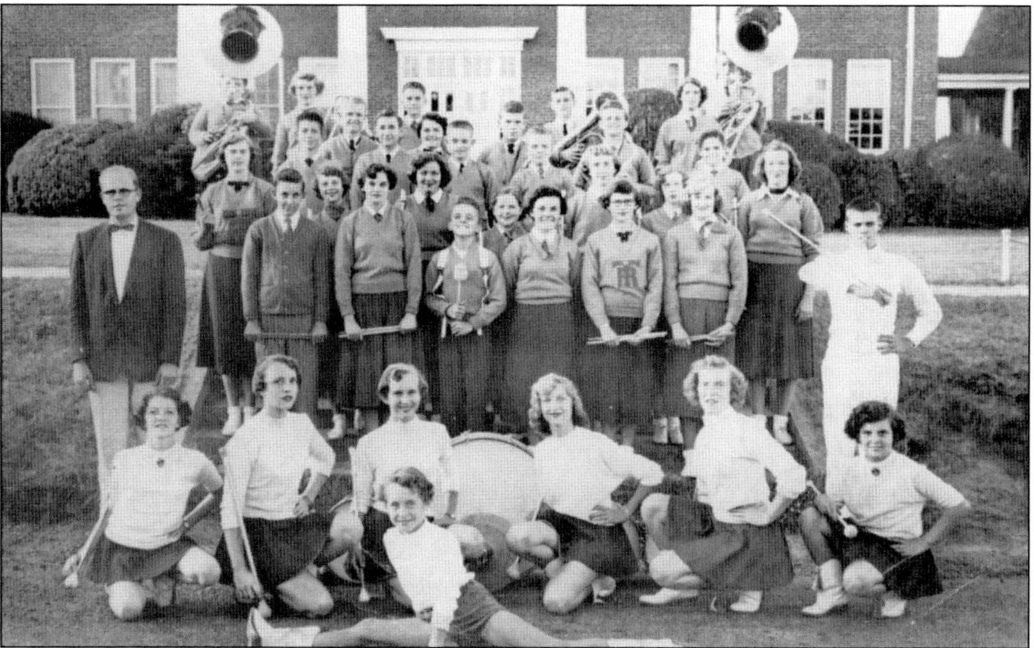

The first Travelers Rest band was formed in 1952, and band members and their parents conducted fund-raisers in order to earn money to buy uniforms. This photograph of the 1955 band was taken before enough funds were earned to purchase uniforms. The band director that year was Lester Watkins (far left), the drum major was Michael Gibson (far right), and the majorettes were, from left to right, Sharon Duke, Dot Styles, Janice Cantrell, Aileen Yates, Joanne Green, and Pat Murphy, with mascot Dottie Vernon in front.

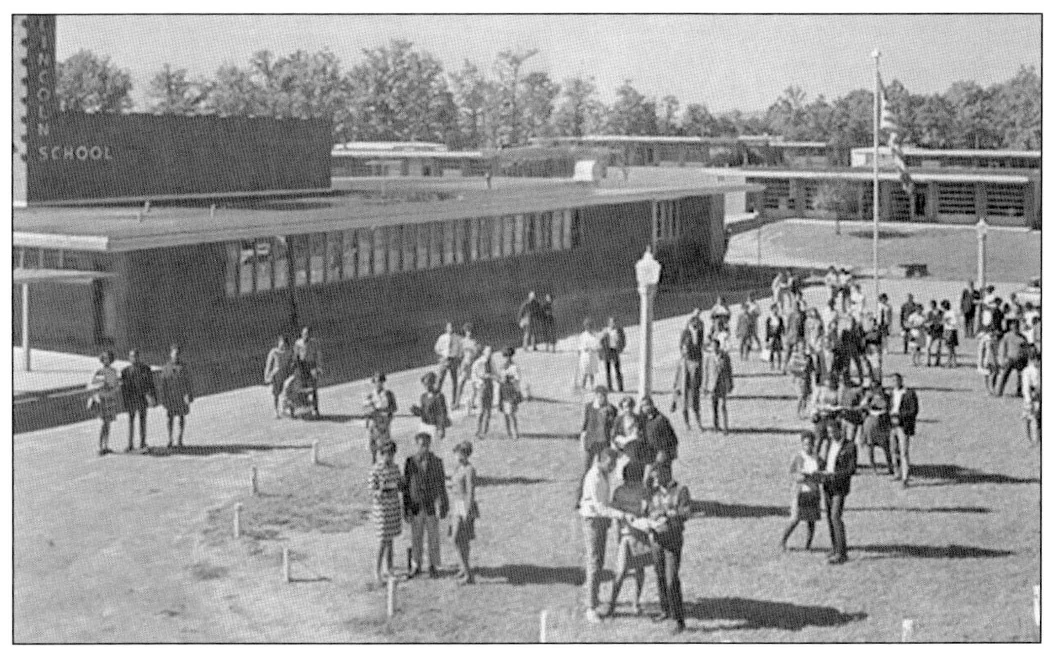

Before integration, most African American high school students in the Travelers Rest area attended Lincoln High School, located at the intersection of St. Mark Road and Highway 290 in the Greer area.

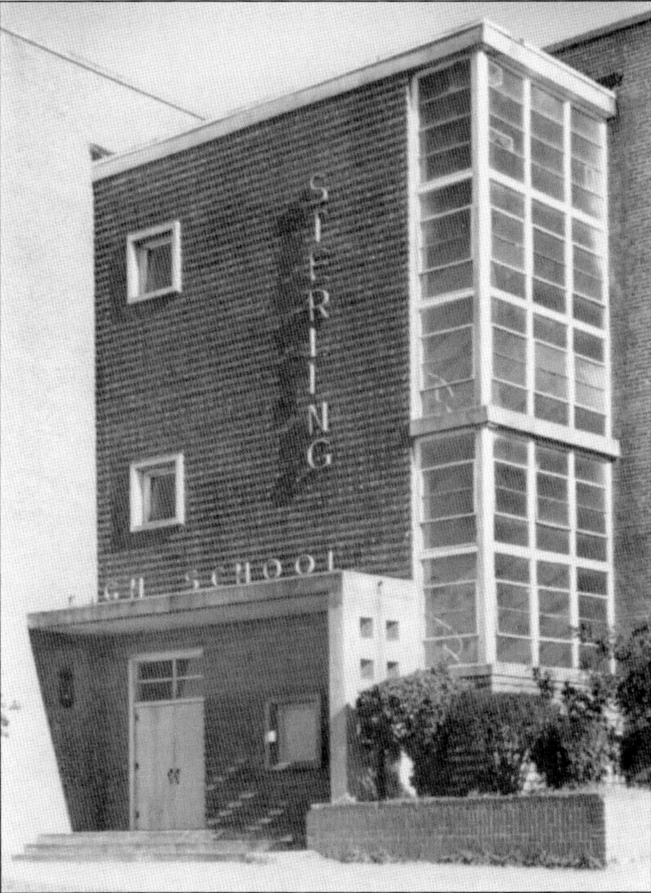

Some African American high school students who could provide their own transportation chose to attend Sterling High School in Greenville prior to integration.

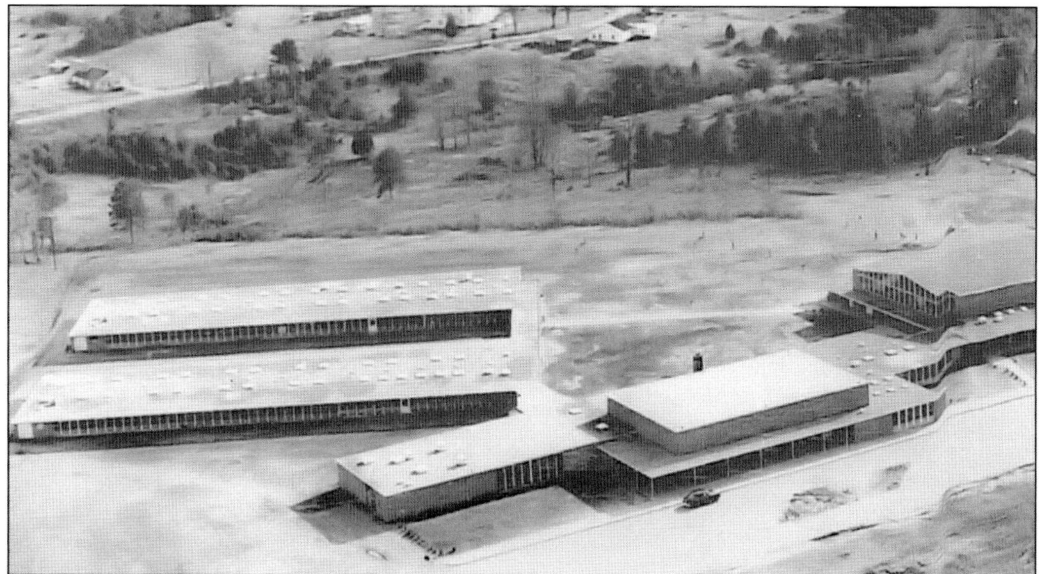

In 1956, a beautiful new building was completed for students moving into the 21st century. This building provided classroom space with proper lighting, heating, and ventilation as well as the adequate facilities needed to carry out a well-rounded educational program. In 2007, this building was vacated, and the high school was moved to a much larger, more modern building at 301 North Main Street in Travelers Rest.

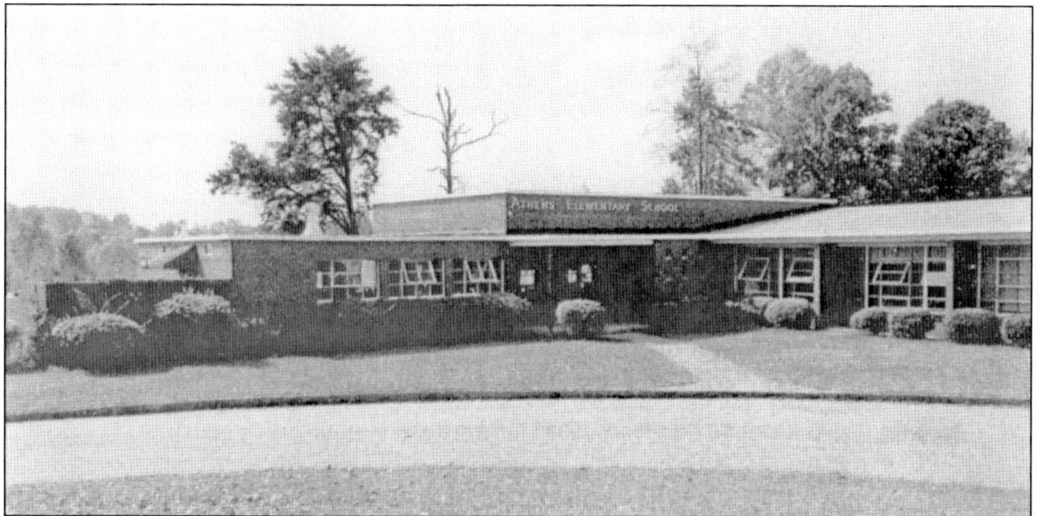

Built on 35.33 acres purchased in 1952 by the School District of Greenville County, Athens Elementary School was completed in 1954. Named for the old Athens section of Travelers Rest, it was the only African American school in the northwestern section of the county. In 1970, during the process of school desegregation, it became a sixth grade center under the leadership of Edris Walker. The school was closed at the end of the 1976–1977 school year due to fallen enrollment. In 1979, it was sold to the City of Travelers Rest, and then in 1981, the city sold the land and buildings to Chestnut Hill, a private hospital. At this time, in 2011, Springbrook Behavioral Health Care operates a residential care facility there. This was also where Wohali Charter School operated before it closed in 2011. (Information supplied by Anita Hudson, Facilities Department, Greenville County School District.)

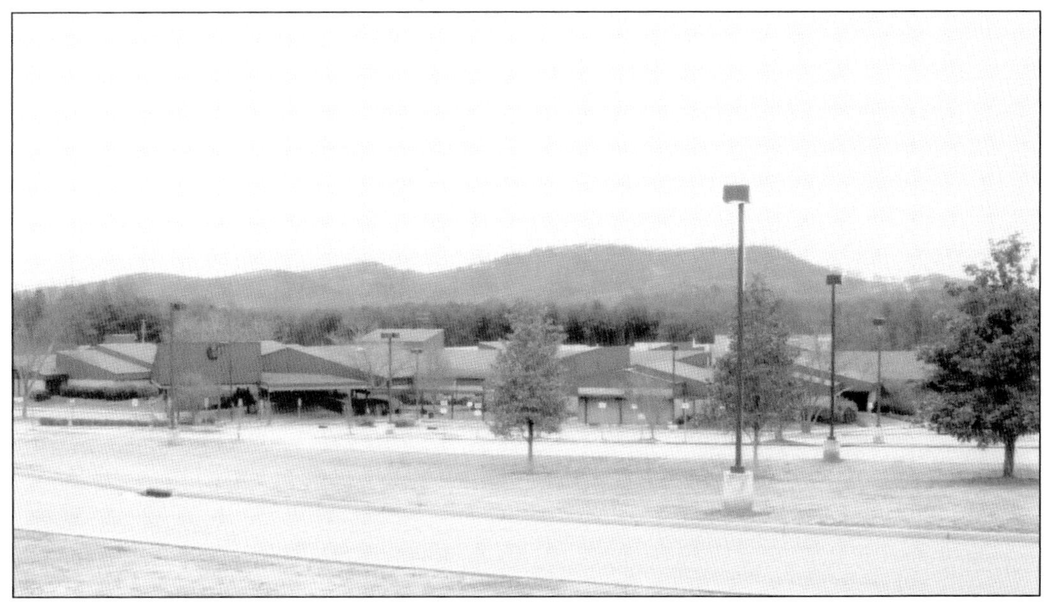

Gateway Elementary School opened in 1982 and is located behind the Bi-Lo shopping center on Hawkins Road. The student body is composed primarily of students from the attendance area of the former Travelers Rest Elementary School on Center Street that was demolished in 1992.

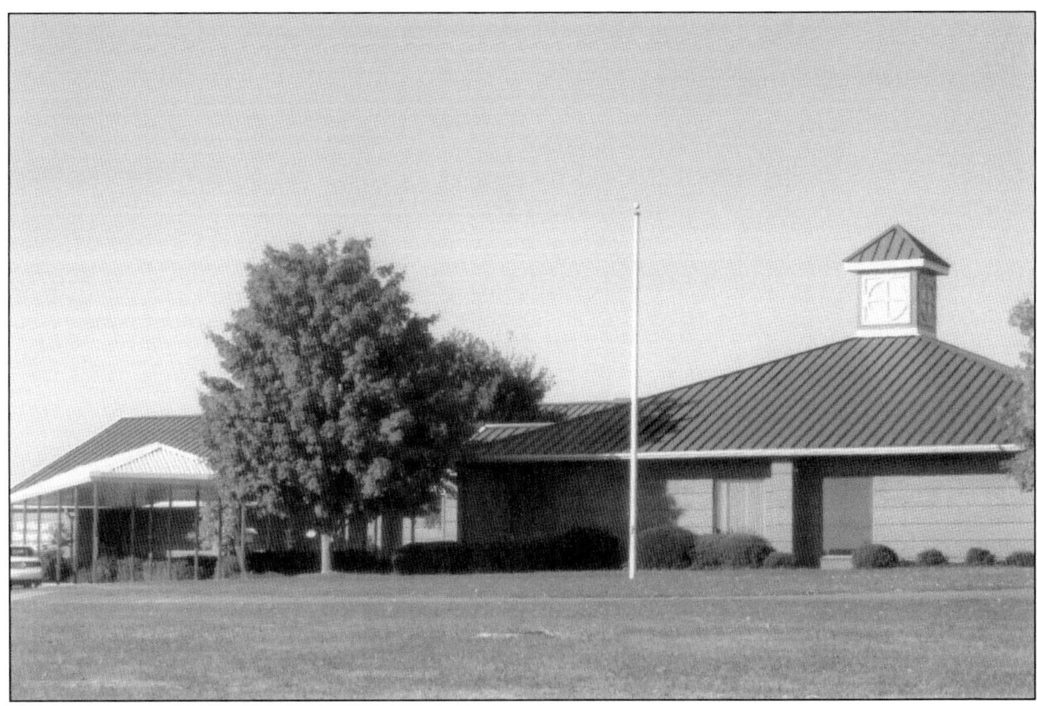

Heritage Elementary School, built in 1994, is located at the corner of Highway 276 and Langford Road, north of Travelers Rest in the Ebenezer community. This land was formerly occupied by a general store and garage.

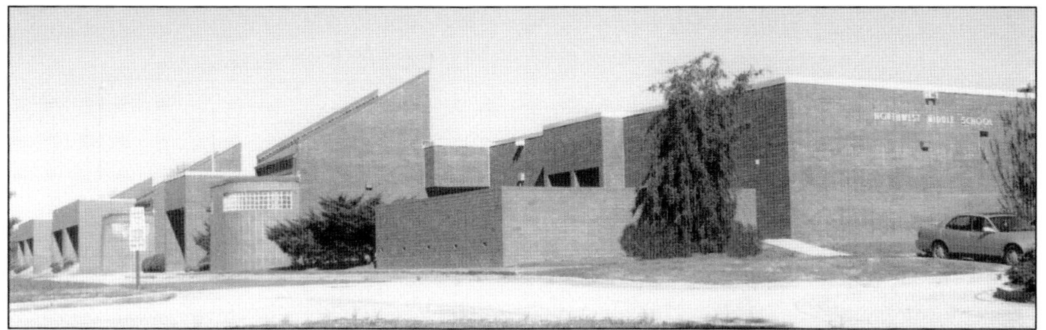

Northwest Middle School opened in the early 1970s and featured a new concept of having open classrooms with very few walls separating them. This school is located across Langford Road from Heritage Elementary School. The open classroom design was eventually abandoned in the 1990s.

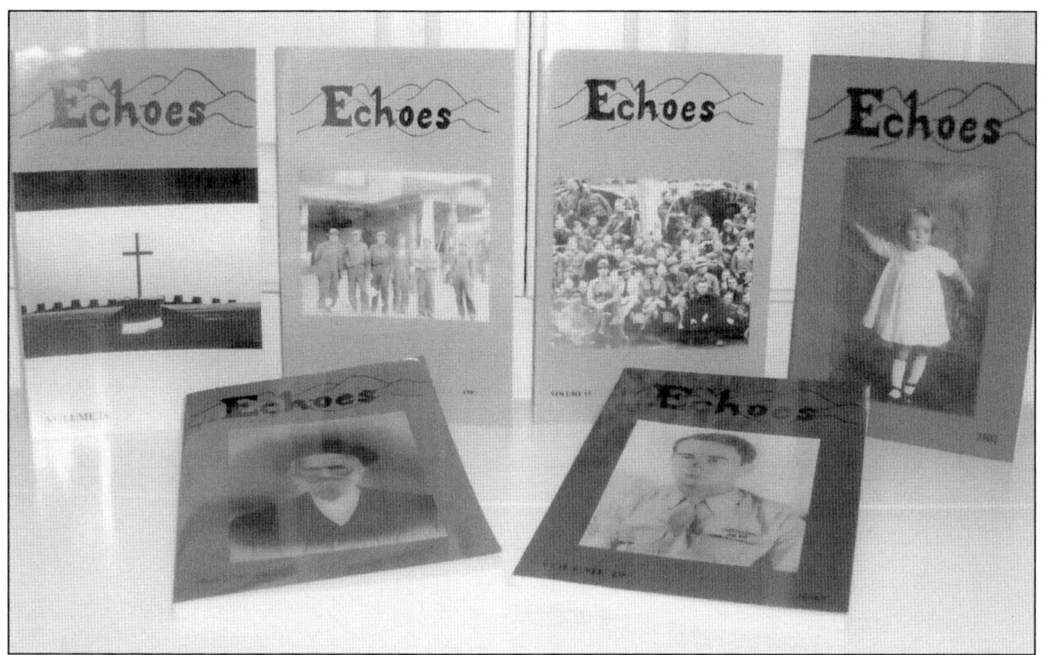

Eighth grade students at Northwest Middle School completed an oral history project every year for 20 years. These students, working in teams, interviewed local residents and researched topics of local historical interest. The result of this ambitious project is a treasured collection of 20 soft-cover books. Thanks to a grant from the City of Travelers Rest, these books will be transferred to CDs so that the valuable information will be accessible to more people.

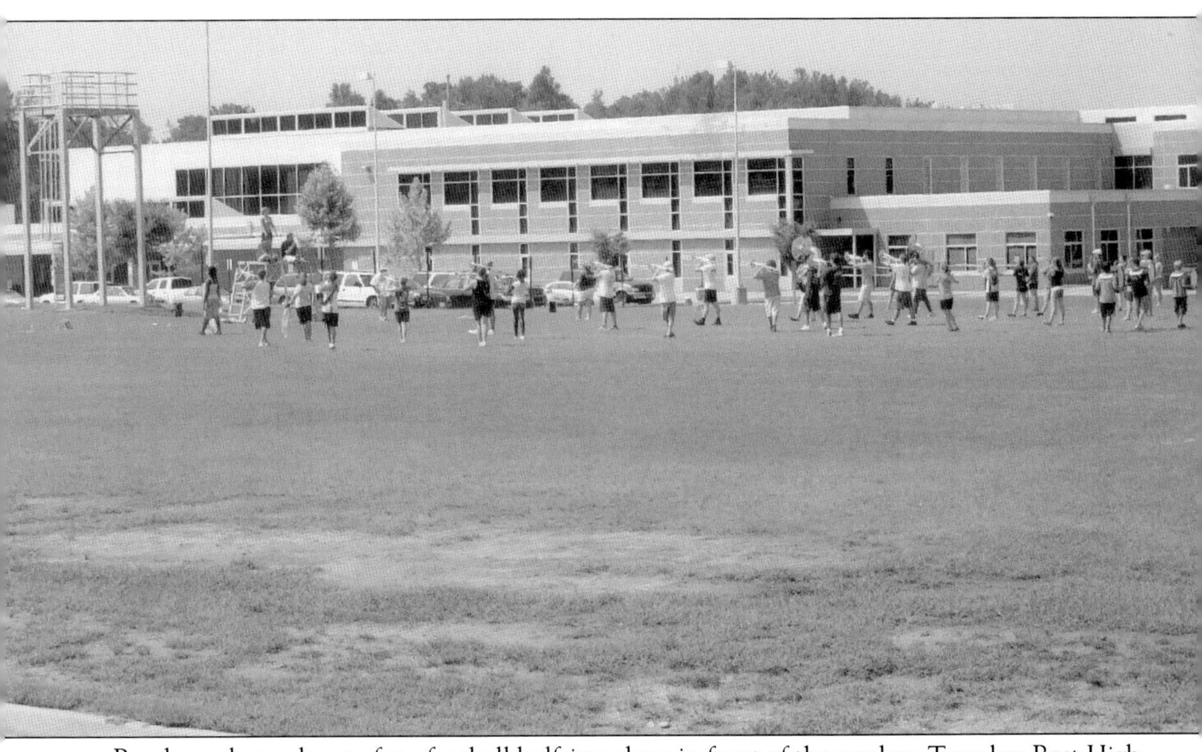

Band members rehearse for a football halftime show in front of the modern Travelers Rest High School, built in 2007. It is located on North Main Street (Highway 276, also known as Geer Highway) on property that was once the Watson/League home.

Five

Businesses

Businesses thrive thanks to the people who continue to work day in and day out to ensure their continued operation. Some of the first businesspeople were farmers and providers of goods to drovers. Travelers Rest, thanks to its location, benefited from the abundance of water, which made it the perfect place for industry. Many cotton gins, sawmills, and gristmills, often operated by just one person, were built in the vicinity of Travelers Rest. As the times changed, the businesses grew, and farmers could be found seeking employment with the mills, especially during the off-crop years. While the city has suffered through the past during down economies, commerce itself continued to thrive. With the onset of newer technology and the outsourcing of jobs overseas, the town has been forced to adjust where business is concerned. Additional banks opened, and larger franchises have moved in. Thanks to a new revitalization effort by the County of Greenville, within whose jurisdiction Travelers Rest is located, businesses are changing; yet glimpses of the town's businesses from the past can still be seen in the present along the streets of Travelers Rest.

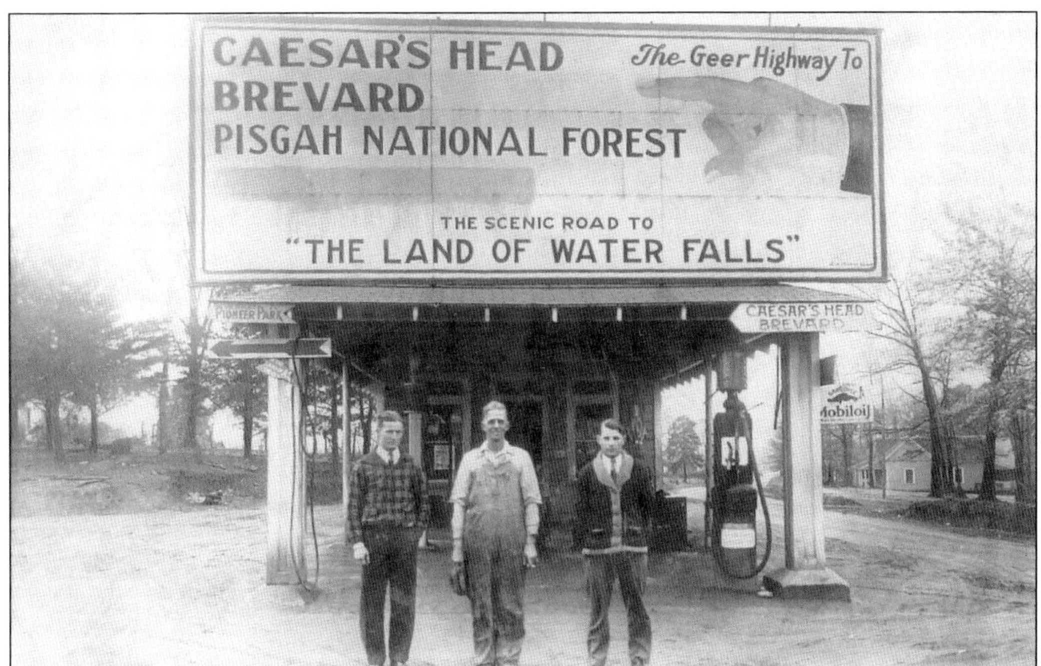

The sign above this old service station located at the junction of present-day Main Street and Poinsett Highway in Travelers Rest indicates that the new Geer Highway will certainly take the traveler to the choice mountain locations. Two of the men in front of the station are Hugh Southerlin (left) and Allen League (right). According to Mann Batson in *A History of the Upper Part of Greenville County, South Carolina*, the highway, built in the 1930s, was named for businessman and president of Furman University Dr. B. E. Geer, who was most influential in the construction of the major road to Caesar's Head. Furman University owned Caesar's Head at that time.

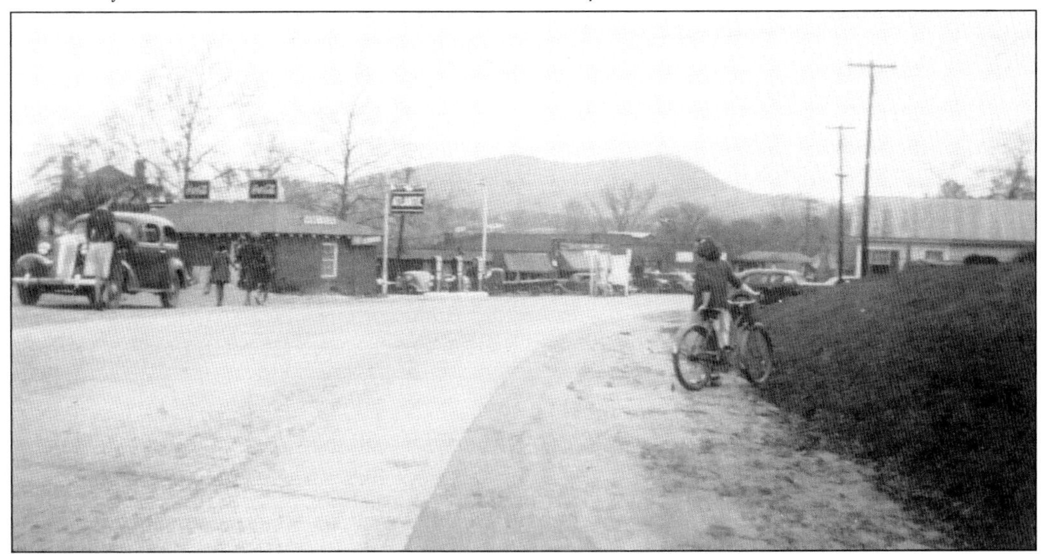

This photograph shows the back of the Holtzclaw Atlantic service station at the junction of present-day Main Street and Poinsett Highway. Paris Mountain formed the backdrop of the business section of Travelers Rest. Other operators of this service station were Ellis Wheatley and James Willis. It was torn down when Main Street was widened.

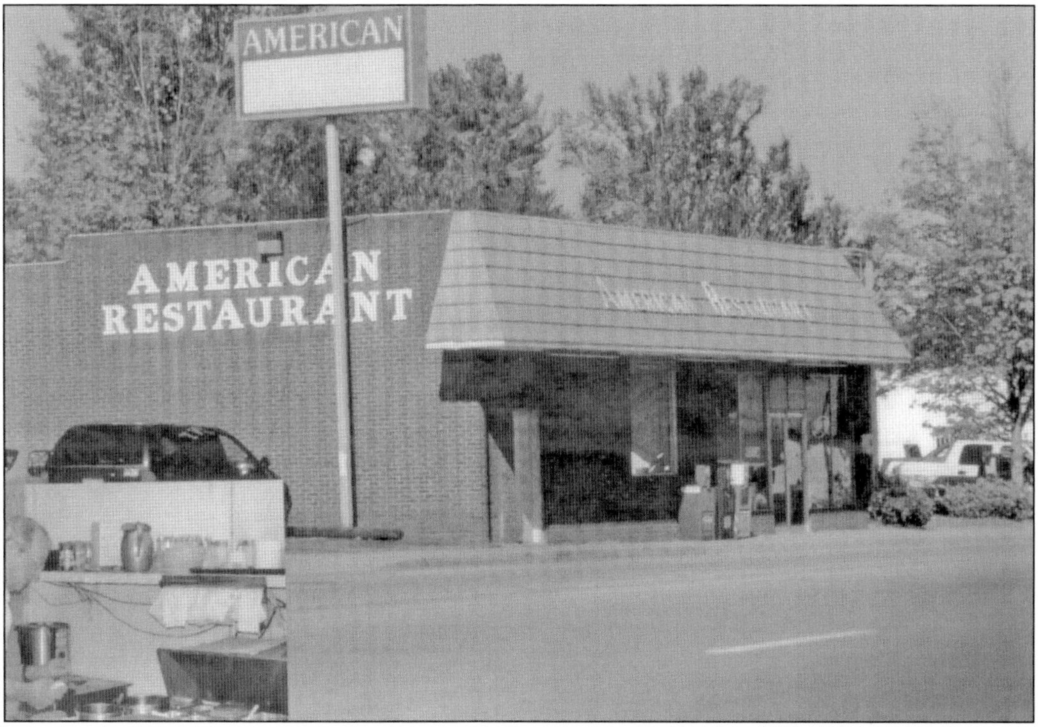

In 1932, Arthur Williams Sr. erected a new building on Main Street called the American Café. In 1943, it was purchased by Roy Styles, and in 1945, Troy Styles purchased the business. Troy Styles Jr. followed his father and operated the restaurant until it closed in 2009. Local citizens used the names café and restaurant interchangeably.

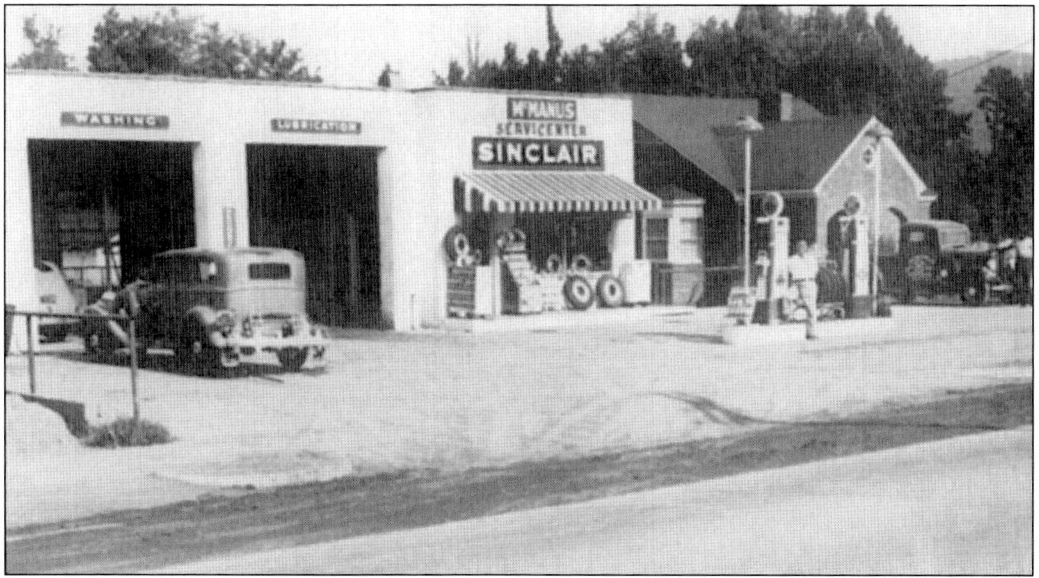

The service station on South Main Street was in business for many years. At the time this photograph was taken it was the McManus Sinclair station, and at one point it was owned and operated by Ray McAlister. The building has been used an EMS base, a beauty salon, a motorcycle shop, a car-detailing business and, as of 2011, a barbershop.

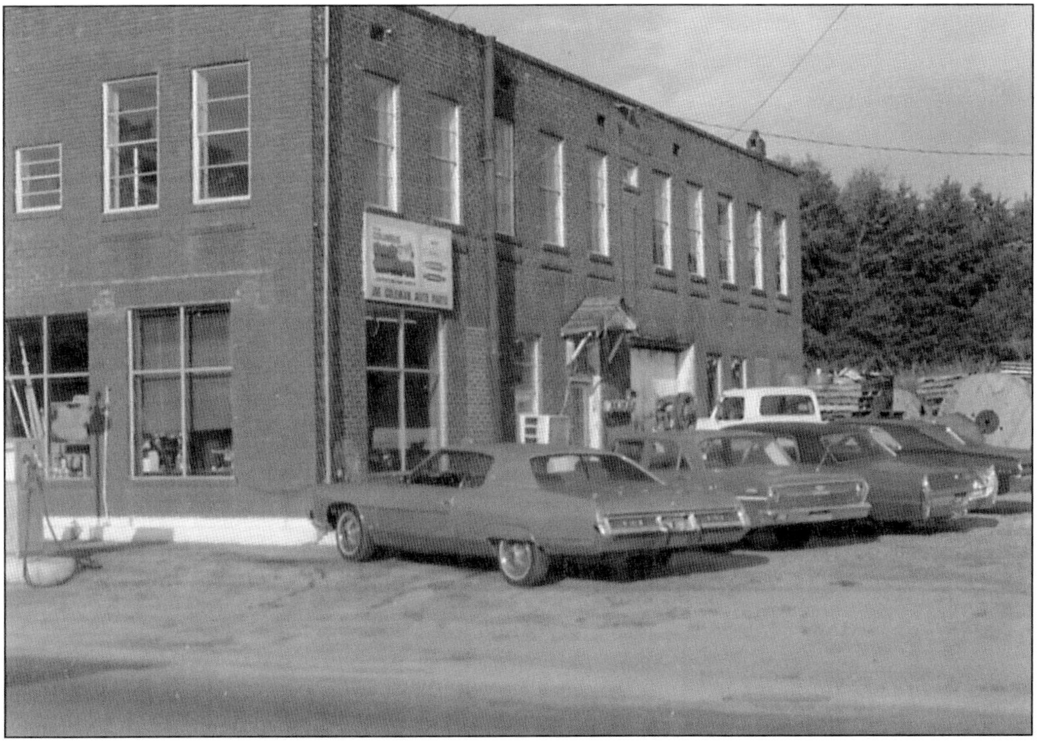

Mildred Goodlett stated in *Travelers Rest at Mountain's Foot* that the Joe Coleman Auto Parts Firm and the Joe Coleman Iron and Metal Company were both established in 1931. In 1941, the auto parts firm moved into the Stamey Building on Buncombe Road (now Main Street), and in 1952, Millard Drake became co-owner. The iron and metal company played a vital role in the war effort during the 1940s, shipping nearly 1.7 million pounds of scrap metals, 220,000 pounds of nonferrous metals, and 110,700 pounds of scrap tin for this critical national need. The firm was honored by the U.S. War Production Board in 1942.

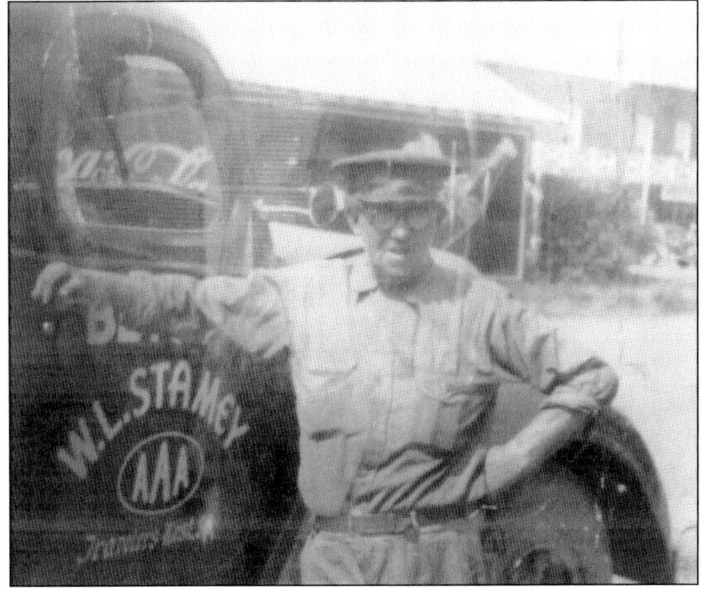

Luther Stamey set up a successful business in Travelers Rest in 1920. He later built a two-story brick building next door to George Coleman Motors on Buncombe Road (now Main Street). Stamey, a skilled mechanic, constructed a wrecker using an old truck and a wooden frame. This homemade wrecker was called "Old Betsey." The wrecker and Stamey were familiar sights in Travelers Rest as well as a larger area of the Carolinas in the years from around 1920 until 1955. Betsey could do jobs when other wreckers failed.

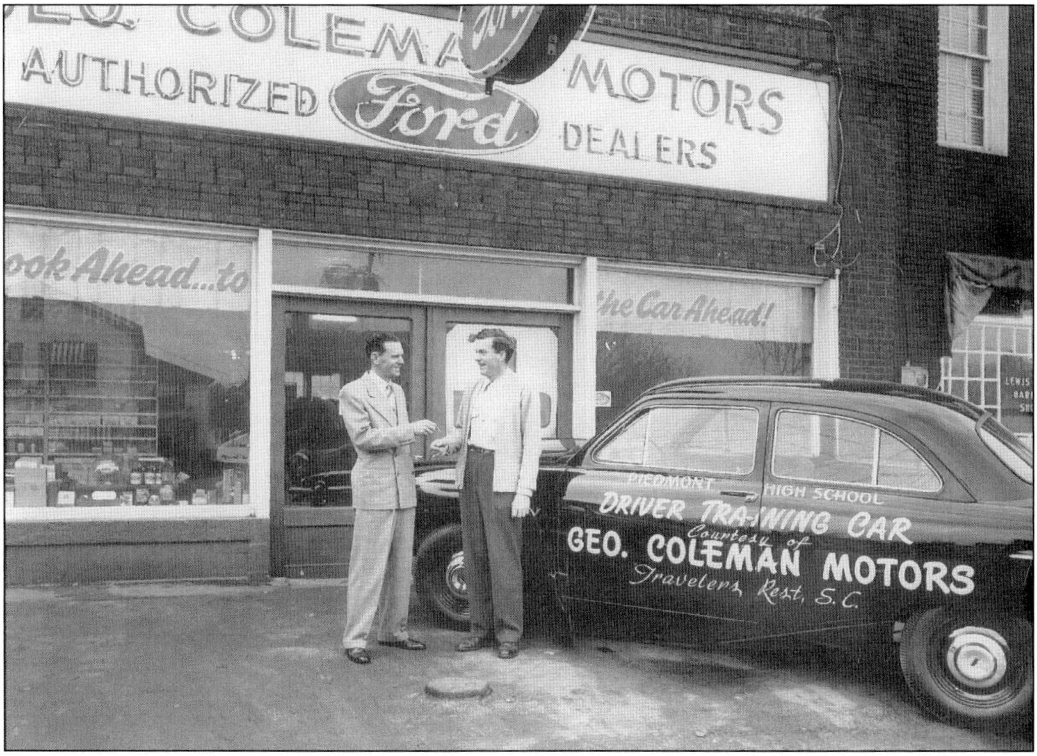

The Coleman-Benson Ford Dealership opened in 1930 in a brick building (above) built by Earle Benson and George Coleman Sr. on Buncombe Road (now Main Street) in Travelers Rest. Benson sold his partnership in 1934, and Coleman continued operation in this location until 1963, when he relocated the business to the new Highway 25 Bypass (below), according to Mildred Goodlett in *Travelers Rest at Mountain's Foot*. The original building was demolished, and the site is now a municipal parking lot. George Coleman Motors has been owned and operated by three generations of Coleman family members: George Sr., George Jr., and Greg. This is the oldest business in Travelers Rest owned and operated by the same family.

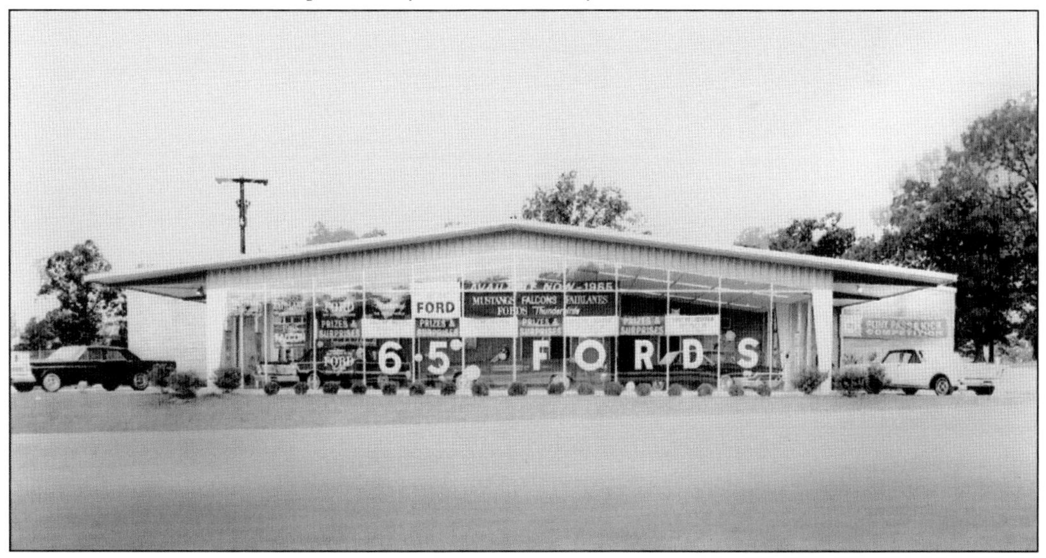

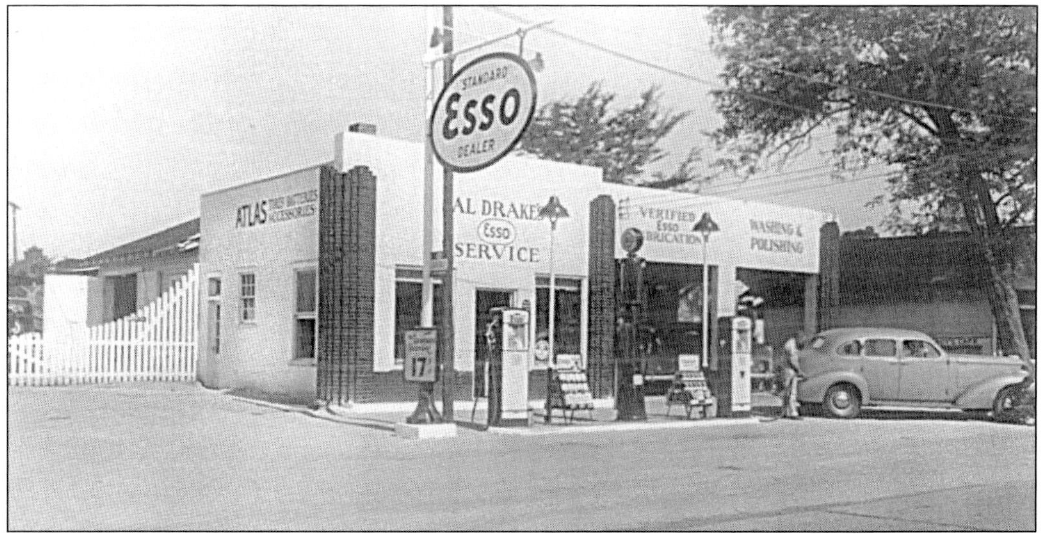

This photograph shows Al Drake pumping gas at his Esso service station, which was the first modern full-service station in Travelers Rest. A recapping shop was located at the rear of the building on the other side of the white picket fence. The entrance to the women's restroom was on the side of the station and was equipped with a heated commode seat. Drake was also responsible for keeping the first fire truck in Travelers Rest at the Esso station. A siren on the roof announced fires for the volunteer firefighters. The service station phone was used to receive calls concerning fires, and Drake almost always drove the fire truck.

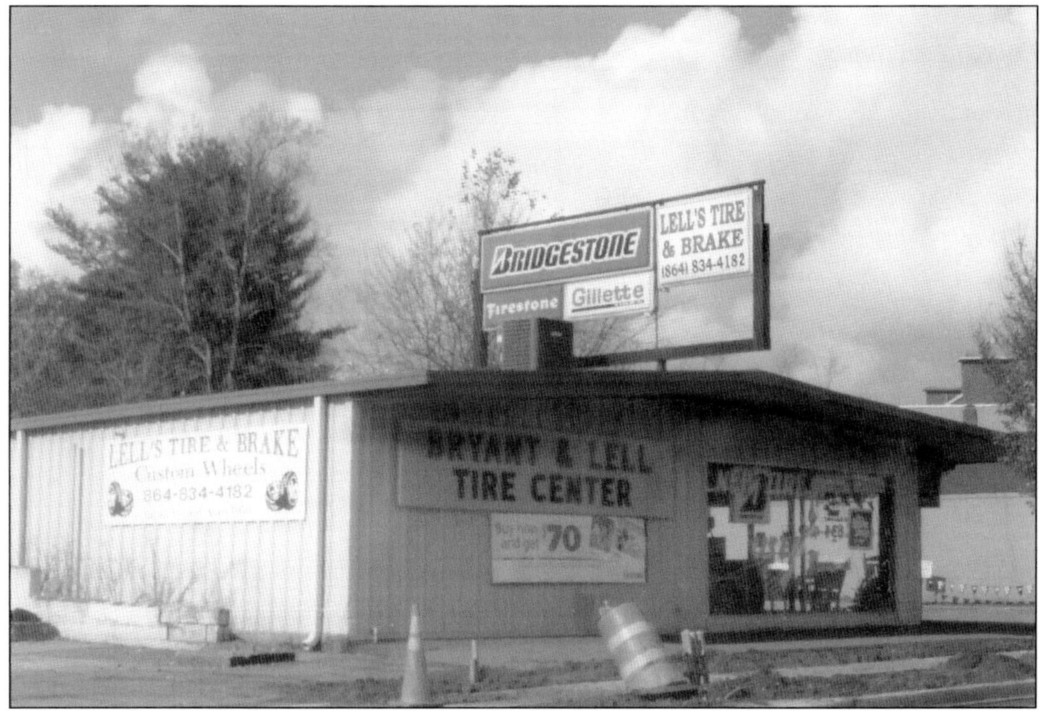

B. E. Bryant and Jerry Lell opened the Bryant and Lell Tire Center at 35 South Main Street in 1960 on the site of the Drake's Esso station. The business has been known as just Lell's Tire and Brake since Bryant retired in 1980.

Alvin Blane Batson came to Travelers Rest in April 1931 as a distributor of Esso products for the Standard Oil Company. His gasoline and oil territory extended as far as the North Carolina state line. His plant was located near the site occupied by the North Greenville Food Crisis Ministry on South Main Street from 2003 to 2011. He retired from the business in 1958.

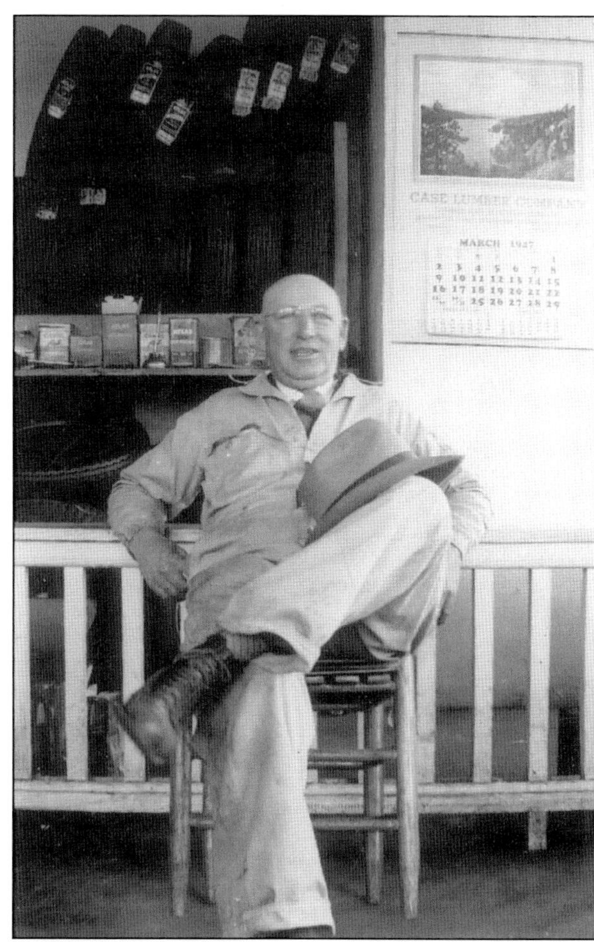

The building at 27 South Main Street was built in 1930 by Marshall Garrett and was operated as a hardware store first by Garrett, then by Dick Williams, and later by Raymond Williams. In 1945, Garrett Furniture opened with brothers Alton, Jack Jr., and Calvin Garrett (Marshall's nephews) as owners. Garrett Furniture was in business in this location until Calvin's retirement in 1997. The building later served as home of the Shops at 27 South Main, and in 2011, Leopard Forest Coffee Company, several specialty shops, and businesses occupy this historic building.

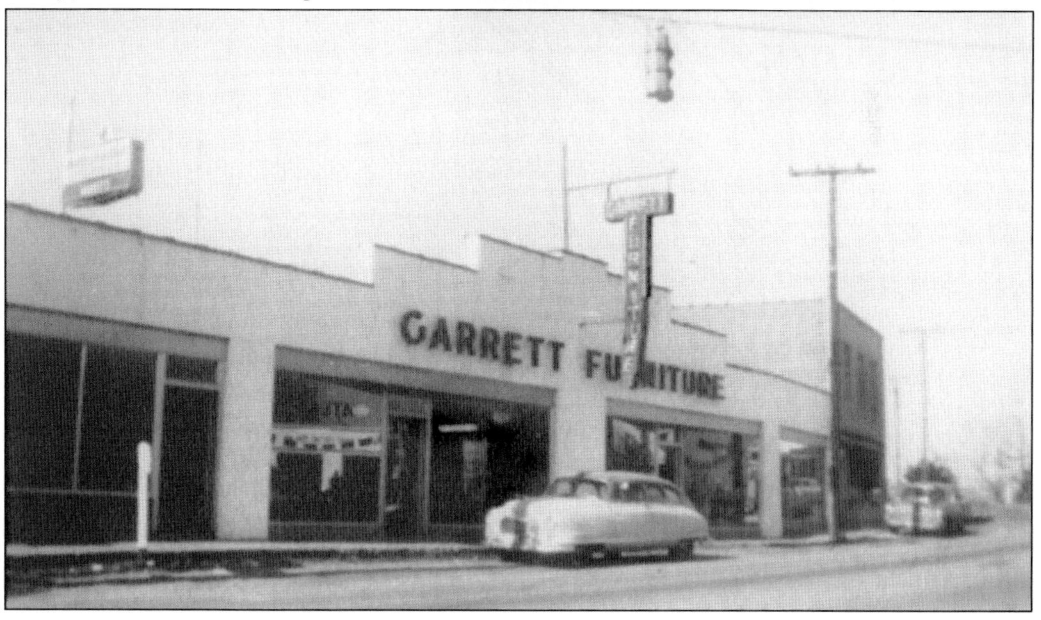

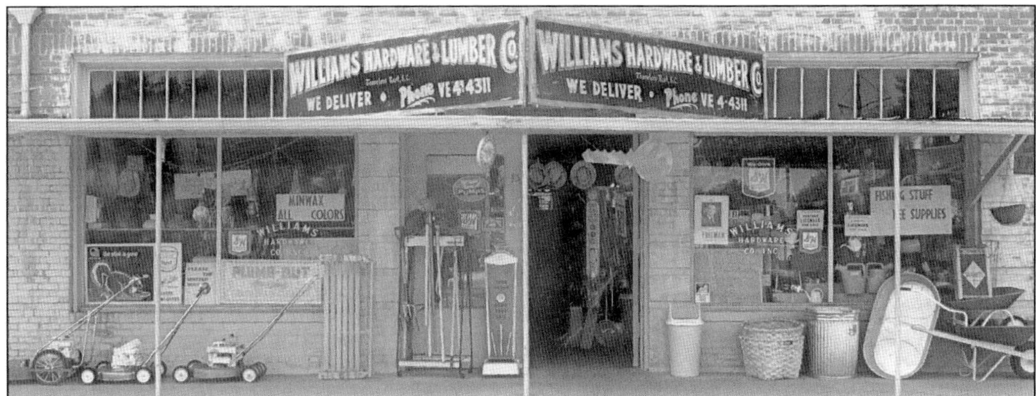

W. R. "Dick" Williams Sr. opened a hardware store in the Garrett Building in Travelers Rest in 1933. Raymond Williams joined his father in the business in 1936. Ten years later, he built a hardware store at 13 South Main Street and established a lumberyard and planer mill adjoining the store. After Raymond's death in 1980, the hardware store was owned and operated by several people, and it became the home to a music store for several years. In 2009, sisters Joyce and Nancy McCarrell renovated the building and opened a fashionable gift shop and restaurant called Café at Williams Hardware.

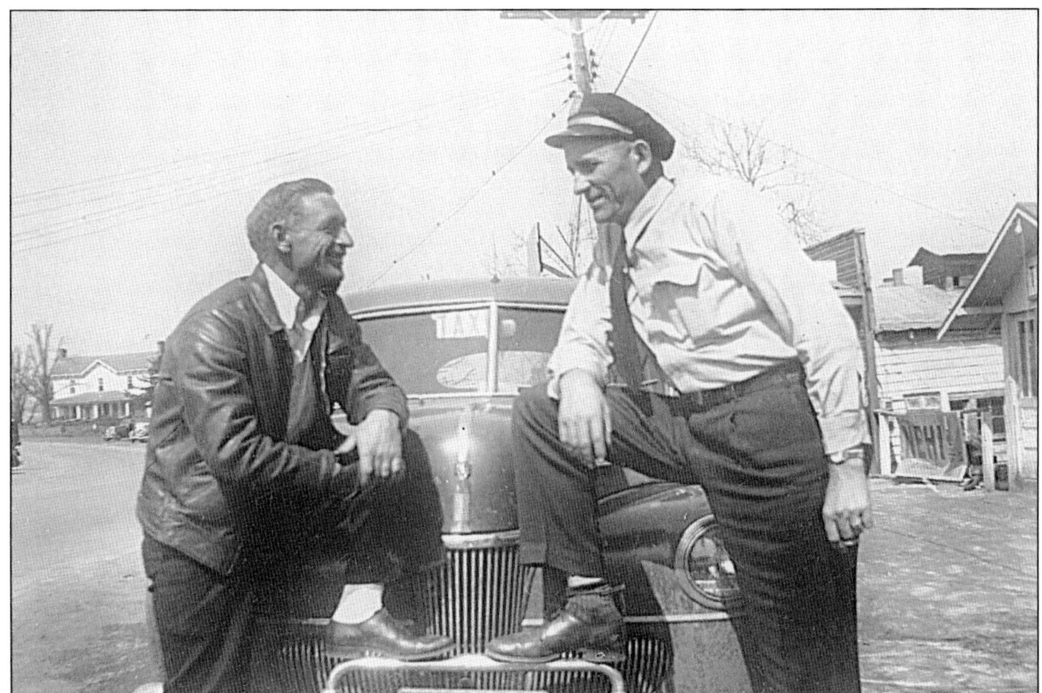

In the early 1950s, many people needed transportation but were unable to own an automobile. Travelers Rest was fortunate to have a taxi service started by J. D. Duncan. B. B. Nix (right), standing with Algie Gilreath, took over the taxi service and operated it in the 1950s. As B. B.'s son Wayne Nix recalls, most calls for the taxi were to take groceries home or to go buy spirits. People who did not own cars would walk to the grocery store, then call Nix to take them and their groceries home. The two cars that Nix used as taxis were a 1947 Kaiser/Frazier and, later, a 1952 Plymouth. For a ride home from the grocery store, the cost ran from 75¢ to $1. A ride to Greenville cost $2.50.

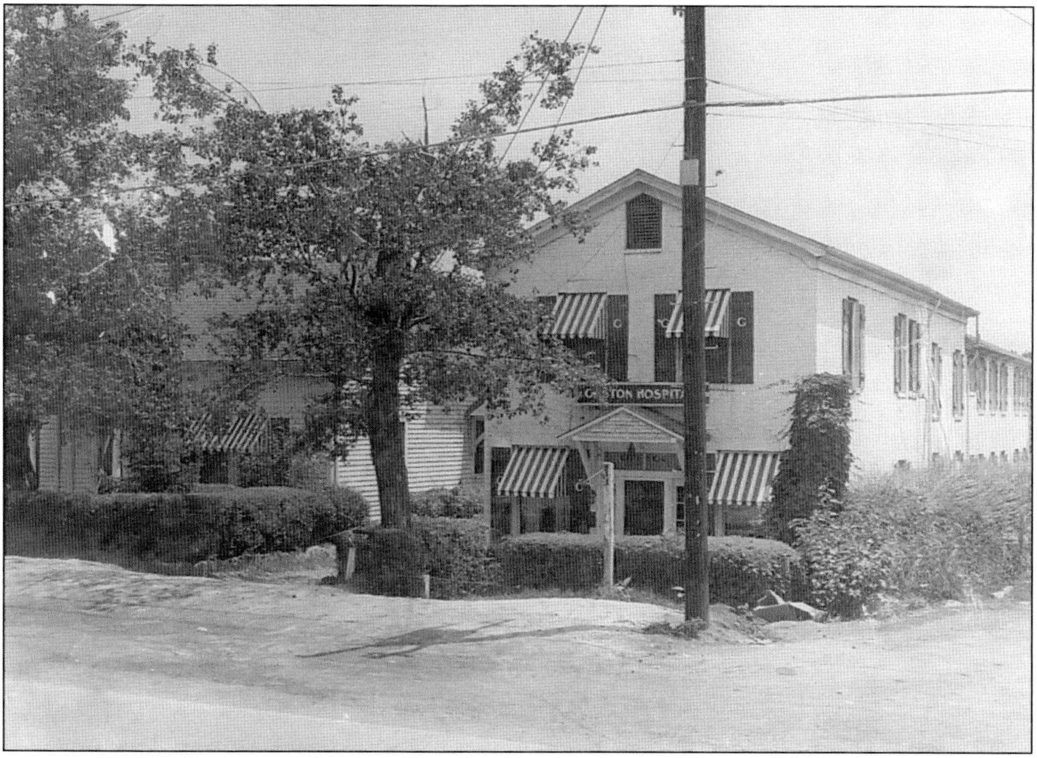

In 1930, Dr. Stobo Roseborough Gaston bought the office formerly owned by Dr. Charles Benson and converted it, and the adjoining house, into the small Gaston Hospital (above). In 1939, he made an addition that provided bed care for 15 patients. Dr. Gaston died in 1957.

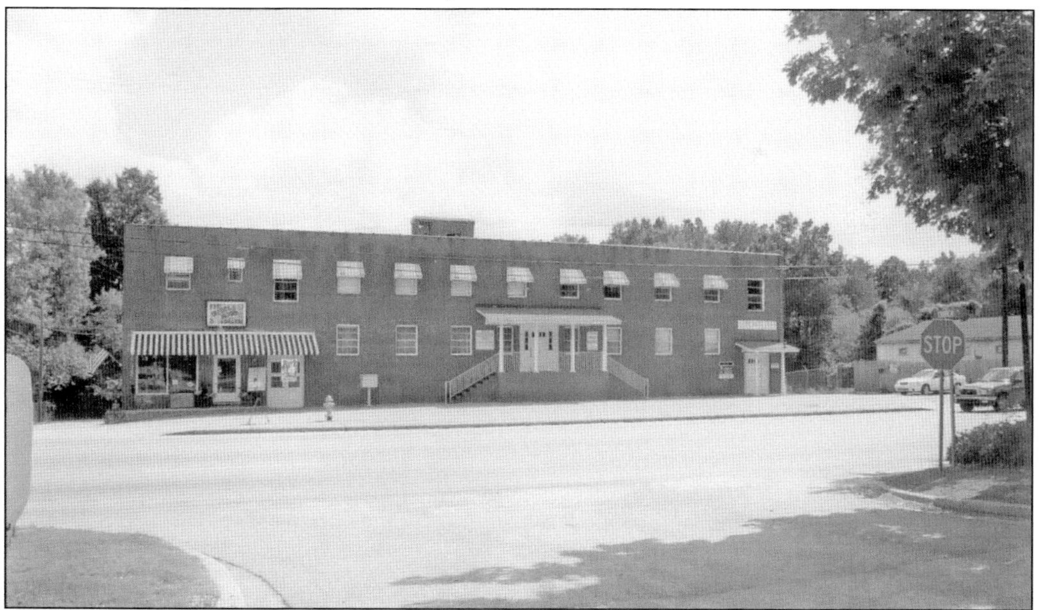

This building was home to Hope Haven, a treatment center for alcoholic patients. Later, various offices were located in the building. Gateway Baptist Church and Wiggle Room Art Gallery currently occupy this location.

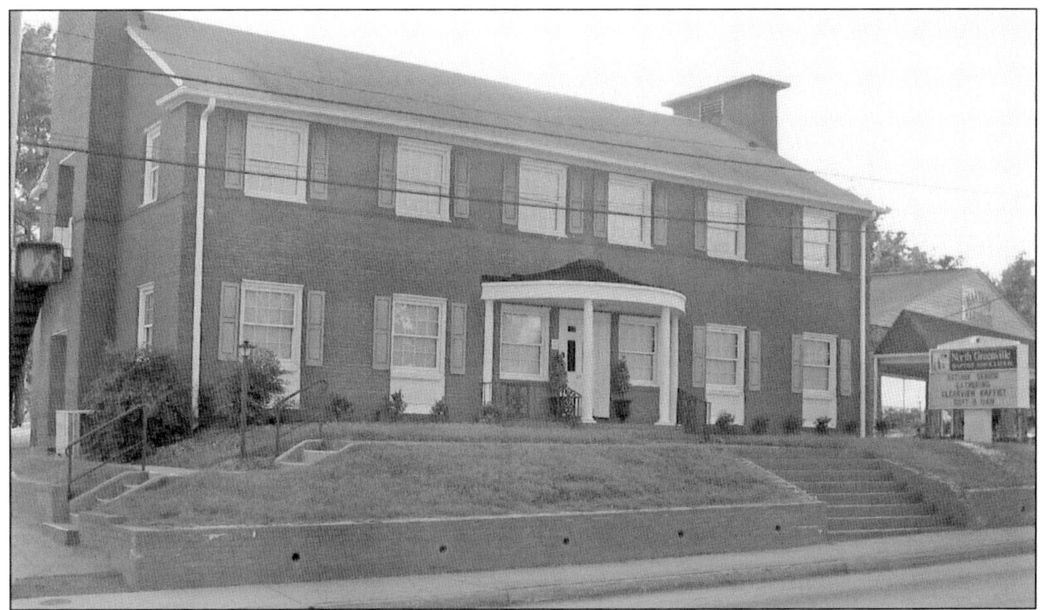

This Williamsburg-style Travelers Rest landmark built by brothers Dr. Thomas E. Coleman and Dr. Stanley Irvin Coleman Sr. was completed in April 1940. Together they operated a general hospital for seven years, and Dr. T. E. Coleman continued to operate the hospital until 1956. In 1960, the building was sold to Travelers Rest Savings and Loan, with the Coleman doctors maintaining offices in the rear of the building. From 1961 to 1971, a branch of the Greenville County Library opened upstairs in space provided by the savings and loan. In 1978, North Greenville Baptist Association moved offices into the building and remain there in 2011. In 1983, the North Greenville Food Crisis Ministry moved into the rear upstairs room and remained in this location until 2003, when the ministry moved to 37 South Main Street.

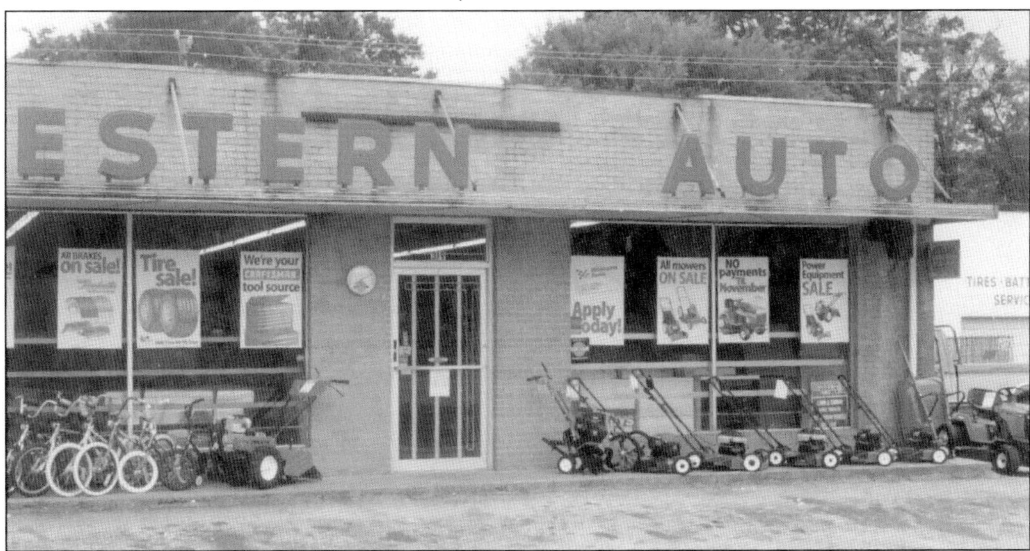

A. I. Edwards opened the Travelers Rest Western Auto store on South Main Street in April 1950. At his retirement, Wayne Nix assumed ownership of the business and continued its operation until January 2004. Trillium Arts Center now occupies the building where Western Auto was located.

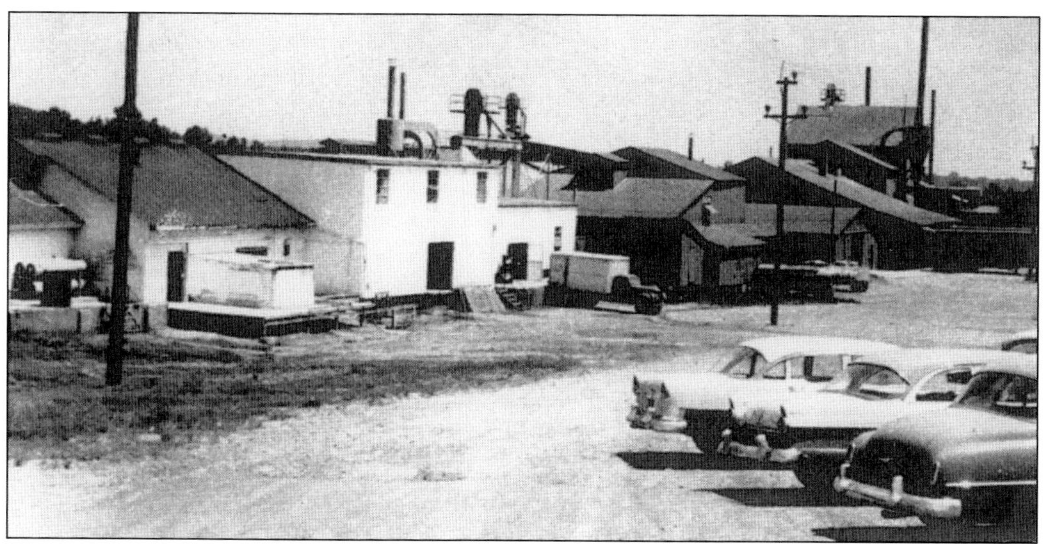

The Zonolite Division of W. R. Grace and Company located to Travelers Rest in 1946 to mine a mineral called vermiculite from deposits near Tigerville. This ore was processed to make lightweight insulation. After 1956, the plant became home to the design group of W. R. Grace. Unfortunately, the vermiculite also harbored small amounts of asbestos, and in 1960, the EPA halted its use. All buildings were demolished in 2010.

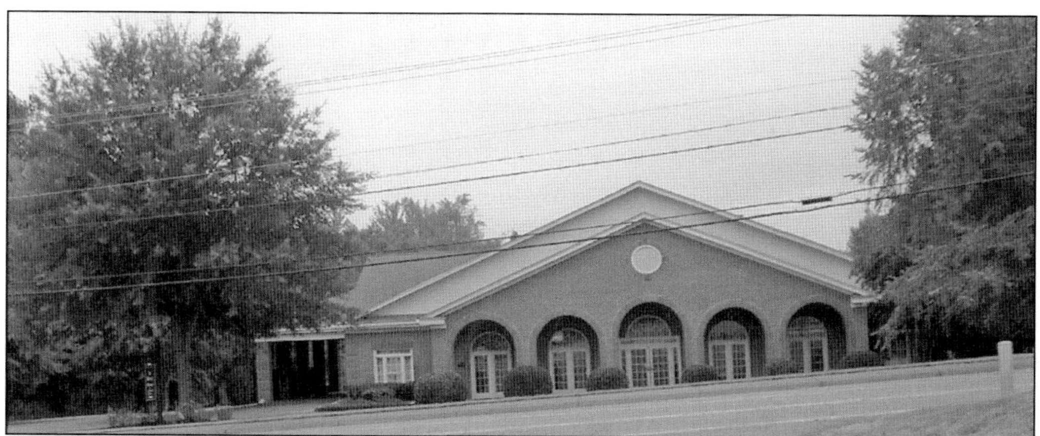

In 1948, Harold Stilwell opened a mortuary on Main Street across from George Coleman Motors, and the following year, he moved the business to the Love home, built in the 1800s, on North Poinsett Highway. Several years later, he and Joe Johnson built a new building across the road, where the business remained until James O'Dell assumed ownership in 1958. In 1963, O'Dell moved the mortuary to the Jim Anderson home at 104 South Poinsett Highway. Townes Howze joined the business in 1972 and operated the mortuary in this location until 1997, when it was moved to the large, modern facility shown at 6714 State Park Road. In 2009, Raymond and Brynda Brown purchased the mortuary from the Howze family.

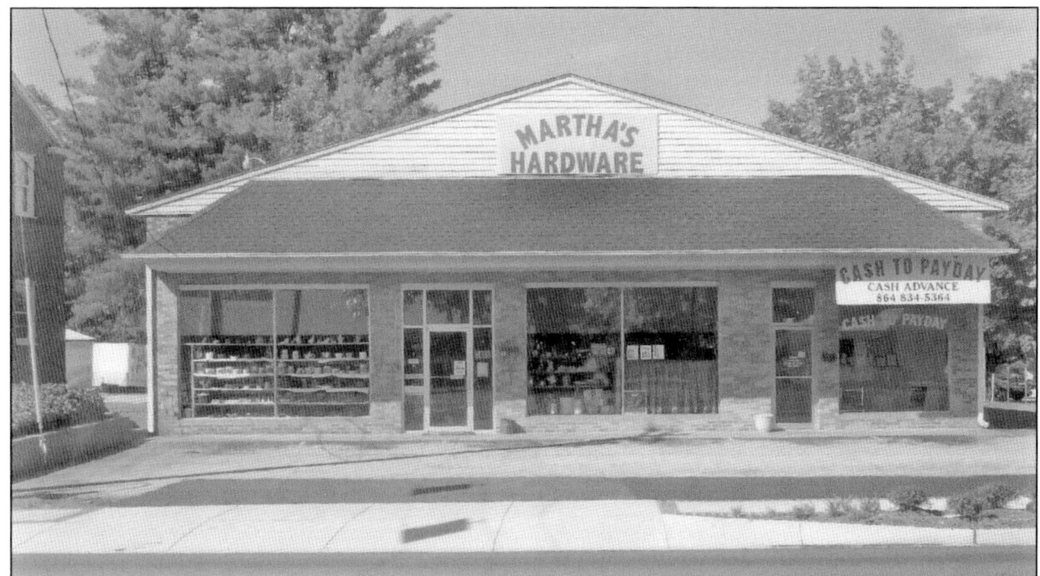

In 1948, Hubert Stokes and Roy Farnham opened a hardware store in a building owned by the Peterson family at the corner of Highway 276 and McElhaney Road. In 1960, they moved into a new building they constructed at 21 South Main Street. In 1981, Calvin and Martha Cox became owners of the building and the business. Martha became sole owner in 1983. In 1996, the name was changed to Martha's Hardware.

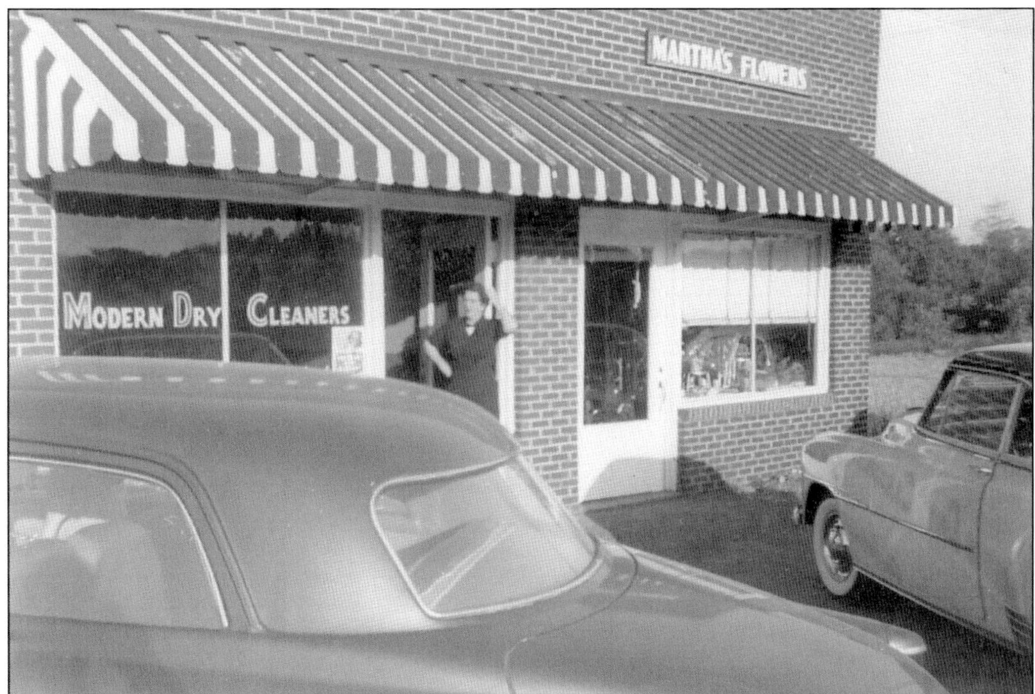

Diagonally across Geer Highway (South Main Street) from Williams Hardware were the businesses of Modern Dry Cleaners, owned and operated by Mae and Vollie Bishop, and Martha's Flowers, owned and operated by Martha Edwards. These were the first two businesses of their kinds in the Travelers Rest area.

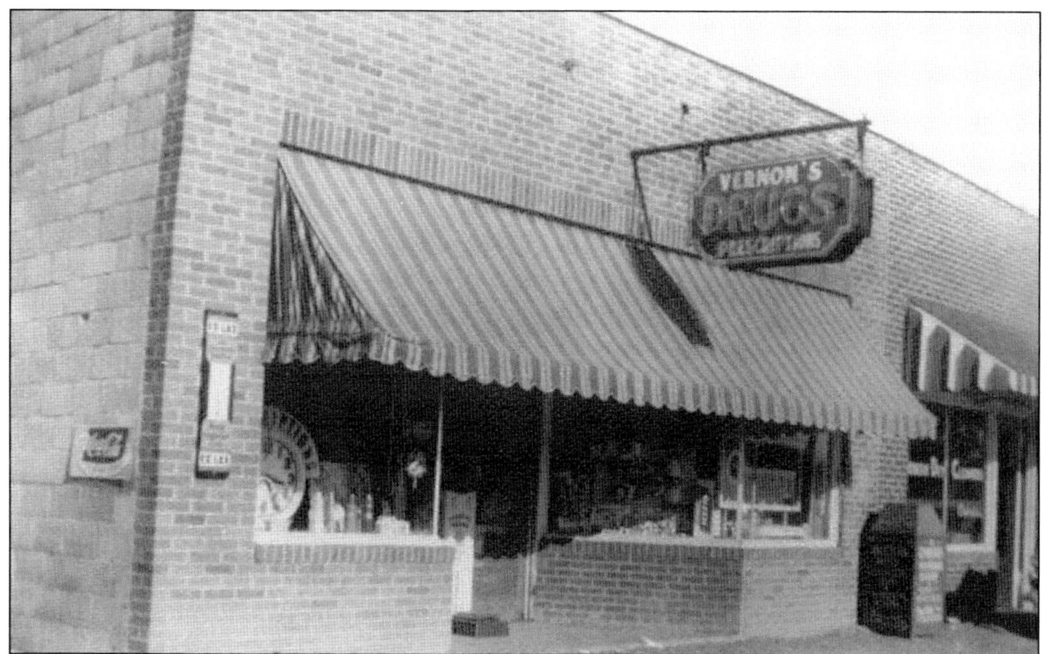

Paul Vernon owned and operated Vernon's Drug Store. He purchased property from C. B. Goodlett and built a drugstore (shown here) that opened on October 16, 1946. Later, Vernon built a larger store two doors above the first building and reopened his business there. The second drugstore opened in January 1964. It later burned, and the business did not reopen.

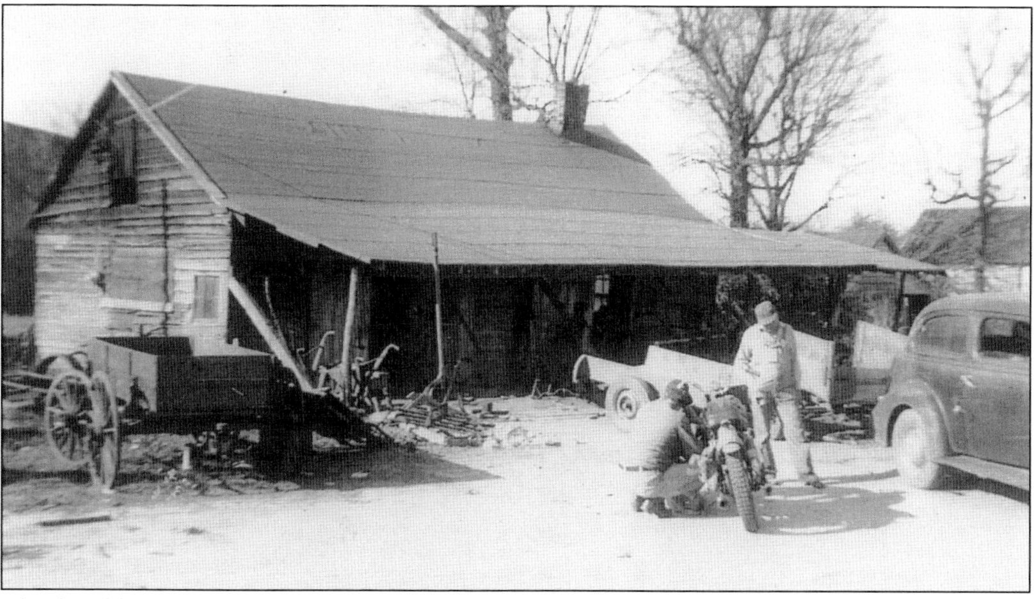

The first blacksmith shop in the village of Travelers Rest was opened in 1869 by Jesse Tate in the area where Sunrift Adventures located in 1995. Mildred Goodlett stated that this location was convenient to the "waggoner" travel of the mountaineers and hog drovers. In 1916, Dr. Earle "Doc" Smith opened a blacksmith shop in the same location and remained there until 1957, when the building was torn down. He then set up a repair shop at the rear of his home on McElhaney Road, which he operated for many years.

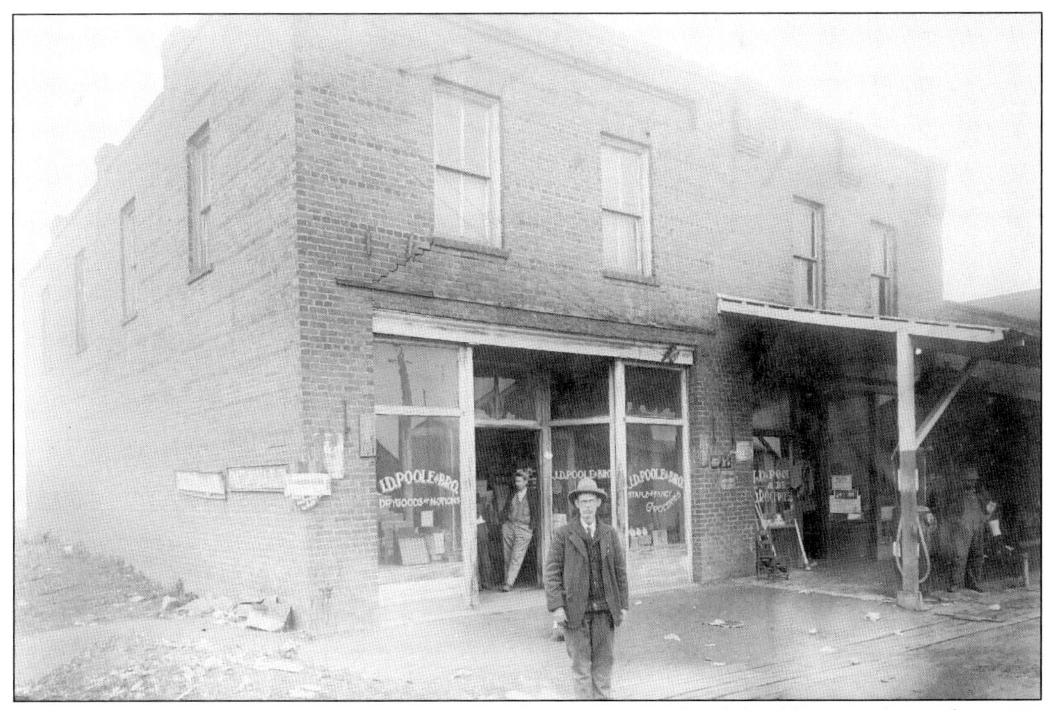

According to Mildred Goodlett, John Roe built a two-story brick building in the early 1900s at the intersection of McElhaney Road and Highway 276. This 1926 photograph shows Jesse Poole in front of the store he operated with his brother Jeff Poole. The lower floor was a general store, and the upper story was a Masonic Hall for a number of years. Tragically, Jesse Poole was struck and killed by an automobile as he walked across Highway 276 (Main Street) in 1930. A number of tenants occupied the building through the years, including the Peterson Hardware Store, Stokes-Farnham Hardware Store, and the medical practice of Dr. John Holliday and Dr. Landrum McCarrell. The building was owned by Grover Brown, and Cromer Childs operated a general store there for many years. The building was finally razed in April 1999, and a car wash is now located on the site of the old store.

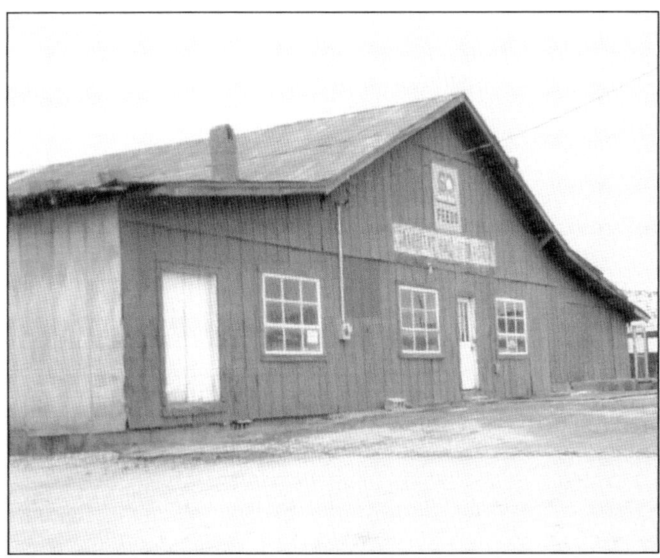

In 1941, James Clark and Harold Drummond opened Travelers Rest Milling Company in J. C. Roe's old building, which had been operated as a livery stable, on McElhaney Road. B. E. McAlister joined the business in 1943, and in 1948, the business expanded into the old Anderson fertilizer store across the road. The name was changed to Travelers Rest Feed and Seed and remains an active, vital business owned and operated by Judy and James H. "Buddy" Clark Jr. In 2011, the site of the original building is occupied by the Travelers Rest Family Practice.

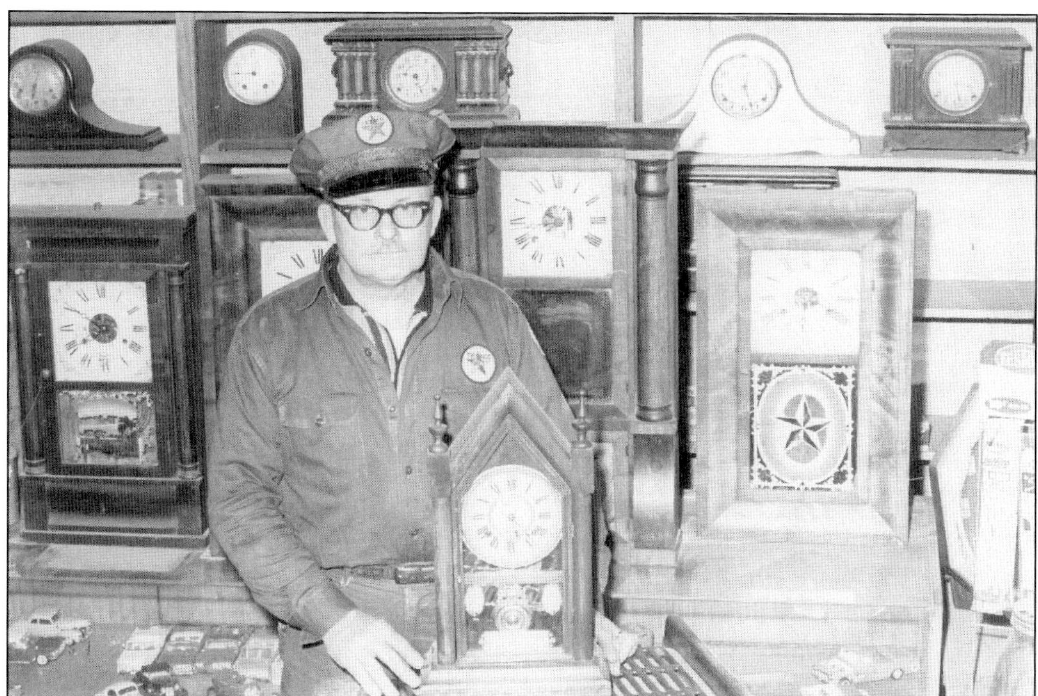

Jack Thacker operated a full-service Texaco station on Highway 276 from 1956 until his retirement in 1987. Thacker was a collector of clocks and also owned several pet parrots. His service station was next door to the ice plant, which provided much-needed ice and cold watermelons in the summertime in the years before ice could be made by home refrigerators.

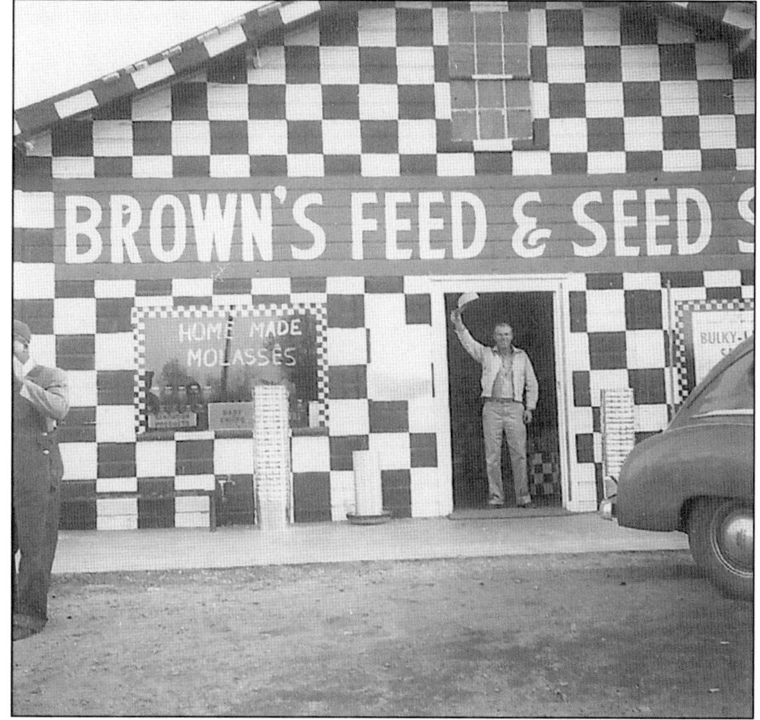

This 1955 photograph shows Grover Brown waving from the door of his feed and seed store in the former Roe Warehouse building at the corner of McElhaney Road and Geer Highway (Main Street). The business was moved across the intersection to the former Blue Ridge Cotton Oil Company building in 1960. The building in the picture no longer stands.

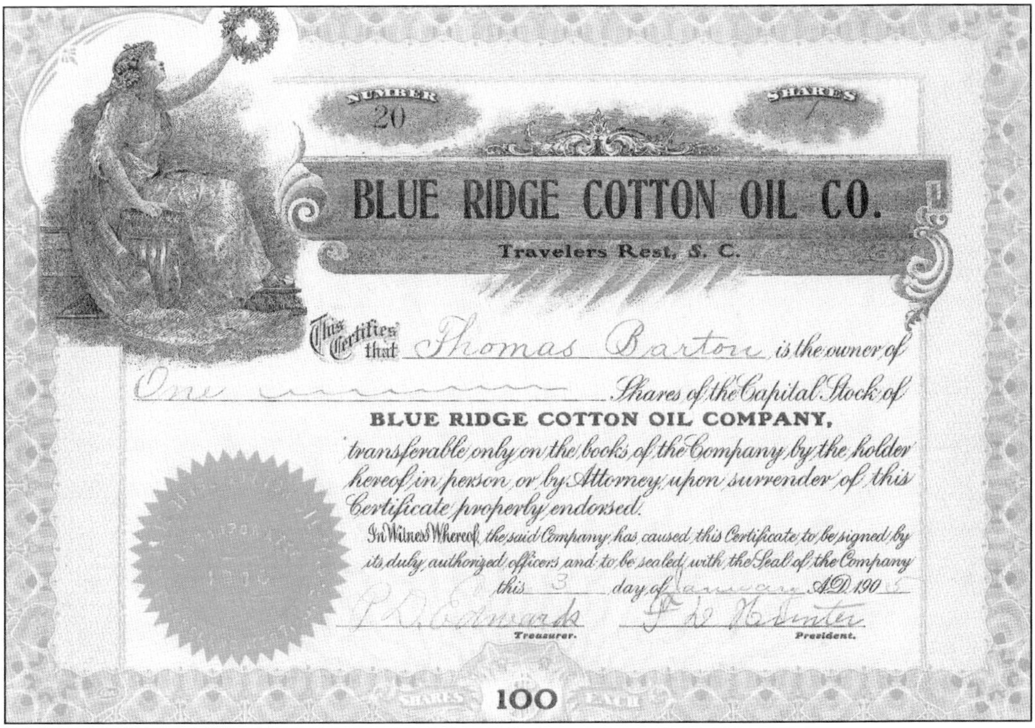

NUMBER 20

SHARES 1

BLUE RIDGE COTTON OIL CO.

Travelers Rest, S. C.

This Certifies that Thomas Barton is the owner of One Shares of the Capital Stock of

BLUE RIDGE COTTON OIL COMPANY,

transferable only on the books of the Company by the holder hereof in person or by Attorney upon surrender of this Certificate properly endorsed.

In Witness Whereof, the said Company has caused this Certificate to be signed by its duly authorized officers and to be sealed with the Seal of the Company this 3 day of January AD 1905

Treasurer. President.

100 SHARES EACH

The Blue Ridge Cotton Oil Company was formed in January 1905 with the "general purpose to manufacture of cotton and oil, cotton-seed meal, cotton seed hulls, and ginnery," according to the company's charter, which was included in Mildred Goodlett's *Travelers Rest at Mountain's Foot*. This oil processing was discontinued prior to 1927, but cotton was ginned at the location for a number of years. In 1960, Grover Brown purchased the building, remodeled it, and operated Brown's Feed and Seed Store, as seen in the photograph below. In 1995, Sunrift Adventures occupied the building and remains there in 2011. This building is located at the corner of Main and Center Streets beside the Swamp Rabbit Trail. (The railroad bed was converted to the Swamp Rabbit Trail.)

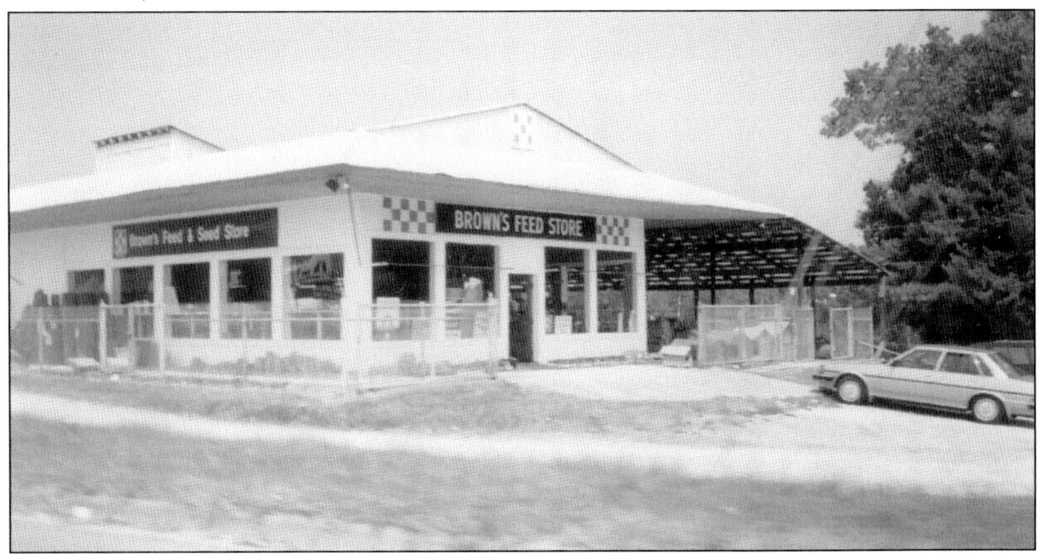

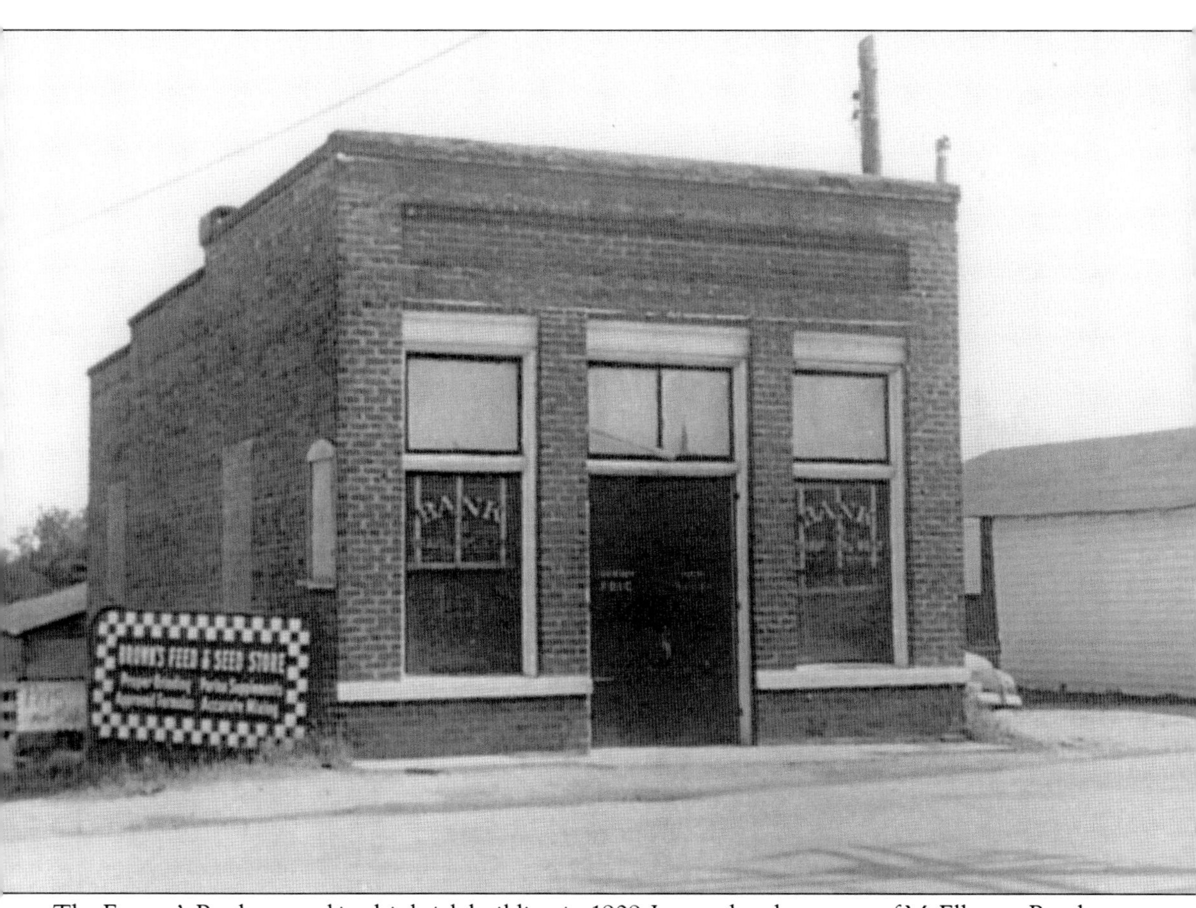

The Farmer's Bank opened in this brick building in 1909. Located at the corner of McElhaney Road and Highway 276, the Farmer's Bank operated until 1932. The Bank of Travelers Rest opened for business in this building 14 years later on March 18, 1946. The small, one-room branch operated Monday through Saturday, making the Bank of Travelers Rest the first bank in Greenville County to offer Saturday banking to its customers on the weekend. The bank assisted customers from 9:00 a.m. until 1:00 p.m. Transactions were made to individual accounts in the afternoons.

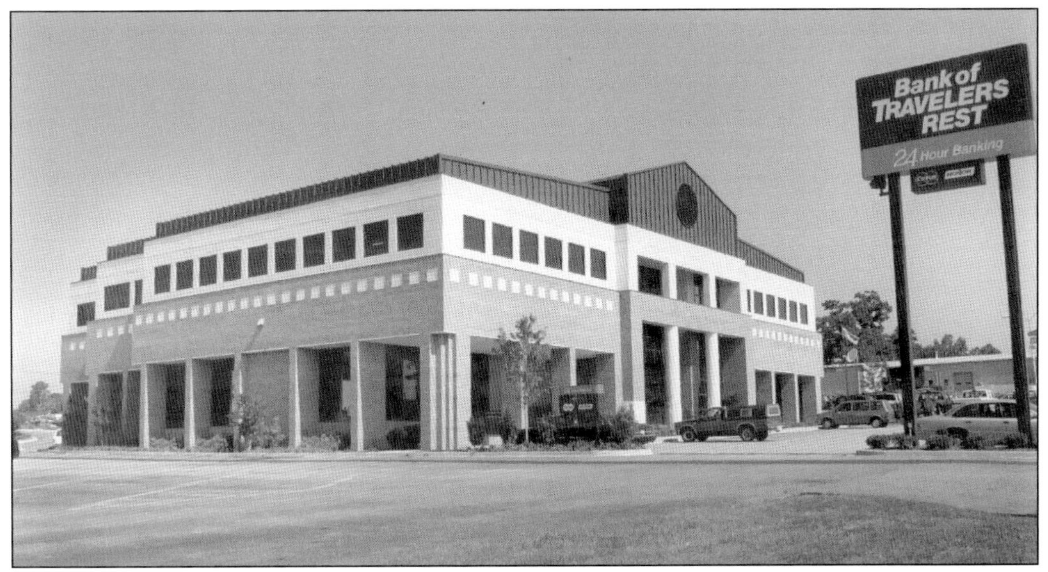

In December 1955, the Bank of Travelers Rest moved to 123 North Poinsett Highway. Modern for its time, the new branch featured drive-in teller windows, 2,000 square feet of floor space, and air-conditioning. In 1977, a much larger office opened at Plaza Drive. This building was remodeled and enlarged, and in 1996, the operations center of the bank relocated here.

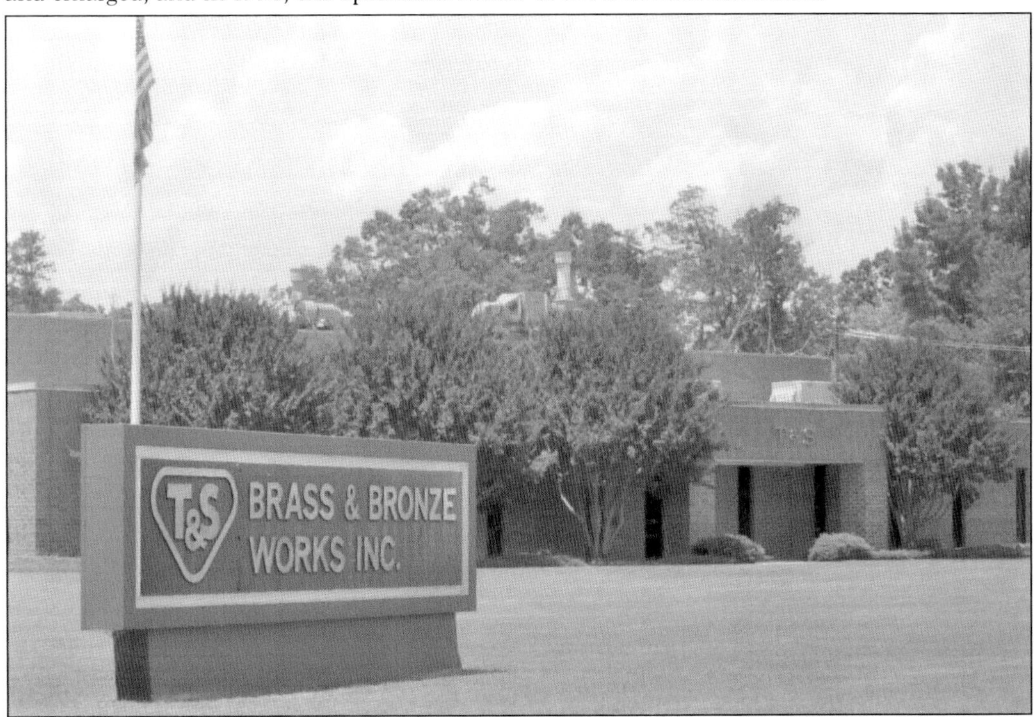

T&S Brass and Bronze Works, Inc., was founded in 1947 and moved to Travelers Rest from Westbury, New York, in 1978. Claude Theisen is president of the civic-minded company, which employs more than 200 people and is located in Saddleback Cove on Old Buncombe Road. T&S manufactures and sells faucets, fittings, specialty products, and accessories for food service, industrial, commercial plumbing, and laboratory markets.

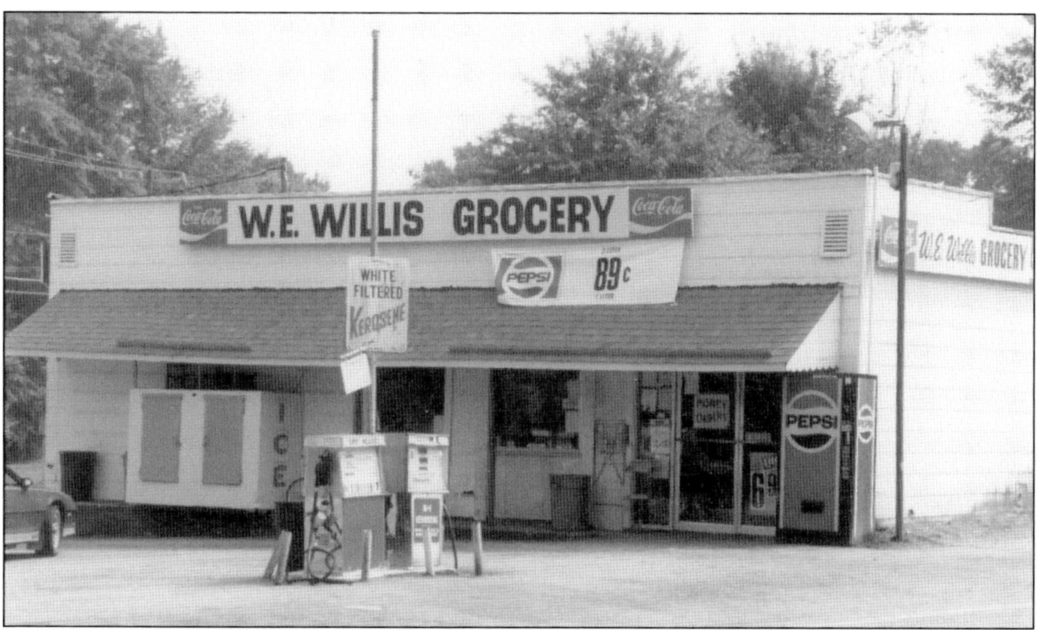

W. E. Willis Grocery, located in the triangle formed by McElhaney Road (Center Street) and Poinsett Highway, has been in continuous operation by the Willis family since the 1930s. J. G. Willis opened the store then sold it to Theron Earle Willis. From the 1930s to 1966, T. E. Willis Grocery was a full-service grocery store offering custom-cut meats and was a popular local gathering place. Theron's son Warren Earle became a partner in 1966 and bought the business at the time of his father's death in 1976. The name was changed to W. E. Willis Grocery, and in 1983, the store became part of the larger company W. E. Willis of Travelers Rest, Inc.

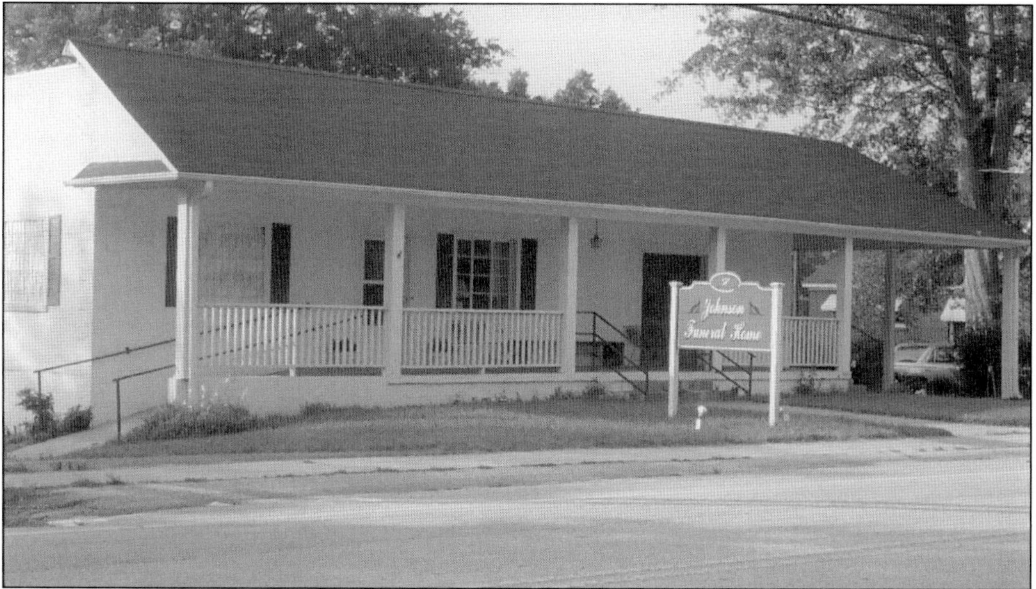

According to Mildred Goodlett, the building at 113 North Poinsett Highway was built by Joe M. Johnson. It was first home to Stilwell Mortuary and then to O'Dell Mortuary. Joe and his daughter Mary Ann Johnson opened Johnson Funeral Home in 1963, and the business has been in continuous operation since that time.

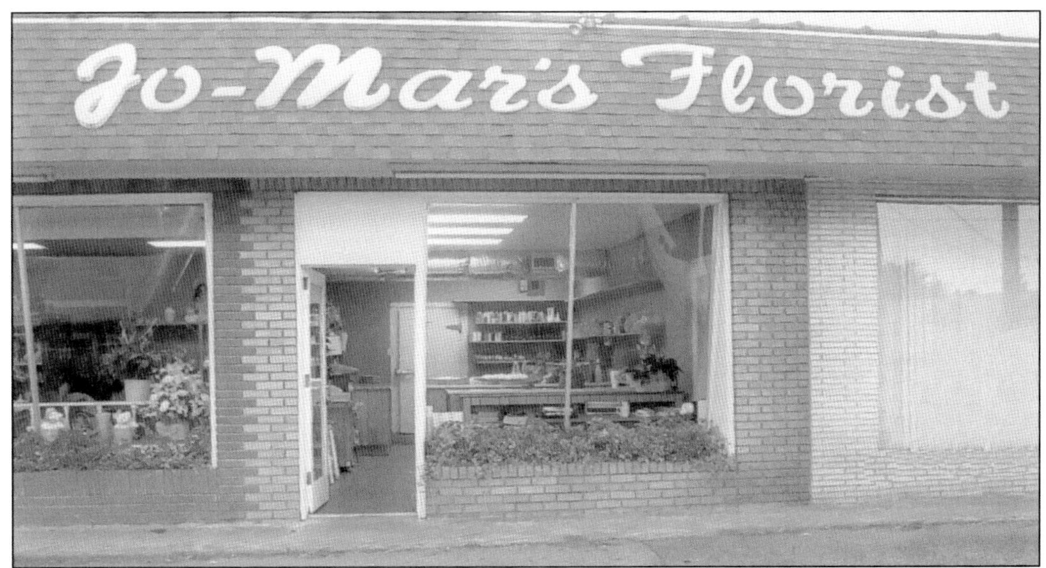

Joyce Clayton Batson and her sister Margaret Reynolds opened Jo-Mar's Florist in November 1970 on North Poinsett Highway. Floral arrangements for all types of events have been prepared by the sisters for over 40 years.

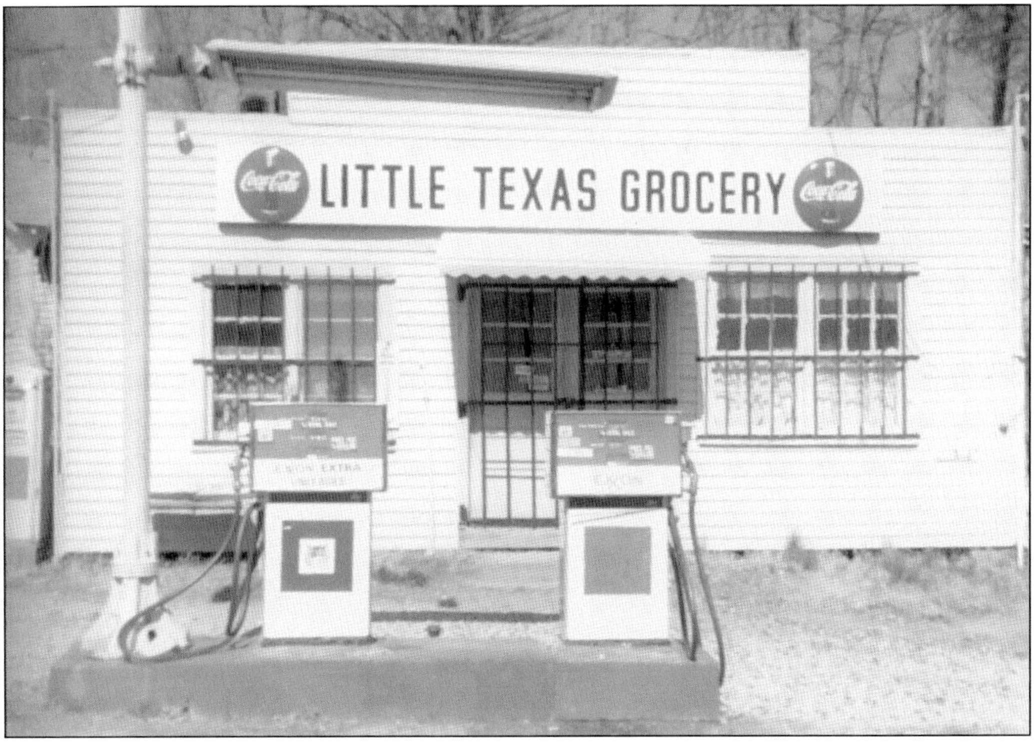

Little Texas Grocery was built by Charlie Davis about 1938, and it was a landmark business in the community. Frank Bridwell operated the store for several years, and Ruth Cheatwood ran the business from 1958 until it closed in December 2009. This general grocery store and the yard surrounding it was a gathering place where people visited, caught up on local news, played checkers, pitched horseshoes, and enjoyed ice-cold Cokes.

Six

Renfrew Bleachery

Renfrew Bleachery was built in 1928 by the Brandon Corporation, and machines from the New England Renfrew Manufacturing company in Adams Massachusetts were used in its operations. During World War II, the bleachery dyed and finished military fabrics. During the 1940s, cooperation between Renfrew and the DuPont Company initiated two textile innovations: continuous bleaching and continuous dyeing units. Visitors from around the world came to Travelers Rest to see them in operation. The bleachery changed ownership several times from 1949 until it was closed in 1988. Renfrew's contributions to the area during the facility's 60 years of operation are too numerous to list. Life in the entire area of upper Greenville County was enhanced as a result of this major textile mill, which employed and provided housing, as well as spiritual and social nurture, to hundreds of local residents. Children of the community were treasured, and activities, organizations, and play space were made available to them. Family bonds were strong, and neighborly concern was woven into the daily life of the members of the Renfrew community.

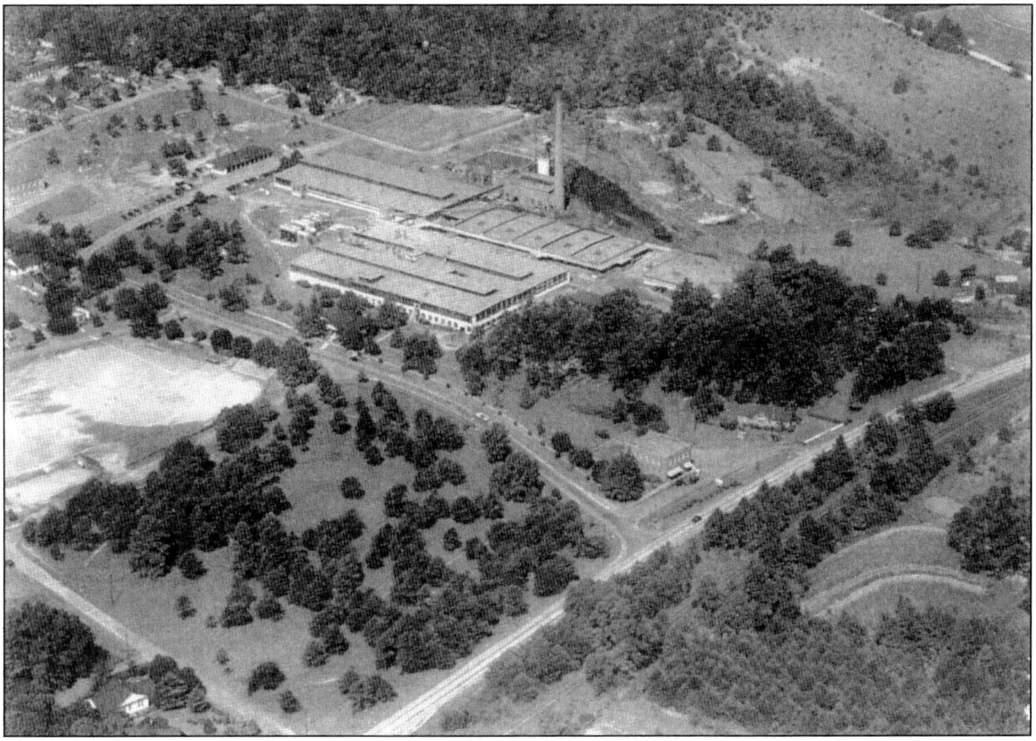

This aerial view of Renfrew Bleachery shows the size and layout of the mill where hundreds of people were employed for the 60 years of its existence. The mill whistle marked time for the surrounding communities, and the smokestack was a familiar landmark, as seen in the image below.

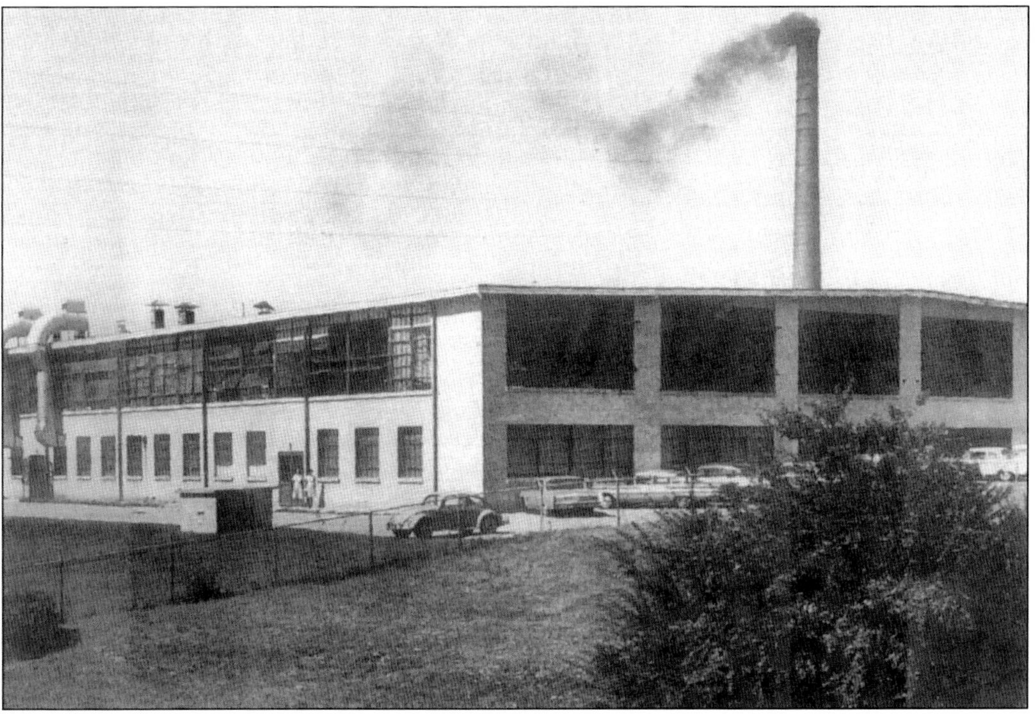

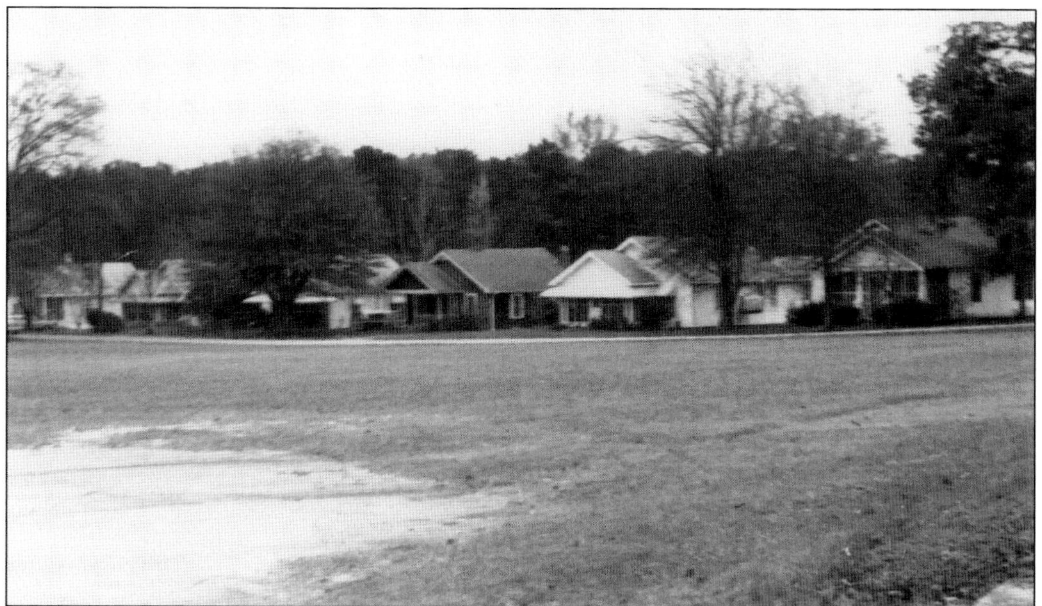

In the foreground of this view of School Street in Renfrew mill village is part of the infield and right field of the baseball park for the Renfrew Rifles of the Piedmont Textile League. The grandstand and dugout are out of the photograph to the left.

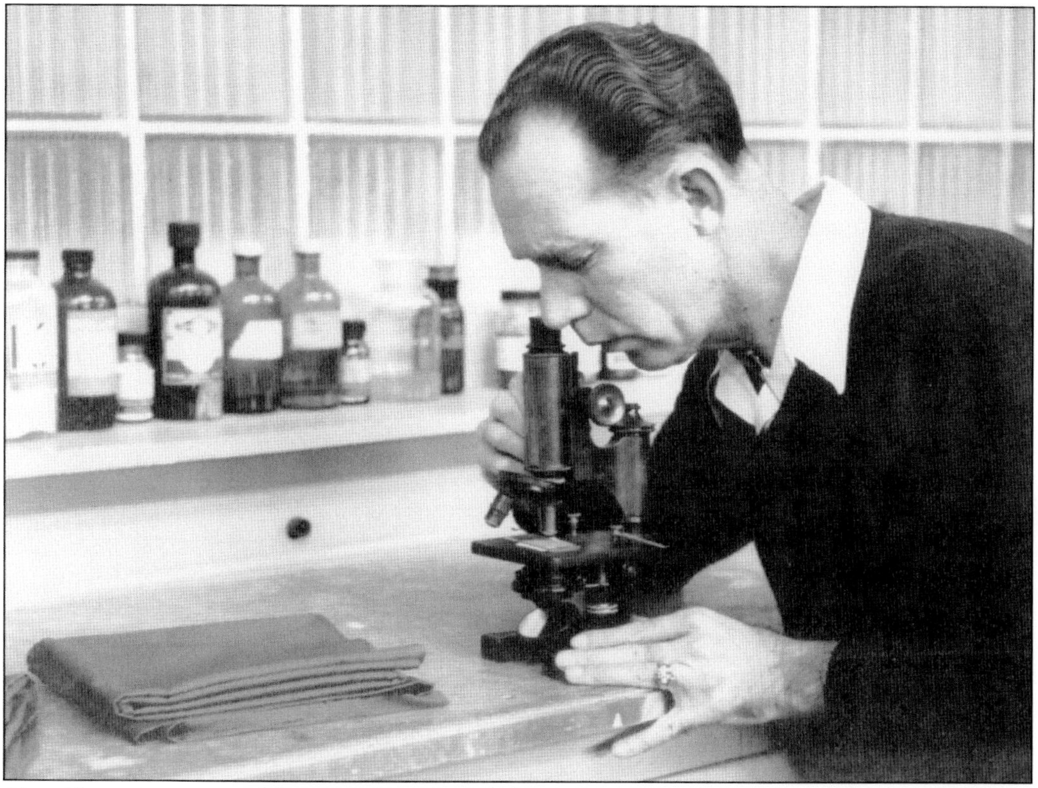

Clint Farmer inspects a fabric sample under a light microscope to better determine the nature of a problem in a defective fabric sample.

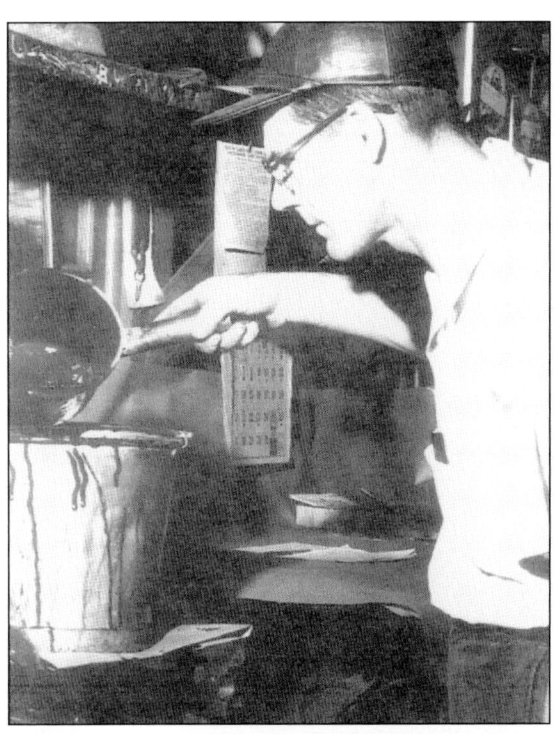

J. B. Duncan is at work in the dye house of the Renfrew plant in the 1960s.

William Ross Sheppard inspects cloth at Renfrew Bleachery to ensure that no defects were shipped to customers.

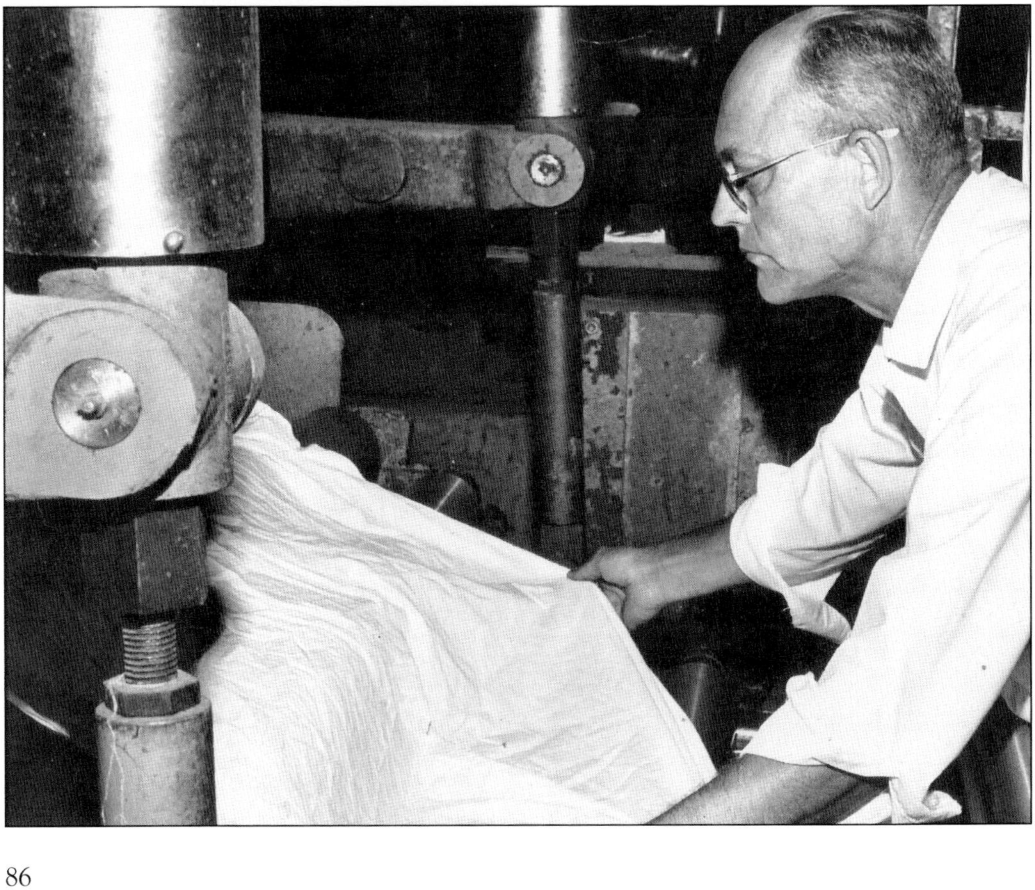

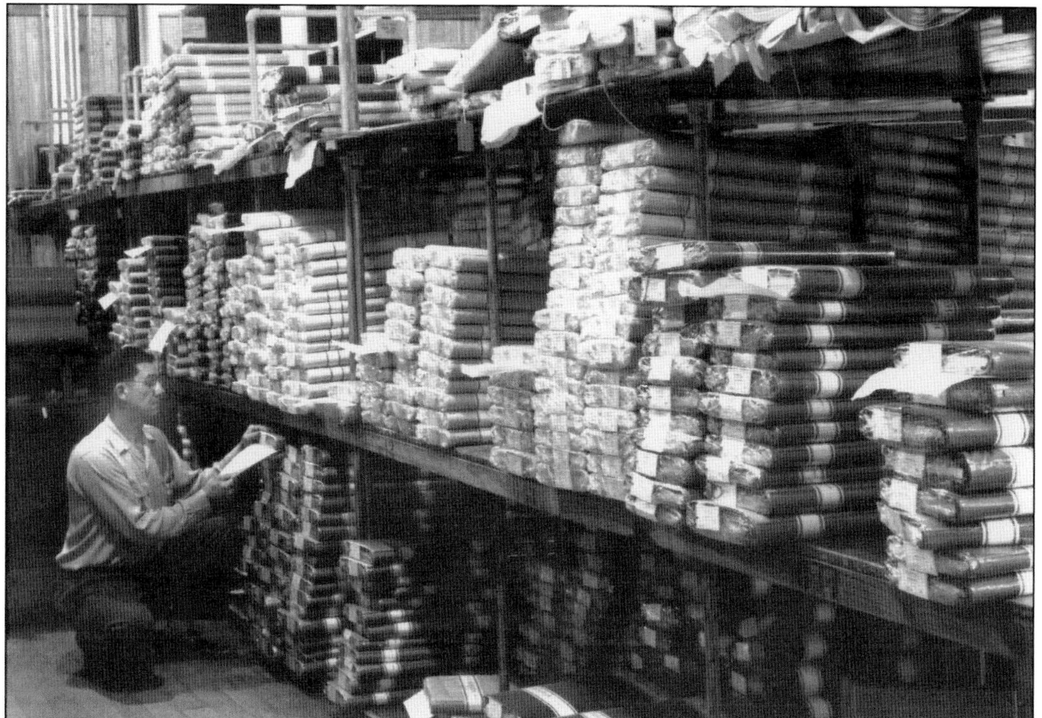

In this photograph from *Echoes*, Volume 13, William Perry Duncan checks cloth that would be sold to customers at the local company store.

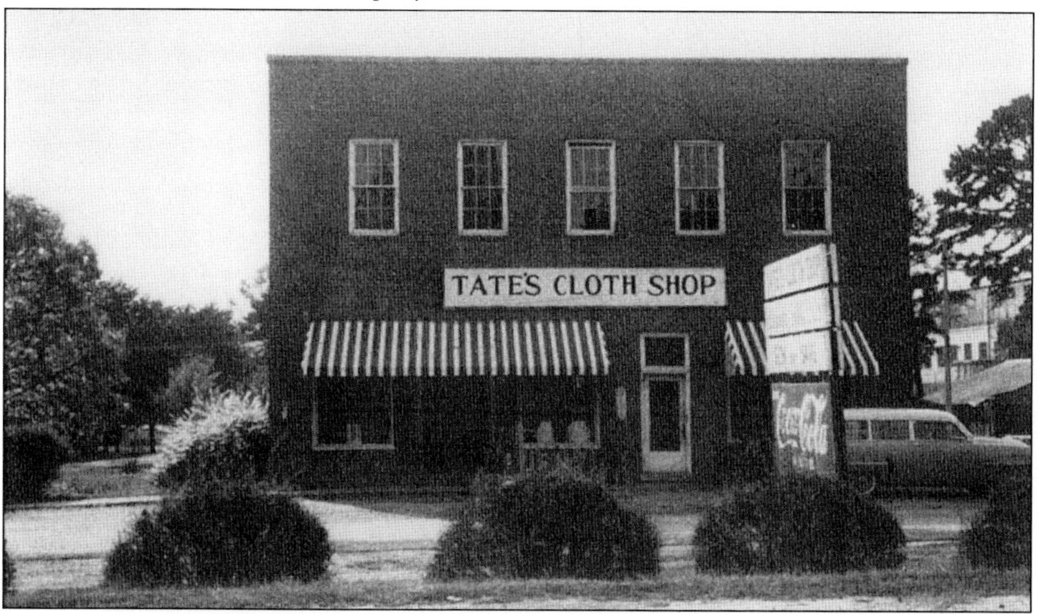

At one time, this building served as the general store for residents of the mill village. People were able to purchase food and clothing without having to leave the village. After the need for a company store ended, Wendell and Kathryn Tate operated a fabric shop here. The building's second floor was known as Renfrew Hall and was used for community meetings, parties, and square dances after high school football games on Friday nights. This building no longer stands.

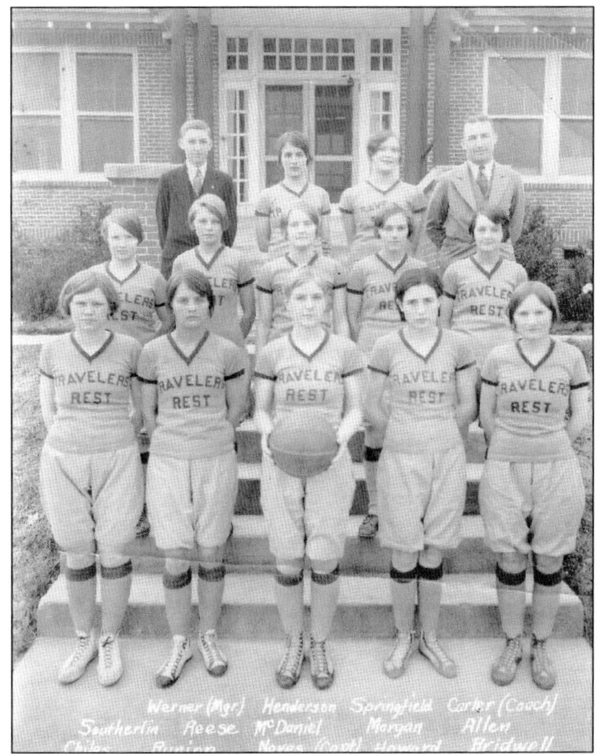

This 1929–1930 girls' basketball team photograph was taken in front of the Renfrew office building. After the Travelers Rest School burned in February 1930, Renfrew Bleachery offered space in houses and buildings for classes and other school activities. Pictured from left to right are (first row) Elizabeth Chiles, Ruth Runion, team captain Daisy Neves, Maggie Howard, and Pauline Bridwell; (second row) Reba Southerlin, ? Reese, Annice McDaniel, Frances Morgan, and Annie Grace Allen; (third row) manager Milt Werner, Faye Henderson, Iva Springfield Simpson, and coach Blackie Carter.

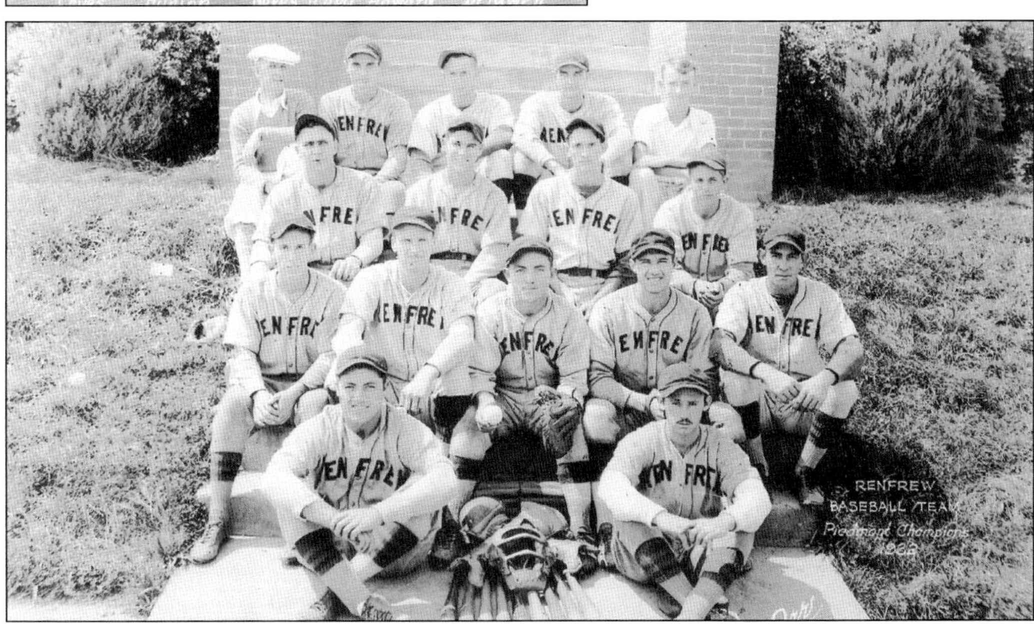

Textile ball was of major importance during the 1930s, 1940s, and into the 1950s. Pictured on the front steps of the Renfrew Bleachery office are the members of the 1932 Piedmont League Champions, the Renfrew baseball team. Pictured from left to right are (first row) Fletcher Heath and Johnny Fox; (second row) Fred Foster, Claude Batson, Chick Heath, Lefty Brown, and Sam Knox; (third row) Ode Medlock, Ted Cabiness, Shag Knox, and George Lindsey; (fourth row) Chester Eddy, Roy Foster, Roy Hogg, Roy Humphries, and James Bishop.

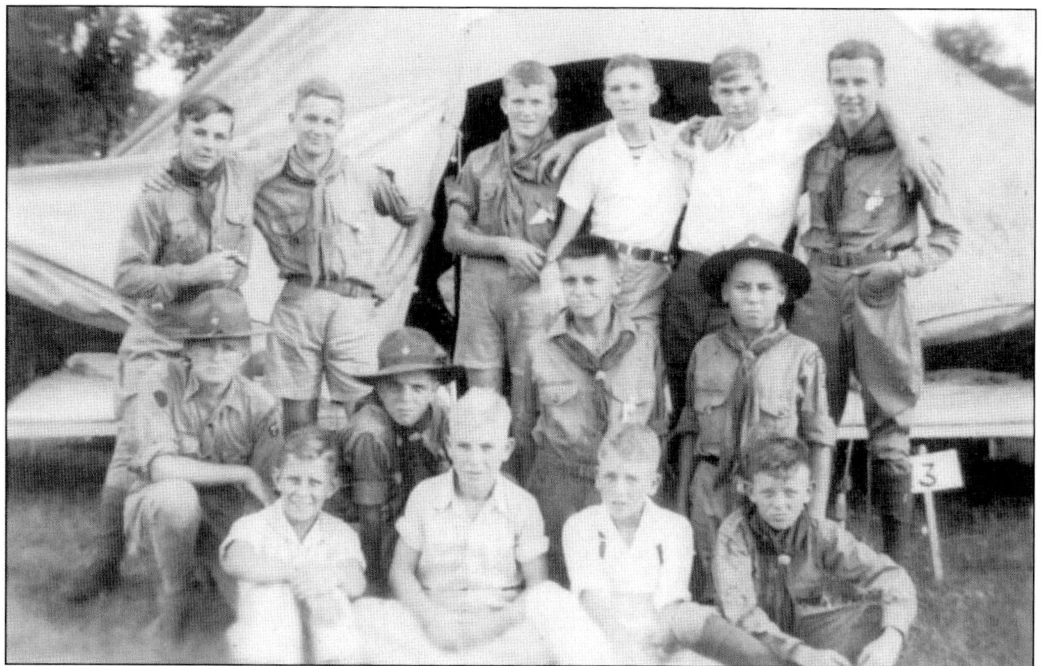

Many young men were active in Boy Scout Troop No. 23 at Renfrew. Seen among the members of the troop in this 1930s photograph taken in front of the boys' campsite are Douglas DeBrabet (first row, second from left), Ford Duncan (first row, third from left), and Roy Lockaby (second row, third from left).

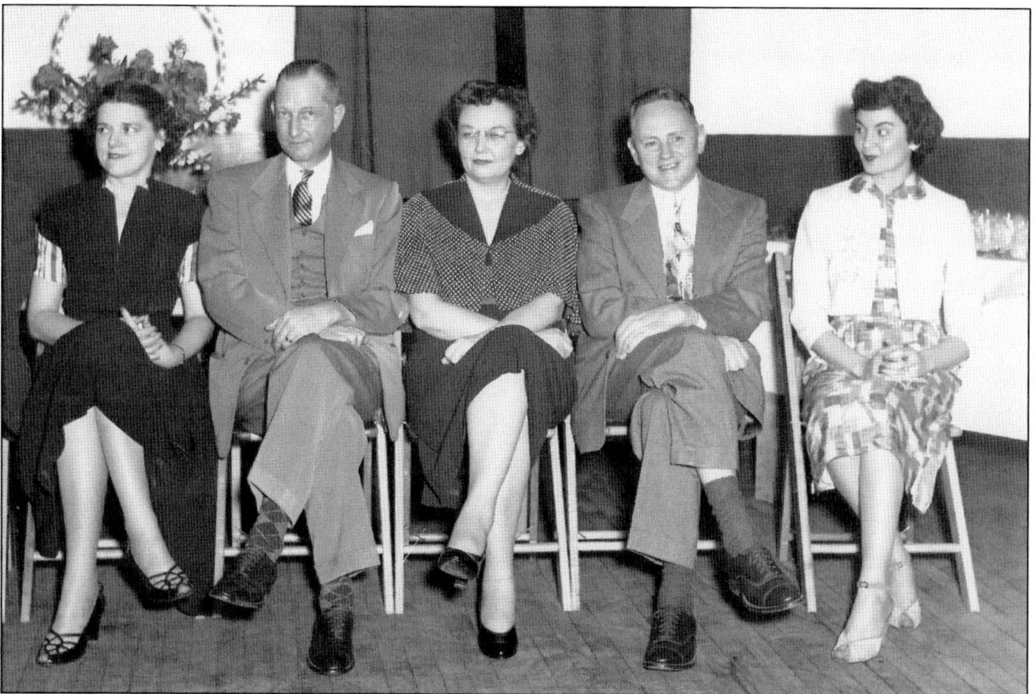

Seated from left to right at a Renfrew social event are business-office employees Hazel Tate Hester, John I. Smith, Ruth Duncan, Roy Anderson, and Evelyn Childs Wood.

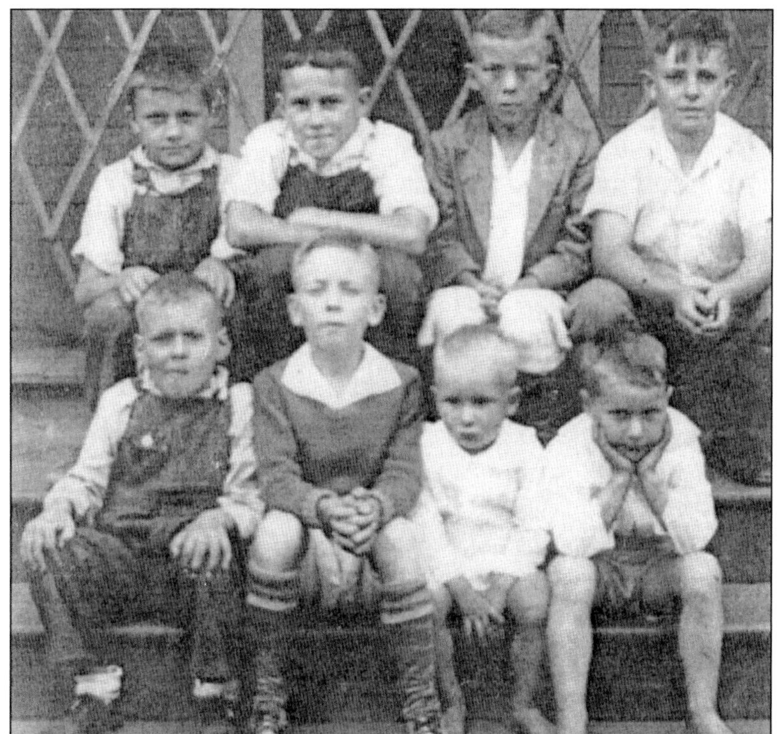

Most families living in the village had several children, so there were always other children to play with. These boys took time out to sit on the steps of one of the houses built by the mill for their employees. Seated here are, from left to right, (first row) Lewis Lockaby, Ford Duncan, Donnie Bridges, and Virgil Bridges; (second row) Roy Lockaby, Boyd Lockaby, Paul Duncan, and Jack Edwards.

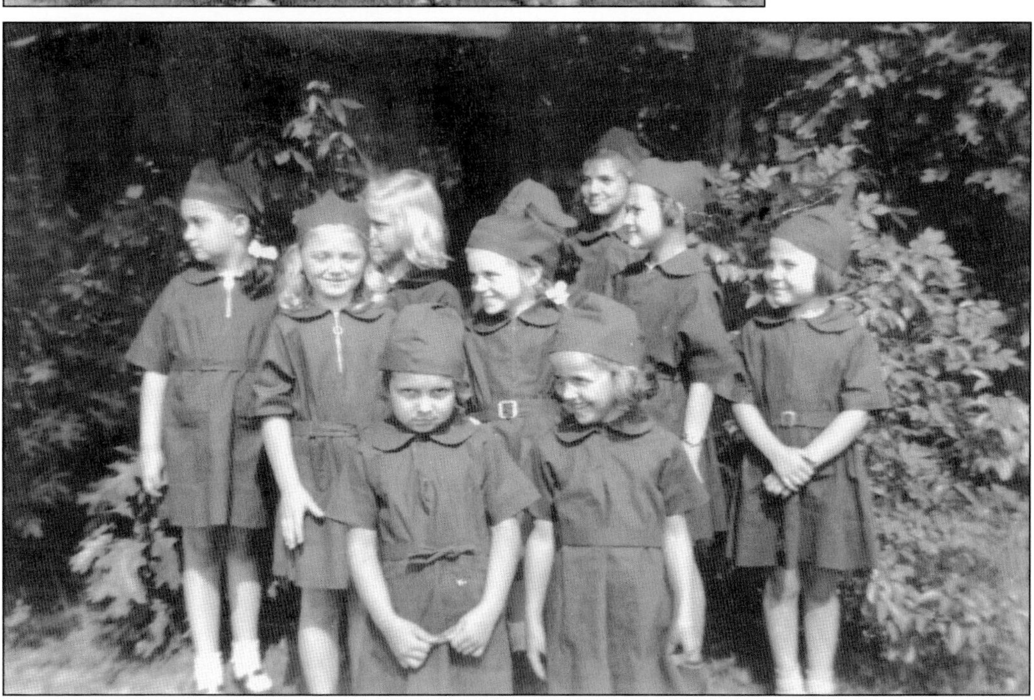

This photograph shows a Renfrew-sponsored troop of Girl Scout Brownies all dressed up in their uniforms. From left to right are (first row) Ann Murphy and Betty Claire Bledsoe; (second row) Nell Anderson, Ann Nuckles, Margaret Lockaby, and Peggy McDowell; (third row) Elizabeth Getaz, Barbara Worrell, and Dora Jane Murphy.

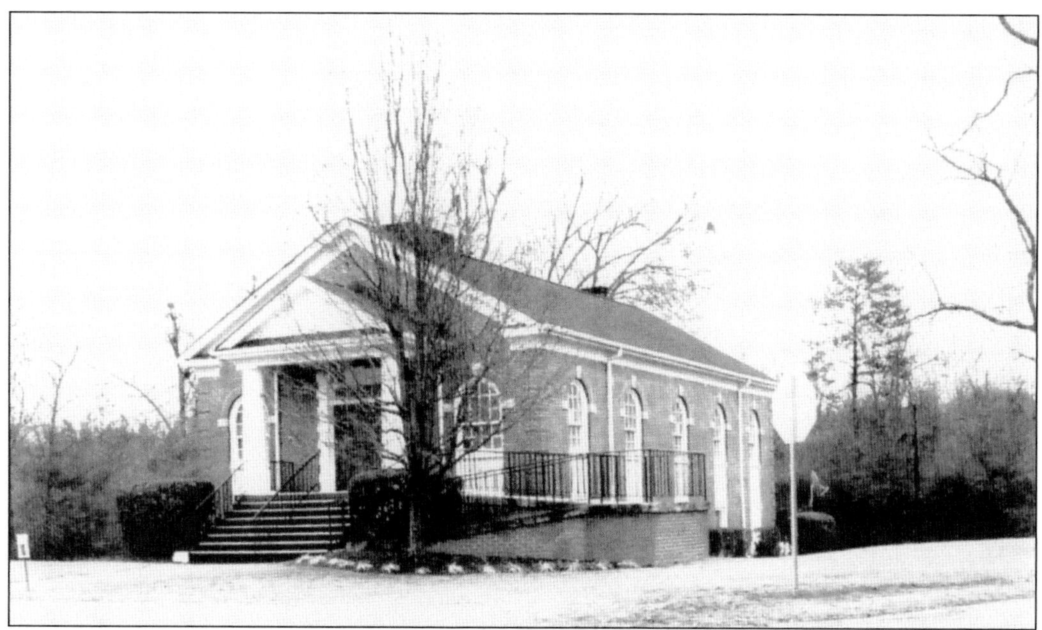

For many years, this Union Church was home to the Renfrew Baptist, Methodist, and Presbyterian congregations. The Baptists built a new church building near the Renfrew main office in 1942, and in 1959, the Presbyterians built a new sanctuary in Travelers Rest on Howard Street (now Wilhelm Winter Street). The building is now home to the New Life Seventh-Day Adventist Church.

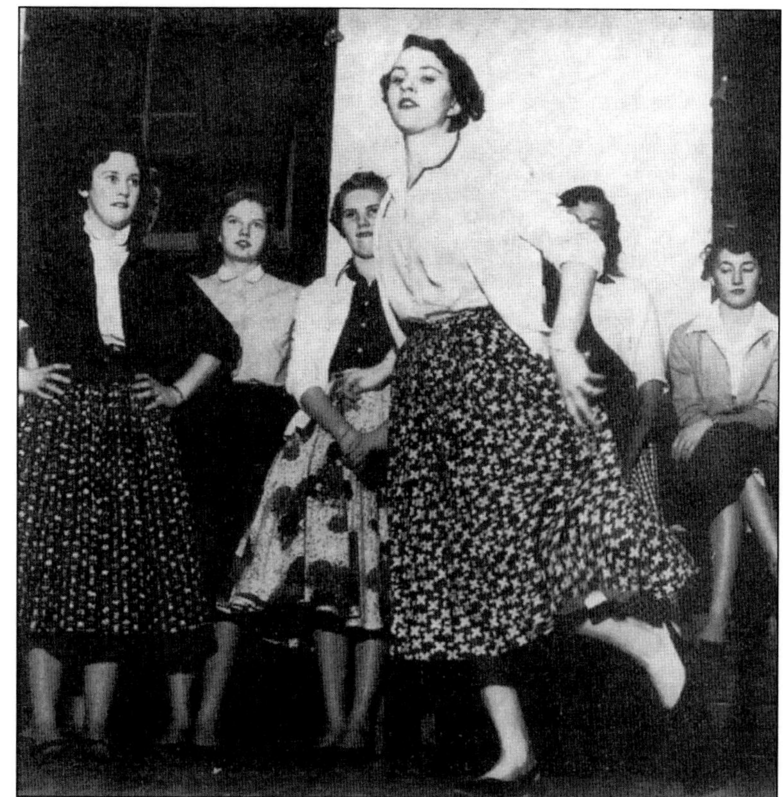

Renfrew Community Hall was the site of parties and dances for teenagers. In this photograph, Dot Styles enjoys a square dance while the other girls—from left to right, Kay Ferguson, Marian Cooper, Becky Farmer, unidentified, and Carolyn Cantrell—look on.

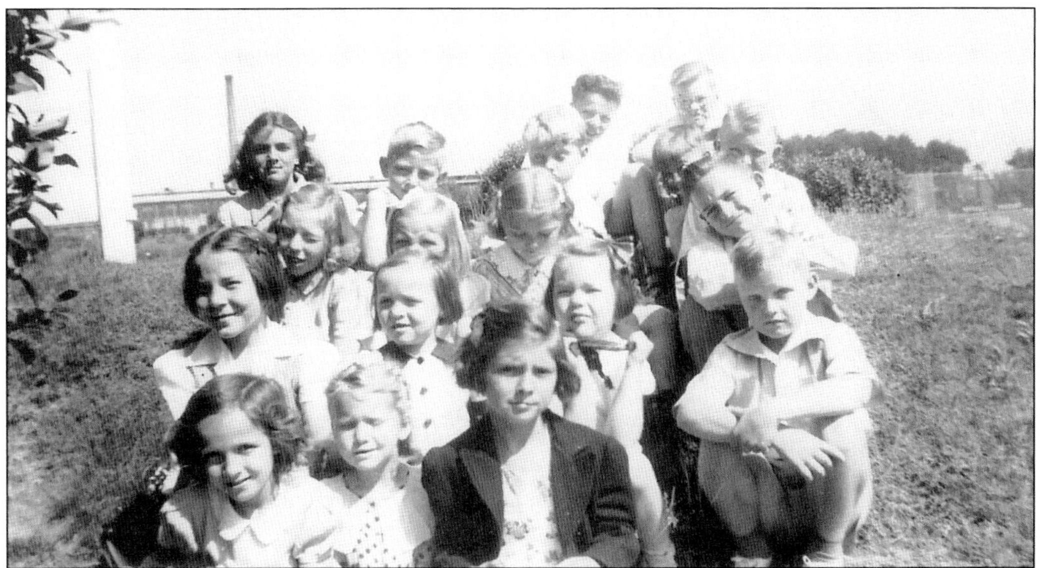

Sitting on the steps in the side yard of the Union Church are, from left to right, (first row) Betty Clair Bledsoe, Catherine Ann Acker, and Ann Murphy; (second row) Peggy McDowell, ? McDowell, Betty Jane Goldsmith, and Charles L. Acker; (third row) Jean McDowell, ? McDowell, Nelle Anderston, and J. B. Granger Jr.; (fourth row) Dora Jane Murphy, Frank Edwards, Larry Farmer, Rembert Jhonson, and unidentified; (fifth row) W. A. Jhonson and Paul Goldsmith. Note the mill and smokestack in the background.

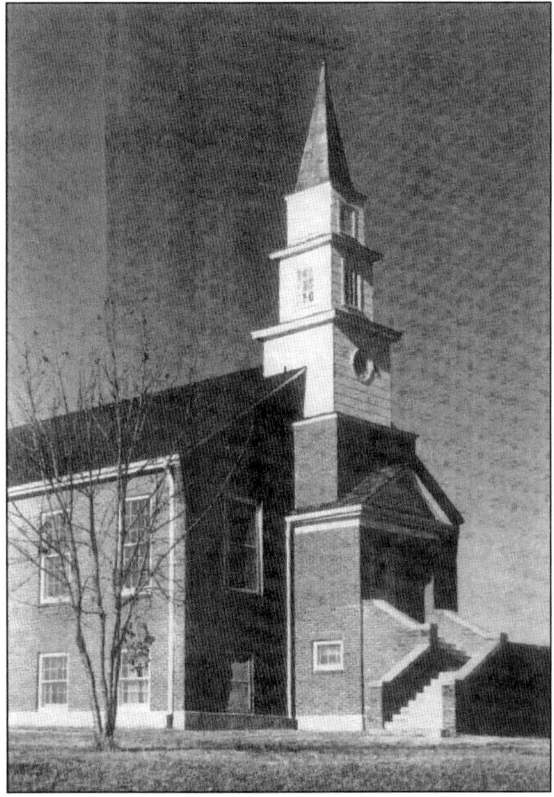

Organized in 1929, this Baptist sanctuary was built near the mill office in the Renfrew village in 1942. In 1956, there was an active membership of 140, and Dr. R. W. Bailes was pastor. Boyce Greer was Sunday school superintendent, Perry Poole was choir director, Ila Mae Rainey was organist, and Evelyn McClure was pianist. In 1985, the congregation built a large new church facing Highway 276.

Seven

MILITARY

Throughout history, militias and military units have served to protect inhabitants as well as their lands and personal property. Travelers Rest created some of its first military units well before the Cherokee Nation ceded over the land. Forts were formed along the frontier for protection from Native American attacks. After the formation of the town, many of the men in the military were experienced warriors, having already engaged in battle during the French and Indian War as well as the Indian Wars of the Carolina Frontier. As the years progressed, the military units continued to grow, moving from bands of rangers to armies of soldiers fighting for state's rights during the War Between the States. Most able-bodied men between the ages of 18 and 45 were required to join the military during the War Between the States to fulfill the solemn duty of protecting not only their own families, but others' as well. The military's impact can be seen throughout the town, and Travelers Rest shares the victories and wounds of battle with every other city. The stories on the following pages represent those citizens of Travelers Rest who have served their homeland and beyond during various times of conflict.

Considered one of the Great Women of the American Revolution, Dicey Langston Springfield was a heroine in every sense of the word. She acted as a spy for the Patriots on numerous occasions and displayed her bravery in many different situations. She married Revolutionary War veteran Thomas Springfield, and they moved to the Travelers Rest area, where they became the parents of 22 children. The medallions pictured here were commissioned by the Daughters of the American Revolution. Each of the large, exquisitely engraved pewter medallions depicts one of 36 special women who played an important role in the Colonials' fight against Royalist forces.

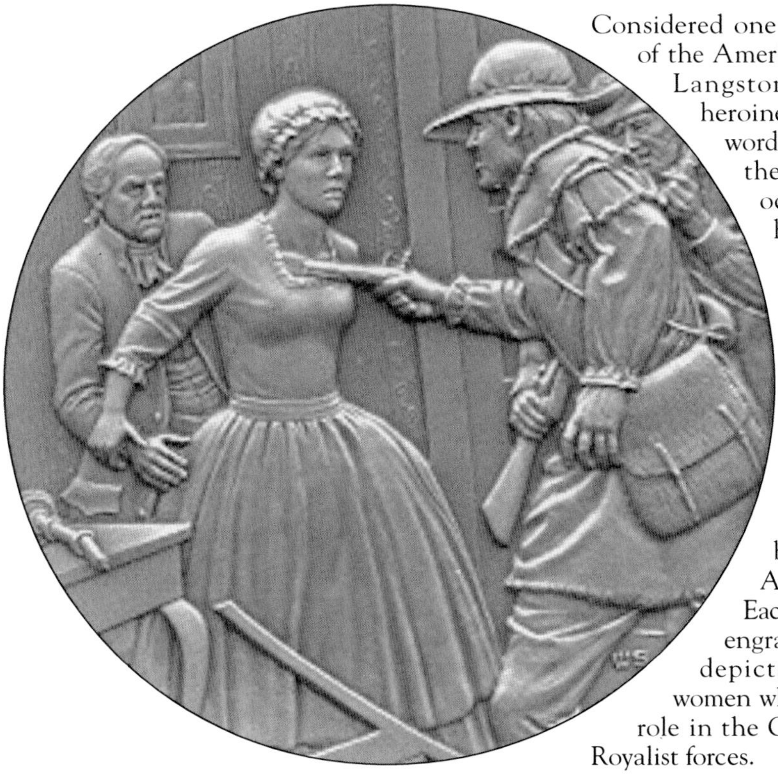

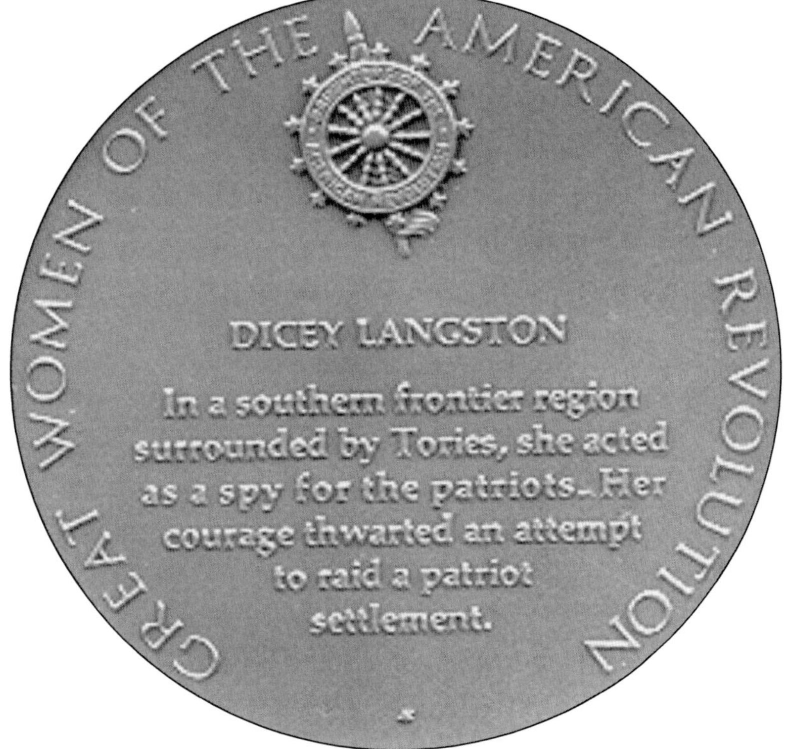

Joseph Delon Cooper (1835–1897) served as a sergeant in Company G of the 16th Regiment of the South Carolina Volunteers during the War Between the States. He served as flag bearer for this unit. According to Steve Batson and D. R. Whittaker in *Cooper Lodge 282, Travelers Rest, SC*, the Cooper Masonic Lodge was named for J. D. Cooper, builder of several local businesses and one of the founders of the Athens community, now part of Travelers Rest.

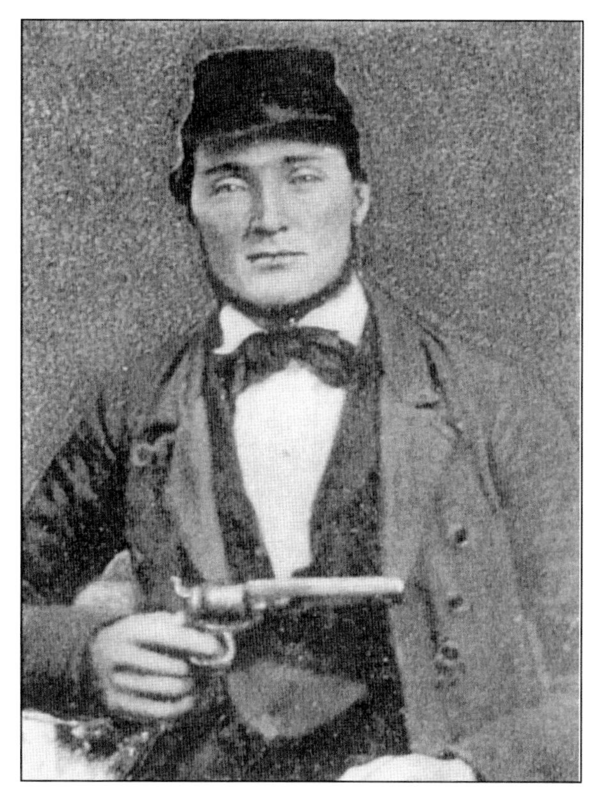

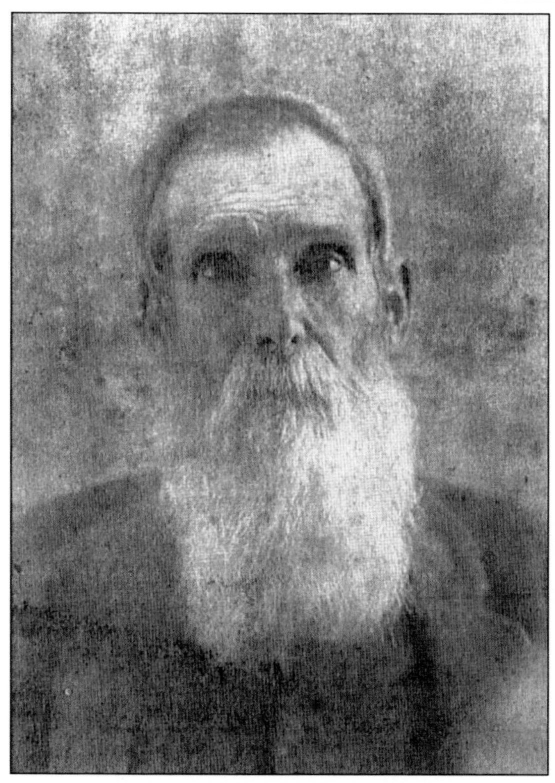

William Douglas "W. D." Batson was a Confederate veteran. He was born in July 1822 and died in February 1909. His body is buried at Reedy River Baptist Church in Travelers Rest.

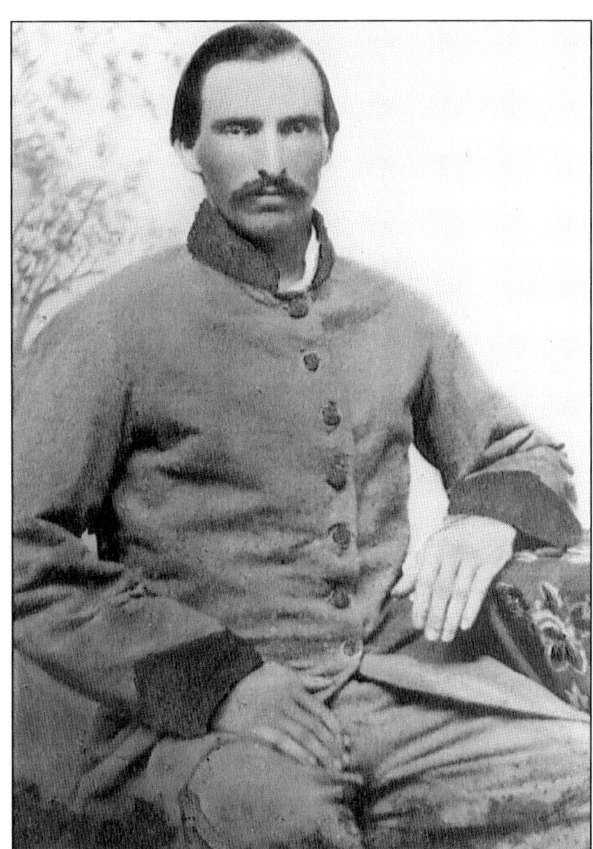

This is a photograph of Confederate Army veteran Aquilla Batson (1832–1863). He died during the War Between the States in Green Pond, Colleton County, South Carolina, and is buried at Reedy River Baptist Church in Travelers Rest. His son, Zion Perry Batson, was one year old at the time of his father's death.

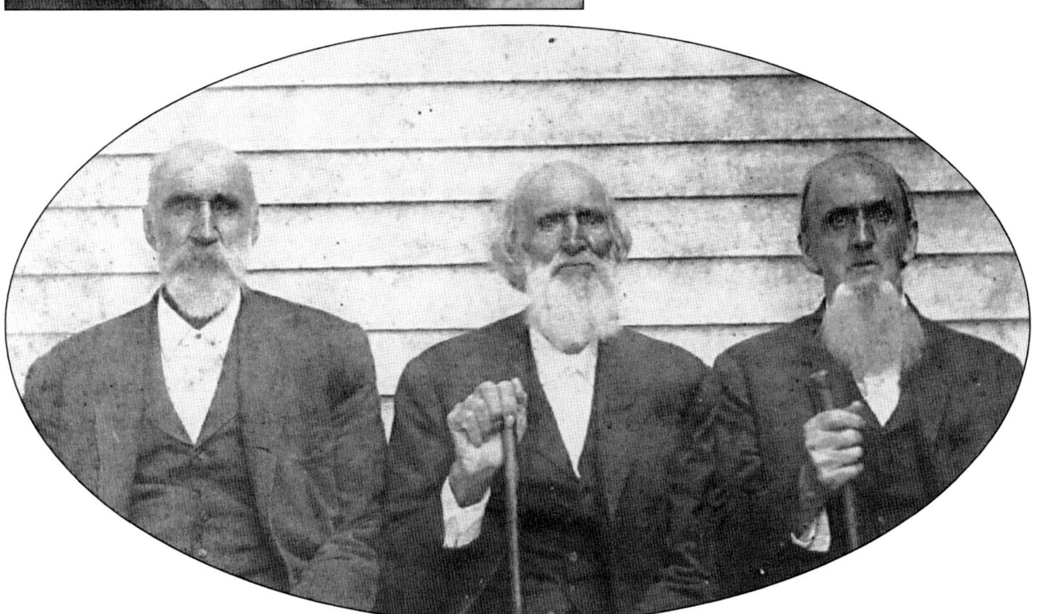

These three brothers from Travelers Rest were veterans of the War Between the States. They are, from left to right, Dr. Franklin Batson, Nathaniel Berry Batson, and John Batson. Franklin and Nathaniel are buried at Ebenezer Baptist Church.

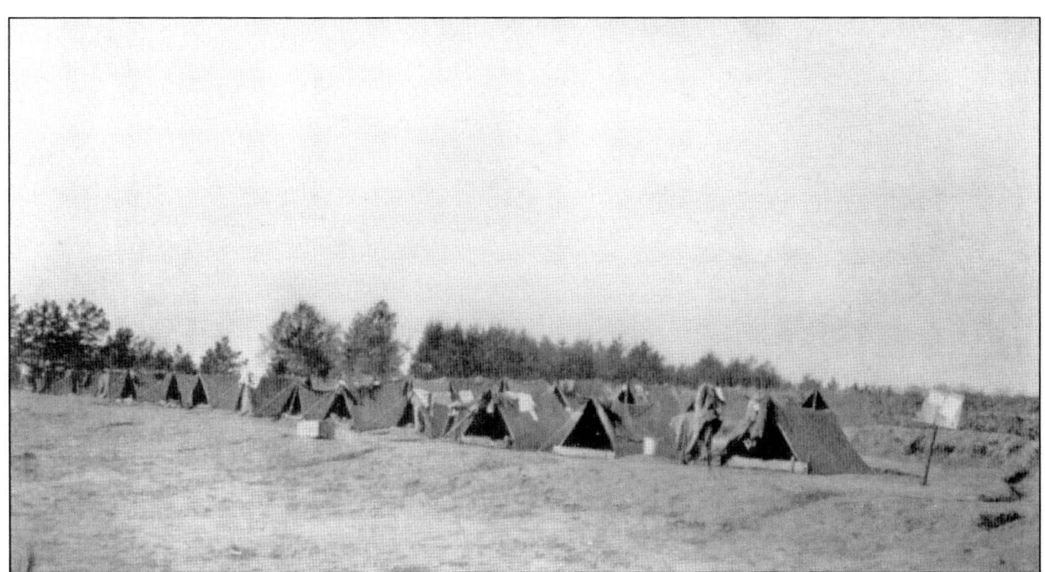

Located above Travelers Rest, Camp Wing was used as a training facility by soldiers from Camp Sevier during World War I. Local residents recall watching the soldiers march through town on the way to the camp, which later became known as Wing's Quarry.

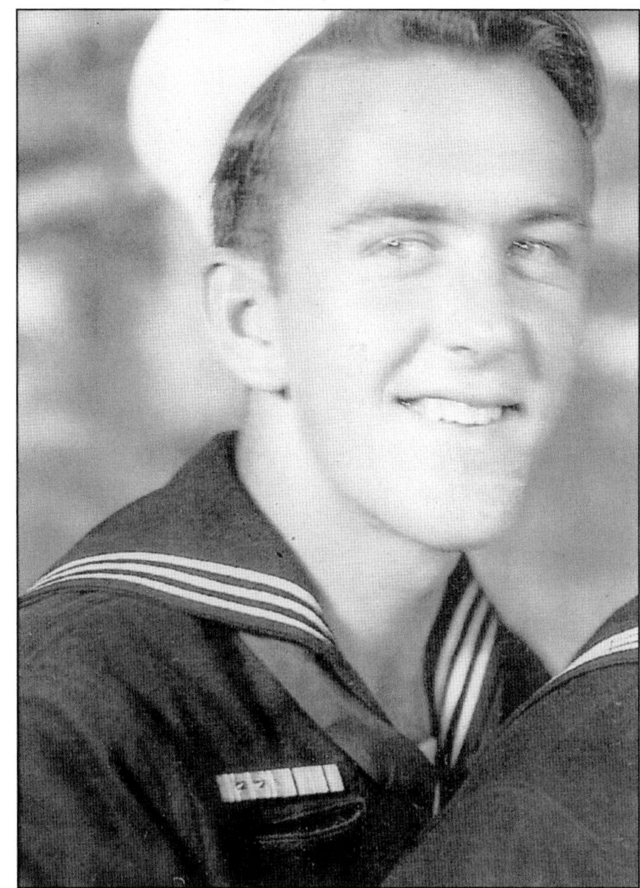

Roy Wood enlisted in the U.S. Navy in 1944 and served on the USS *Topeka* in the Pacific Theater in World War II. His ship participated in the invasion of Okinawa, an operation involving the Japanese island of Kobe, and was in Tokyo Bay when the Japanese surrendered. Wood returned home to Travelers Rest after the war, married Delane Baker, and worked as a mail carrier for 35 years.

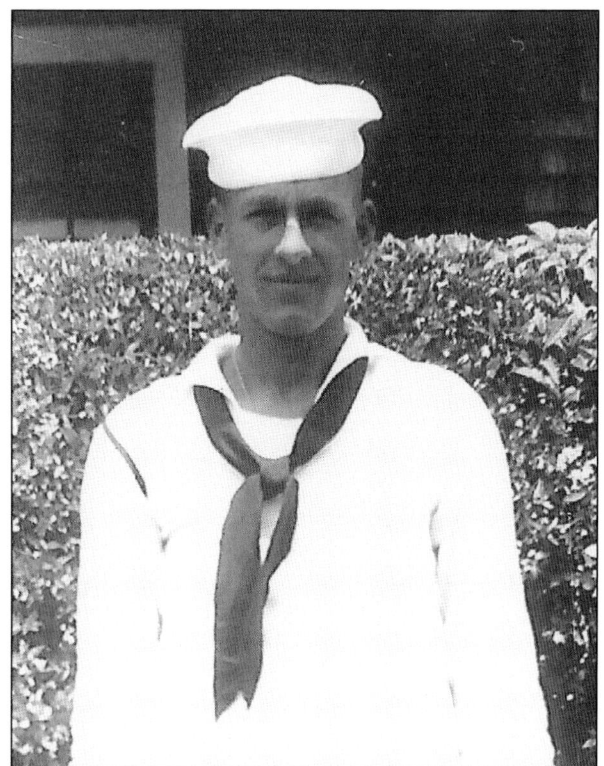

Lewis T. Lockaby served in the U.S. Navy during World War II as a pharmacist's mate, third class, attached to the amphibian crew aboard the USS *Oneida* in the South Pacific. He was in the invasion of Okinawa and took the first occupation troops to Yokohama, Japan; Pusan, Korea; and Singtao, China, at the end of the war in the Pacific. Three Lockaby brothers—Roy (U.S. Army), Boyd (U.S. Navy), and Lewis—served concurrently in World War II. Boyd also served in the U.S. Air Force during the Cuban Missile Crisis.

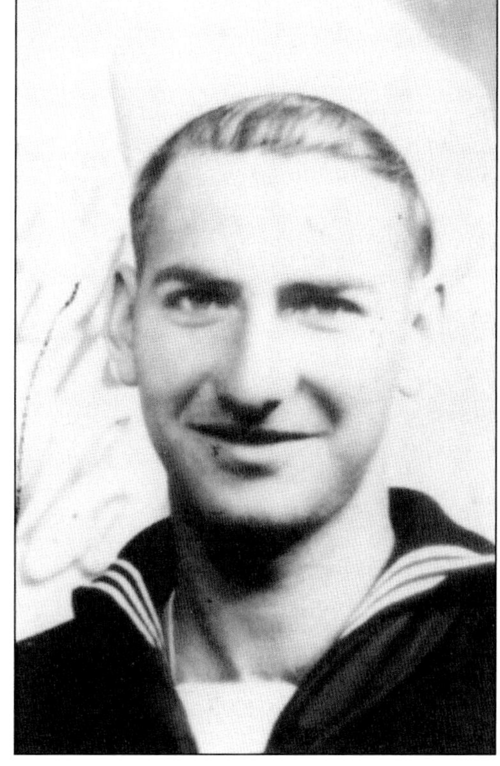

S2c. Hubert Brine Hawkins, born August 25, 1925, to Henry Y. and Annie F. Hawkins, went down on the USS *Samuel B. Roberts* (DE 413) on October 25, 1944, along with 88 other men who also lost their lives when the ship was sunk at the Battle of Leyte Gulf off the island of Samar following a fierce battle with the Japanese. The ship has been called "the destroyer escort that fought like a battleship."

Col. Frank J. MacNees (1908–1981), a native of Minnesota, served in World War II as commander of 435th Troop Carrier Group, flew missions on D-Day carrying troops to Normandy, trained B-25 bomber crews, and served as commander of Donaldson Air Force Base in Greenville, according to Maj. Lawrence J. Gilmore and Capt. Howard J. Lewis in *435th Troop Carrier Group*. Donaldson was once dubbed the "Airlift Capital of the World" for its role in the Berlin airlift, Korean War, and Cold War. Colonel MacNees and his wife, Dolores, retired to Travelers Rest in 1963.

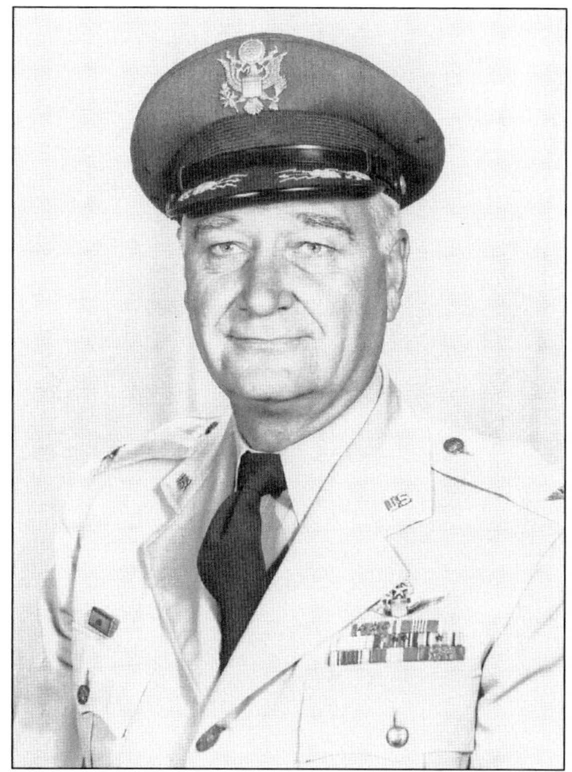

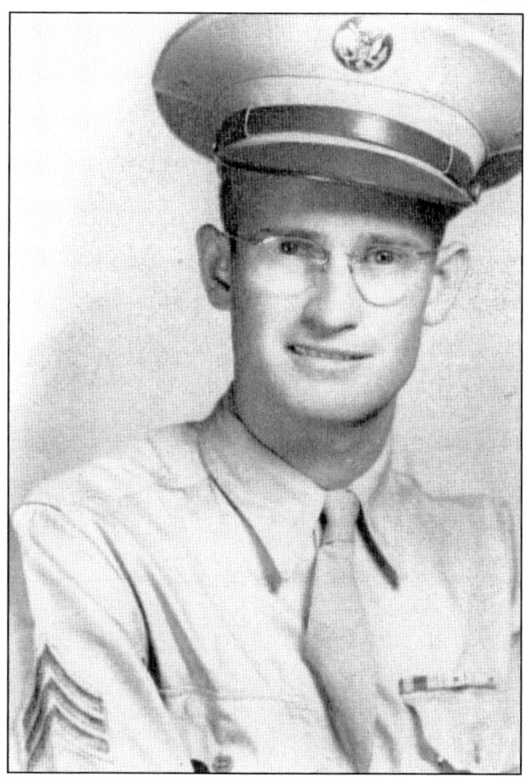

Sgt. Grover Jefferson McGriff was at Honolulu when Pearl Harbor was attacked by the Japanese and later fought in the Fiji Islands and the Solomon Islands during World War II. He was later recalled for the Korean Action and became a staff sergeant of Battery C, 555th Field Artillery Battalion, 5th Infantry Regimental Combat Team in Korea. This battalion was known as the "Triple Nickel Division." Sergeant McGriff went missing on July 14, 1953, and was never found.

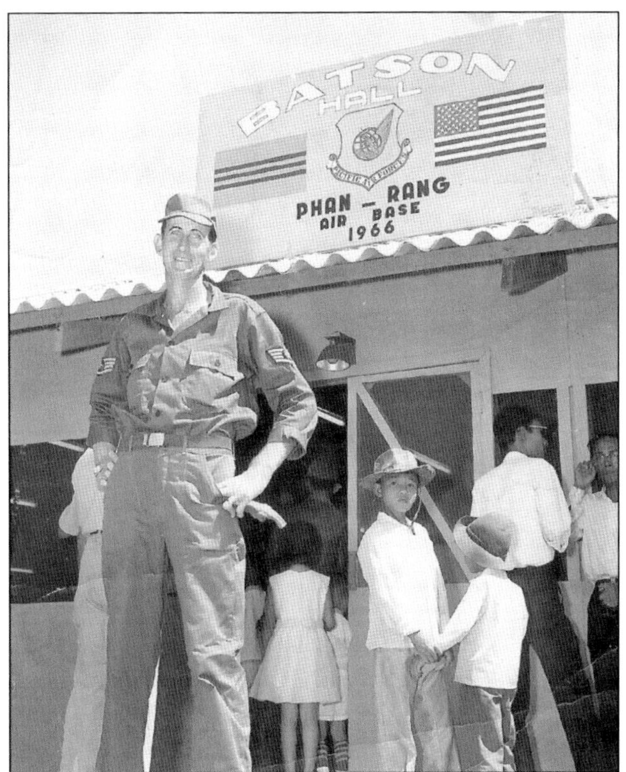

S.Sgt. David J. "Jack" Batson of Travelers Rest, an outstanding baseball player, was a consistent member of the "All-Air Force Team" and twice played on the "All-Armed Services" team. He designed and supervised the construction of a large dining hall at the Phan Rang Air Force Base in South Vietnam. The facility, which seated 1,000 persons, was named Batson Hall in his honor. This photograph was taken during the dedication ceremonies held in April 1966.

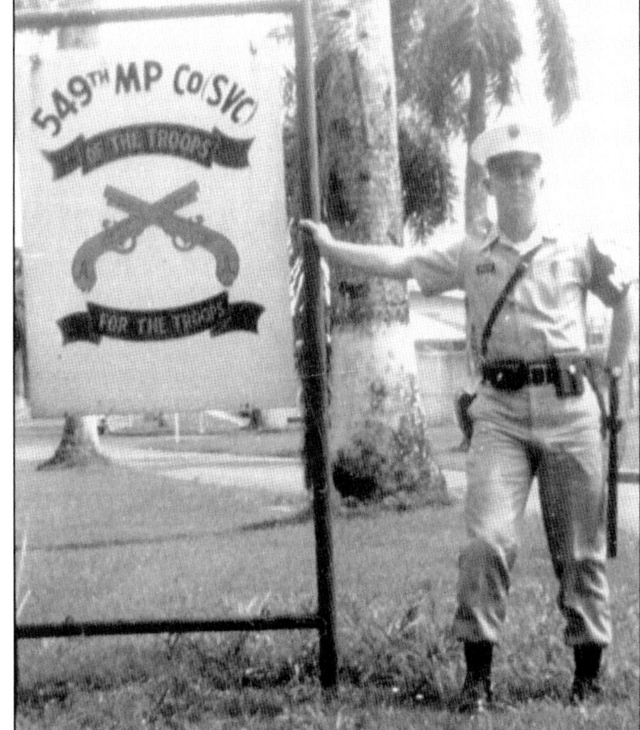

In the 1950s and 1960s, most of Travelers Rest's young men served a tour of duty in the military. In this photograph, Sp4c. Sam Benson poses beside the 549th Military Police Company sign at Fort Davis in the Panama Canal Zone in 1965.

Eight

People

Figuratively, a town, city, or village can exist without people. After all, just because there is no one there does not mean that the place does not exist. It is a speck on the map, a point on the cross-grids of latitude and longitude, but that is all it will be. Without people, cities and towns cannot develop their own characters, their own little quirks, and the traditions that make them unique. Memories cannot be created and histories cannot be written without people. Travelers Rest is just such a town, strong with heritage and overflowing with tradition, thanks in no small part to those who have helped carve it into the little piece of art it has become. Many a hero has lived here, royalty has visited, and loving families have created lives here. With the turn of each page, a new story is told, a new history is created, and a new memory is brought back from the depths of a soul. Take a few minutes to learn about the stories of the lives of the people who have made Travelers Rest into more than just a mark on the map of the State of South Carolina, as each one has made a unique impact on the community.

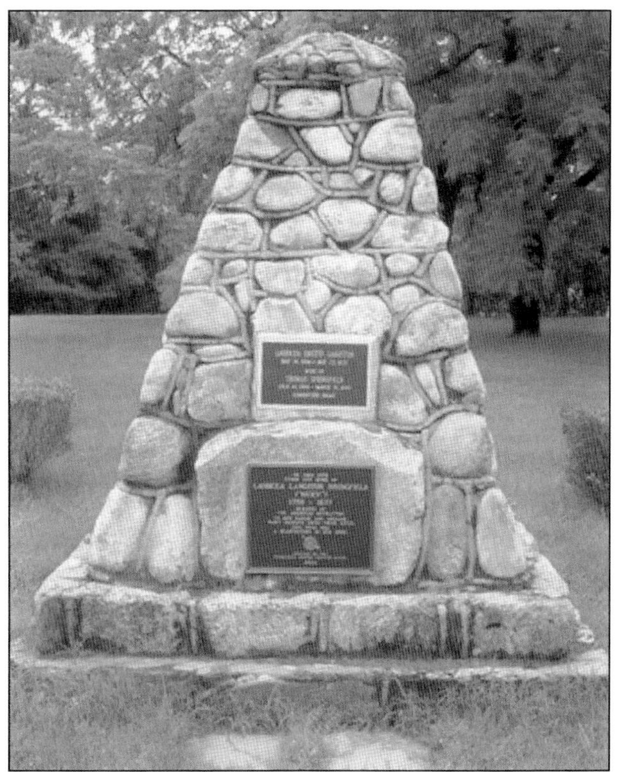

Revolutionary heroine Laodocia "Dicey" Langston Springfield and her husband, Thomas, a veteran of the Revolutionary War, lived in Travelers Rest. Both are buried in a family cemetery that is maintained by their descendants who remain in the community. To honor and recognize her contributions to our country, the Nathaniel Greene Chapter of the Daughters of the American Revolution erected a monument near the Springfields' original home on Tigerville Road.

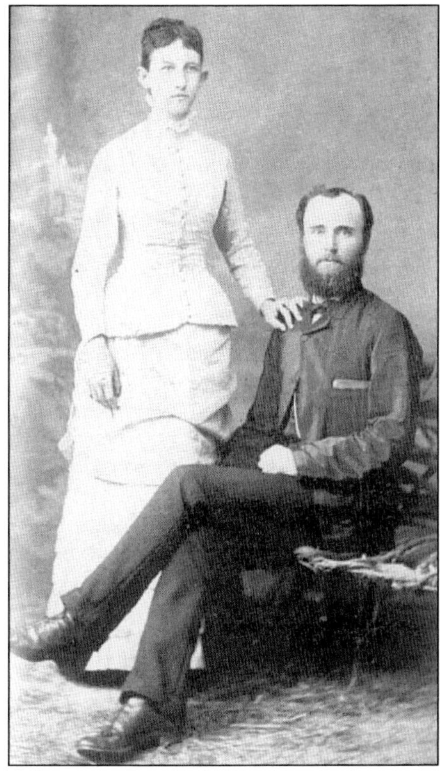

The wedding portrait of Fannie Anderson Goodlett and Dr. Benjamin Franklin Goodlett was taken in 1883. Dr. Goodlett (1855–1929) served the community, from Greenville to the mountains, as a physician for 50 years. In order to care of his patients, he traveled by horseback, then horse and buggy, and later owned and drove one of the first automobiles in the area. After graduating from Greenville Female College, Fannie Goodlett (1864–1939) taught in the schools of Greenville County.

This picture of Stephen Perry Marchbanks and his wife, Rebecca Jones Marchbanks, was taken about 1880. The Marchbanks lived in the house on Old Buncombe Road known as the "Hillhouse Home." Many of their descendents live in the Travelers Rest area.

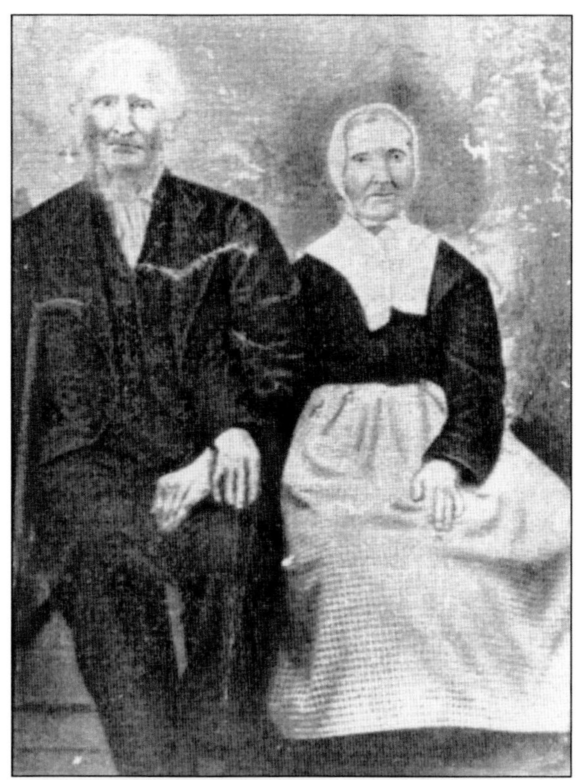

Will Vest and Birdie Campbell were married in Pelzer on November 6, 1898. They moved to Travelers Rest, where they owned a large peach orchard and truck farm in the Little Texas community. They moved to a house on Center Street (formerly McElhaney Road) in 1921. Will Vest operated a gristmill at 8 South Main Street and built a grocery store at the same location in 1926. The store building was relocated to 3 Edwards Street and is now the home of the Travelers Rest Historical Society Museum.

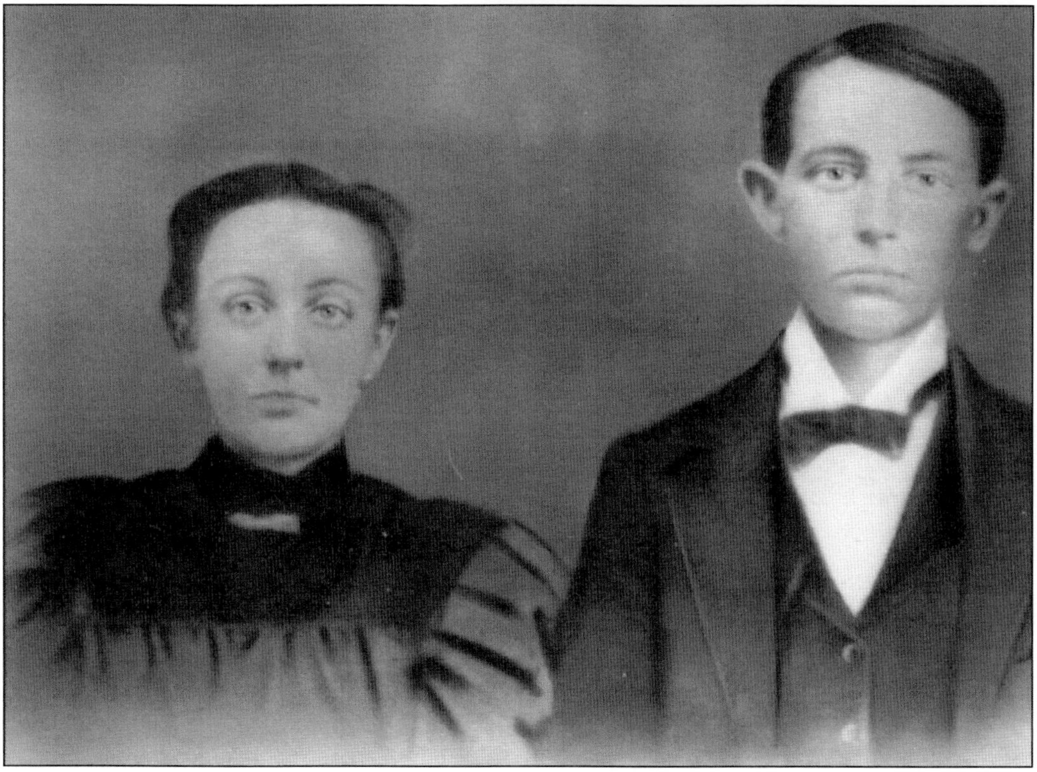

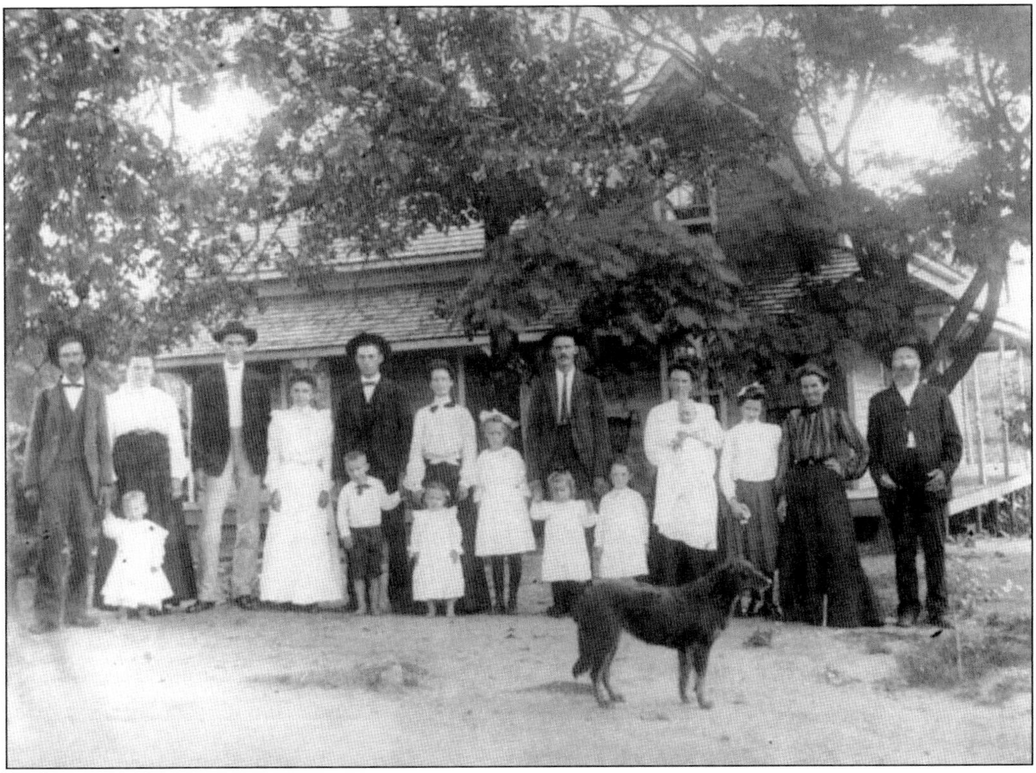

Hezekiah Young "H. Y." Batson; his wife, Frances Cornelia Hall; their children; and their grandchildren were all born in Travelers Rest, South Carolina. The home in which H. Y. and Cornelia lived and reared their children was located on Hawkins Road in Travelers Rest. In 1900, the Batson family moved into the house seen in the photograph, which was located where Stax Original Restaurant stands on Poinsett Highway. This photograph was taken on their daughter's wedding day, August 20, 1905.

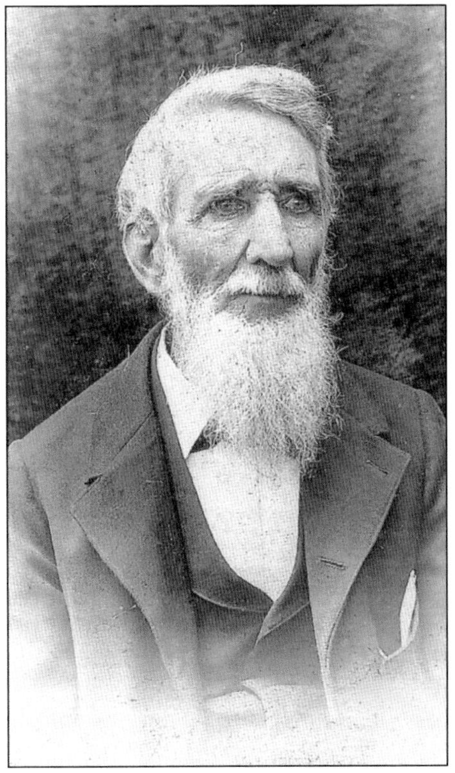

Robert Wright Anderson; his wife, Mary McCullough Anderson; and their daughters moved to Travelers Rest in 1873. They operated what was later known as Spring Park Inn. Colonel Anderson was a land developer, businessman, and farmer. He served two terms as county commissioner, and he was a leader in efforts to see that all children had an opportunity for an education. Anderson also served as postmaster from 1889 until his death in 1898.

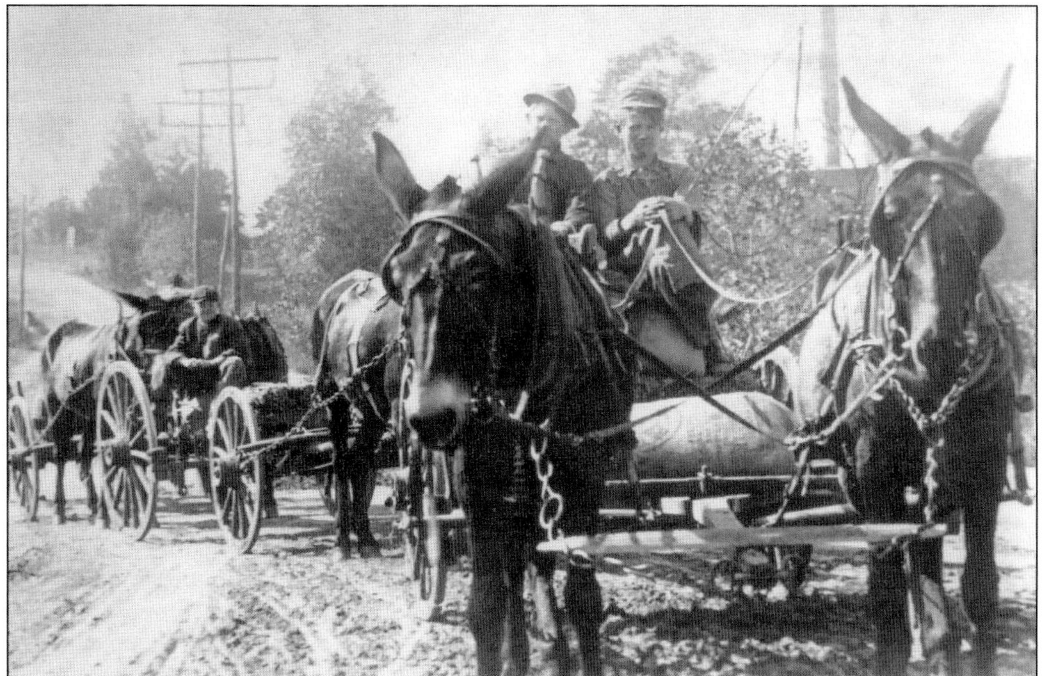

Tom Peterson, Lee Silvers, and G. P. Peterson used wagons pulled by mules to deliver loads of logs and lumber in 1910. This picture was restored from an original photograph taken in 1910, shortly before the three men moved to Travelers Rest. (Courtesy of Ruthea Silvers.)

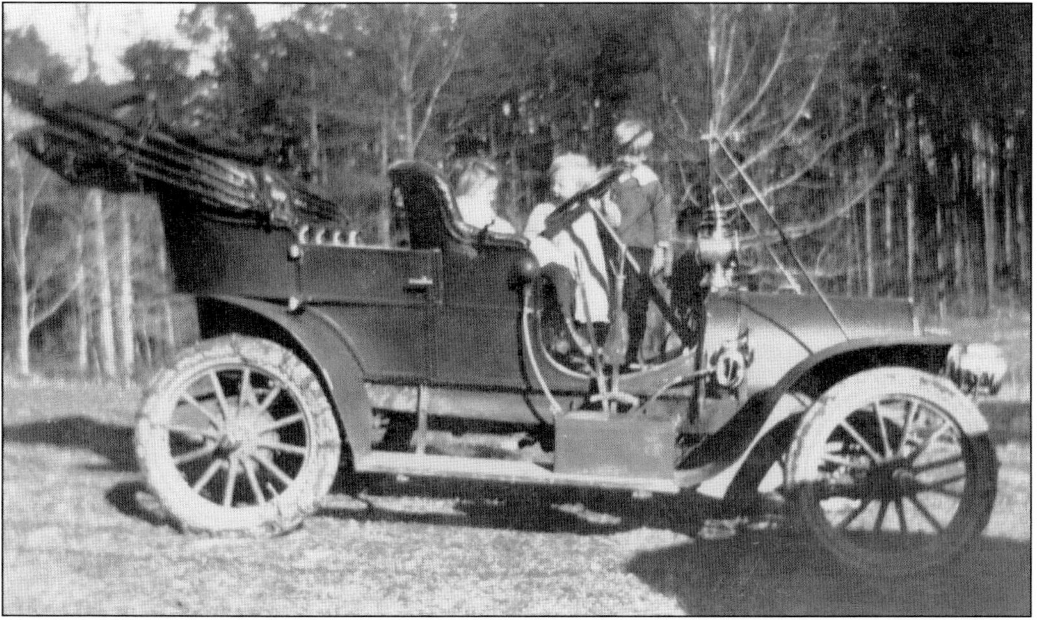

In this *c.* 1910 photograph is the 1904 Franklin automobile belonging to Robert Lee Cunningham, husband of Vannie Smith Cunningham. Three of the Cunninghams' children pose in the car. They are, from left to right, Artie, Paul, and Roy Cunningham. In the 1920s, Robert Lee Cunningham and his son John Clarance would walk down McElhaney Road to near Main Street in the evening to fuel and start a diesel-driven generator that powered the streetlights in Travelers Rest.

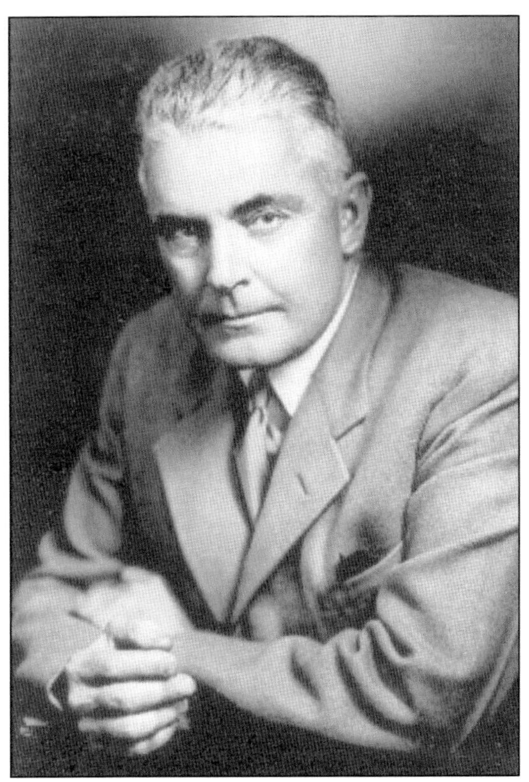

Dr. John B. Watson (1878–1958) was born in Travelers Rest, graduated from Furman University, and earned his Ph.D. degree from the University of Chicago. His influential research and writing pioneered a new movement in psychology, and the impact of his work earned him the title "Father of Behaviorism." He was included as a charter member of the Furman University Hall of Fame, was awarded the LL.D. degree from Furman, and is honored for initiating a revolution in psychological thought. Shown below is a roadside marker located near Renfrew Baptist Church that honors his achievements.

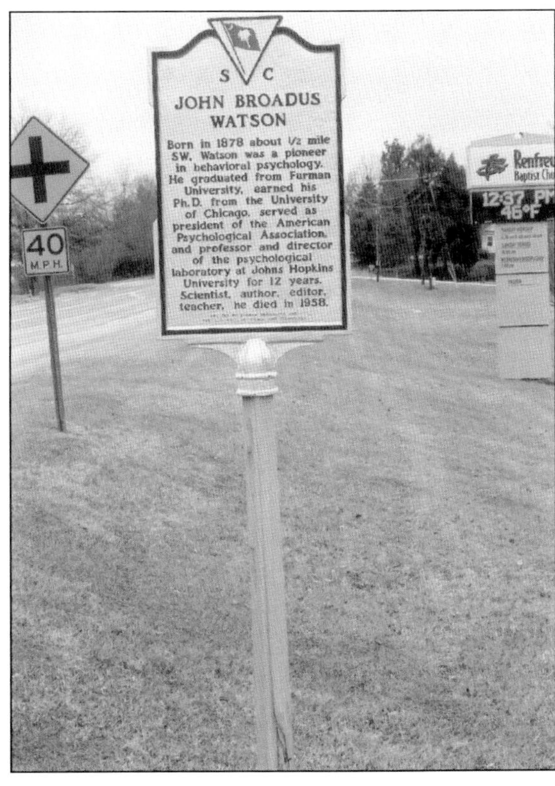

Dr. John Laney Plyler was born in Travelers Rest in 1894. He graduated from Furman University, served in the U.S. Army, earned his law degree from Harvard University, and was named a judge of the Greenville County Court. In 1938, he became president of Furman. In his 25 years of leadership, the Poinsett Highway campus was built and developed. Dr. Plyler was called "the tall, silver-haired educator who guided Furman in its greatest period of growth." He died in 1966.

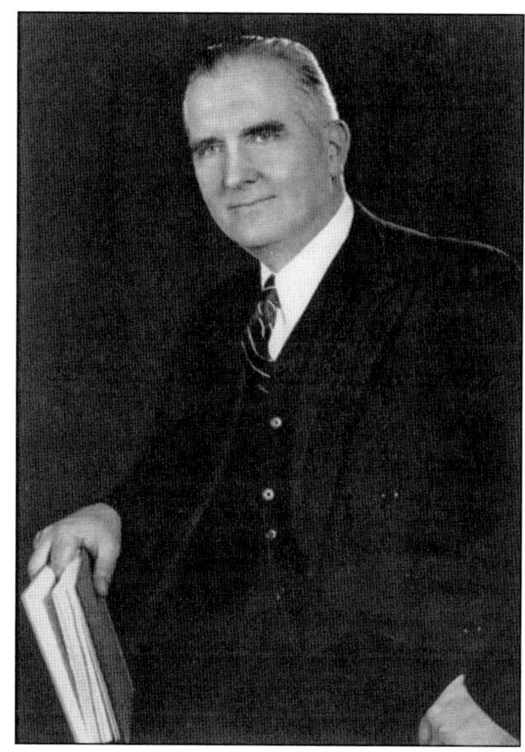

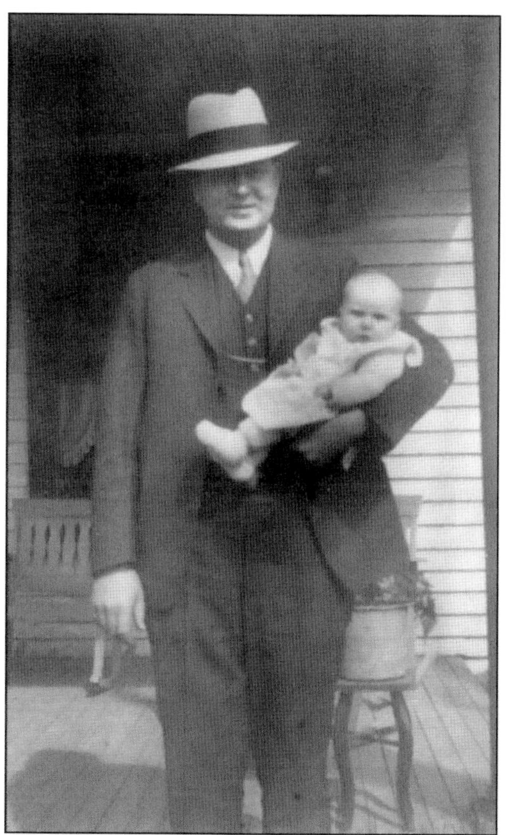

Mildred Goodlett states that Dr. Stobo Roseborough Gaston was born in 1900 and began his medical practice in Travelers Rest in 1928. He founded Gaston Clinic and opened the first part of his hospital in 1930. Dr. Gaston died in 1957. In this 1932 photograph, he is holding infant JoAnn Coleman.

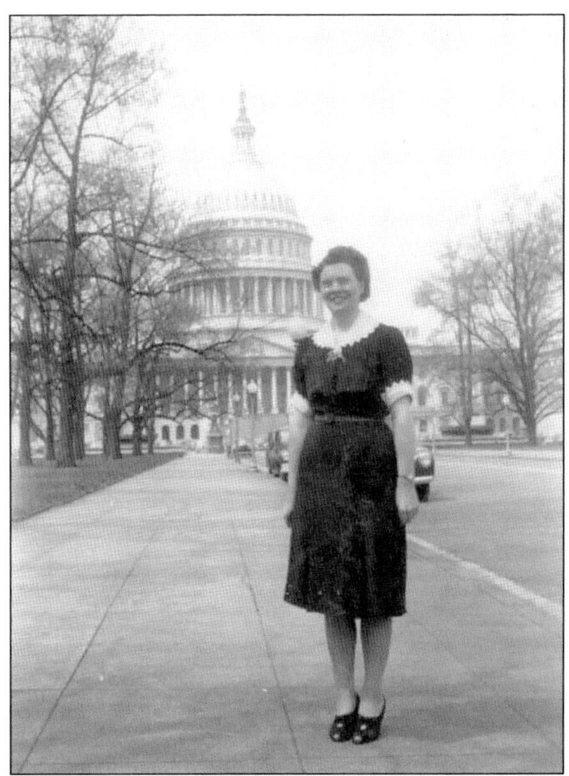

Rhoda McCarrell was born in Greenville County on September 29, 1902. She was the daughter of Vance Washington and Nancy Willis McCarrell. She taught at several schools in the Travelers Rest area, including Pleasant Retreat, Locust Hill, and Travelers Rest. In 1938, she found herself in Washington, D.C., for what she thought would be a temporary job with Congressman Joseph Bryson of the Fourth Congressional District. She stayed on even past her retirement in 1969. In all, she worked for three different members of the U.S. Congress as an administrative assistant. McCarrell died on April 18, 1993.

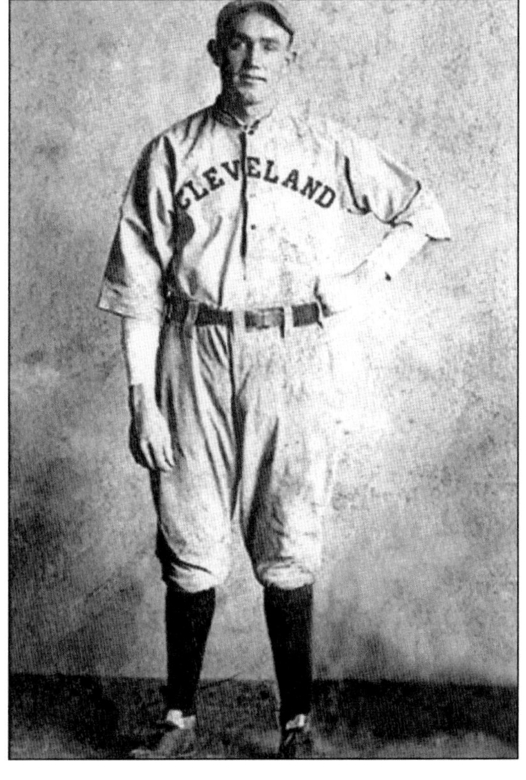

In 1914, infielder Walt Barbare played for the Cleveland Naps with another Greenvillian, "Shoeless" Joe Jackson. In 1918, Barbare played for the Boston Red Sox, where he was a teammate of Babe Ruth. Boston went on to win the American League Championship that year. In 1923, Barbare returned to play Textile League baseball in South Carolina. He was active in various areas of textile ball. He married Mary Howard of Travelers Rest, and they made their home in Travelers Rest for the remainder of their lives.

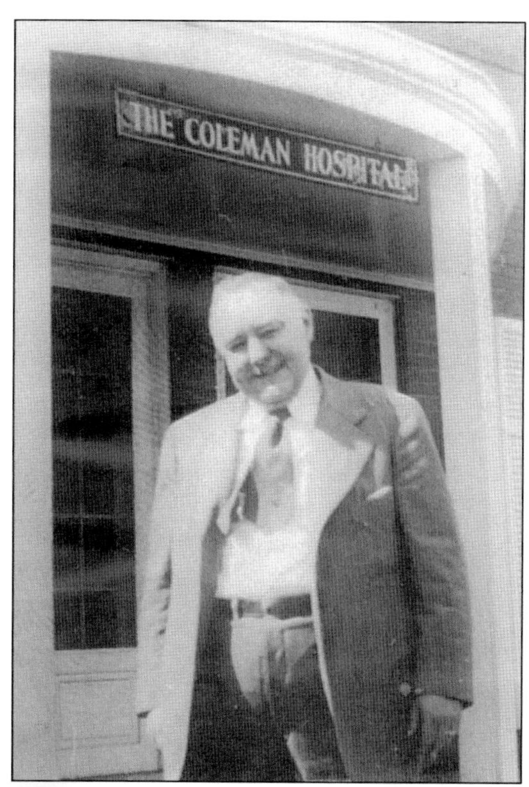

Brothers Dr. Thomas E. Coleman and Dr. Stanley Irvin Coleman Sr. practiced medicine for many years in the Travelers Rest area. According to Mildred Goodlett, they were graduates of the Medical College of South Carolina, and they built a handsome brick hospital building at the intersection of Buncombe Road and Geer Highway in 1940. Seven years later, Dr. Stanley set up a separate office while Dr. T. E. continued to operate the hospital until 1956, after which he devoted himself full time to private practice. Dr. "T" was plant physician for Renfrew Bleachery for 35 years.

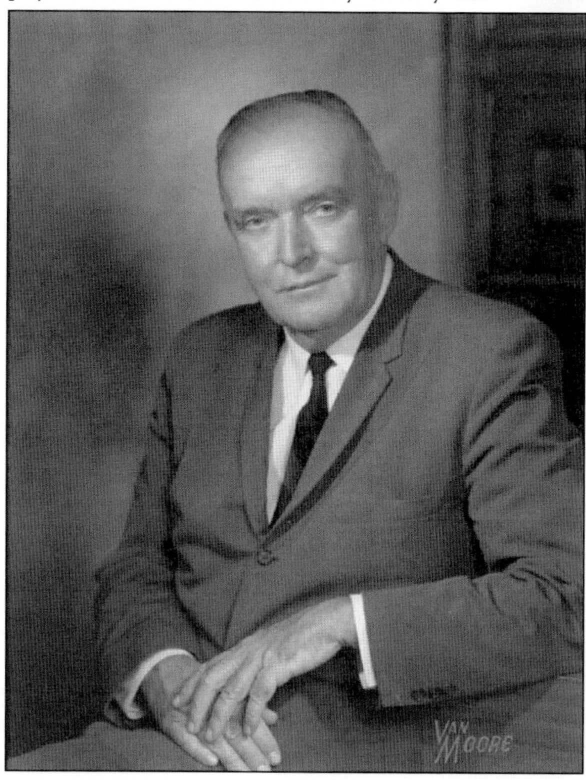

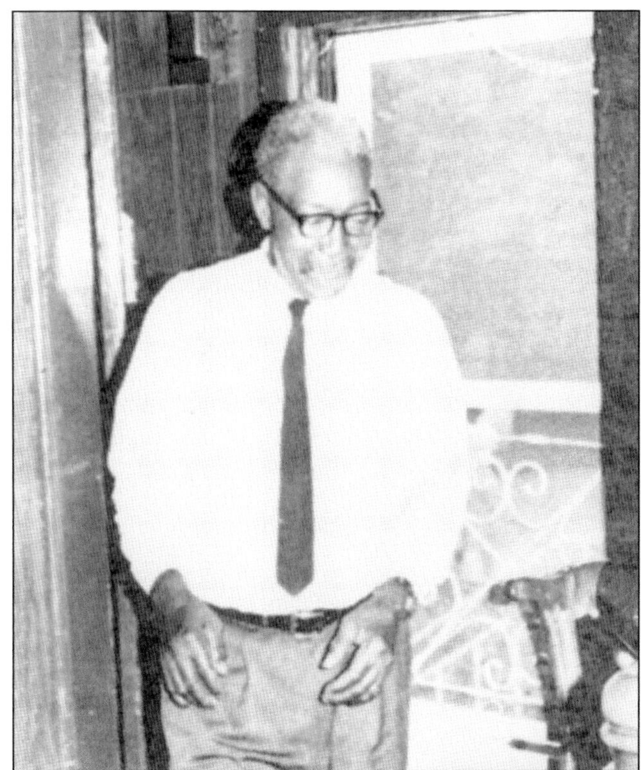

Mass Bowen was a prominent citizen in Travelers Rest for many years. He was the first African American to serve on the city council, and he owned and operated the town's garbage disposal service until the municipality assumed the responsibility after the town's incorporation in 1959.

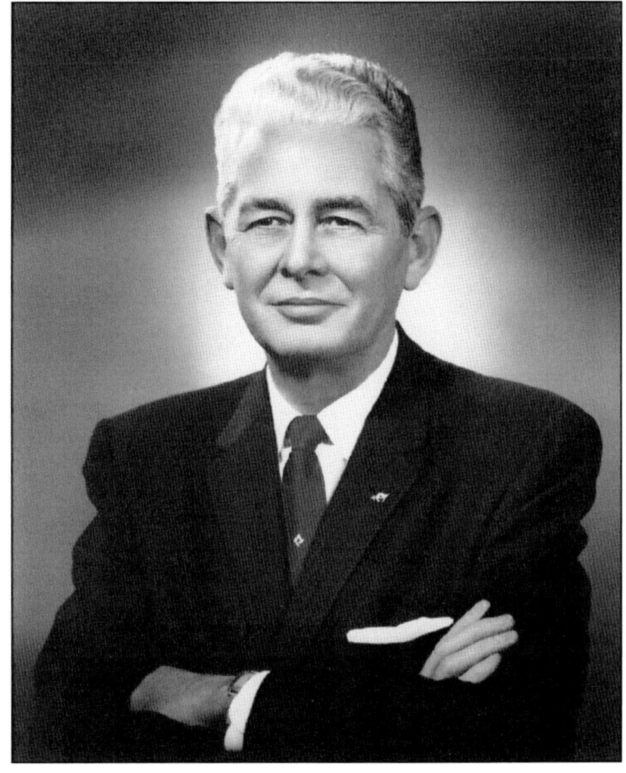

John J. White, a Greenville native, Furman University graduate, and veteran of World War II, began his career in insurance in 1929. White was the first president of the Bank of Travelers Rest when it opened in 1946, and he continued in that position until his retirement. His son Bruce White stepped into the leadership role and remains as president of this vital financial institution that has contributed much to the Travelers Rest area.

Carey and Frances Hatcher Joyner owned and operated Joyner's Variety Store, located in the Anderson Building adjacent to the Dixie Home store on South Main Street in Travelers Rest. Carey Joyner, a jovial, friendly merchant, made sure that customers enjoyed their shopping experience, and people often came from surrounding communities to shop in the popular store.

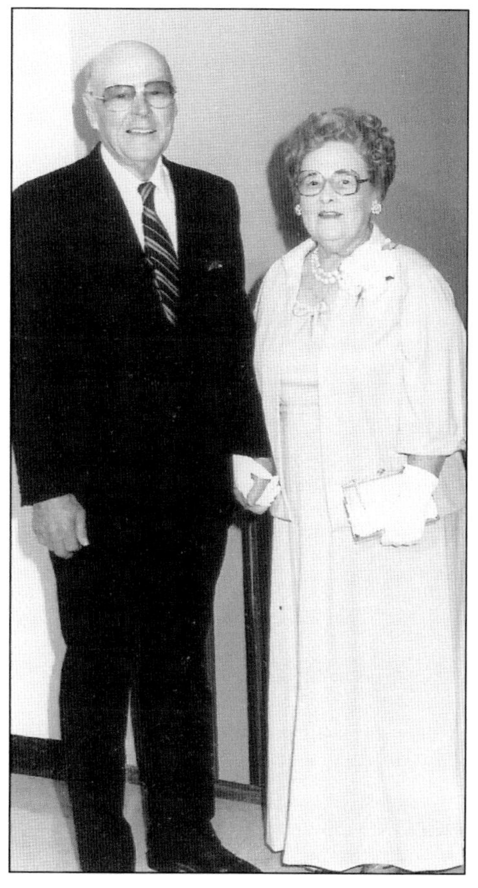

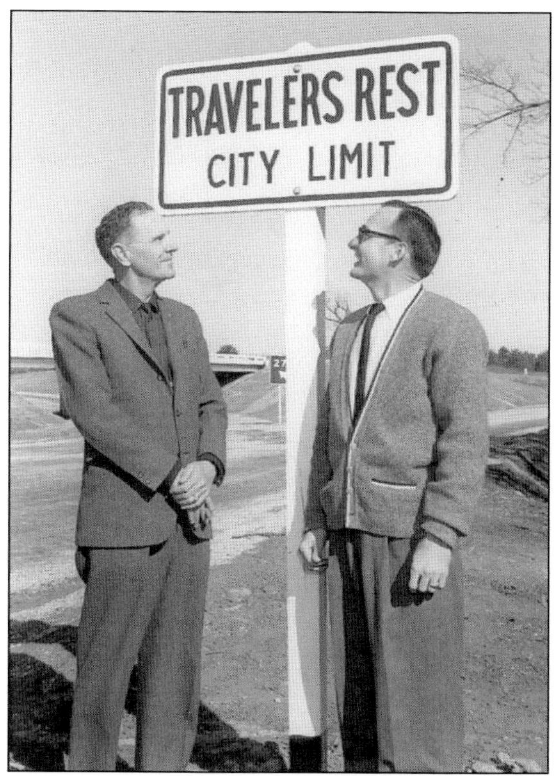

This picture was taken in 1959, shortly after Travelers Rest was incorporated for the second time. In this photograph, Mayor George Coleman (left) and Councilman Calvin Garrett admire a new sign at the city limits.

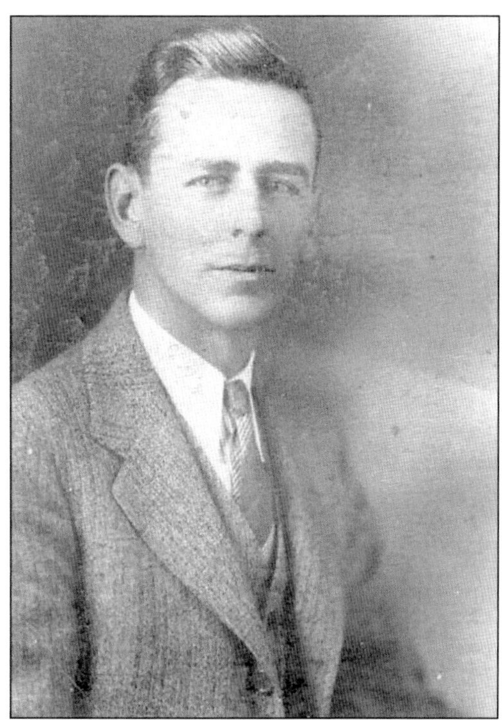

James Stobo Garrett Sr. bought the large building at 27 South Main Street in 1945, and his sons—Alvin, Jack, and Calvin—opened Garrett's Furniture, Inc., in Travelers Rest. The elder Garrett worked as a distributor for Allison-Irwin. His sons were active in civic affairs: Calvin was mayor of Travelers Rest from 1969 to 1971, and Jack Jr. served on the board of trustees of the Greenville County School District for 12 years and was chairperson for two terms. He later served as a member of the South Carolina House of Representatives.

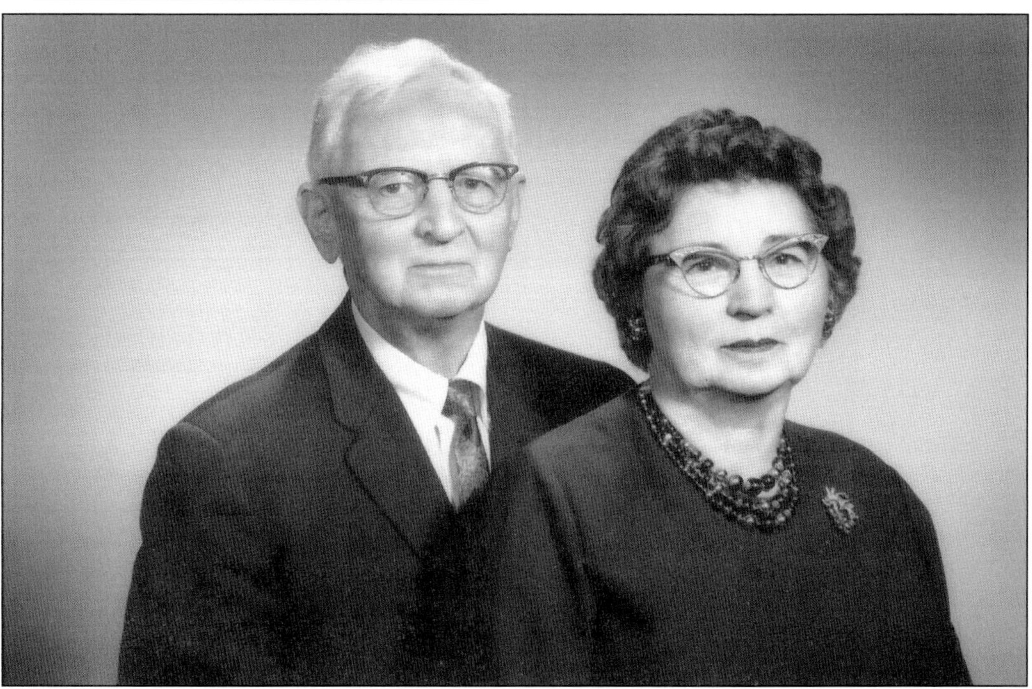

Mildred Wilson Goodlett was born in Newberry, South Carolina, in July 1897 and died in March 1997 at the age of 99. She married Claud B. Goodlett in 1931 and moved to Travelers Rest. They were the parents of two sons—Claud B. Goodlett Jr. and V. Wilson Goodlett. Mildred authored five books on local history and genealogy. One of her books was *Travelers Rest at Mountain's Foot*, published in 1966.

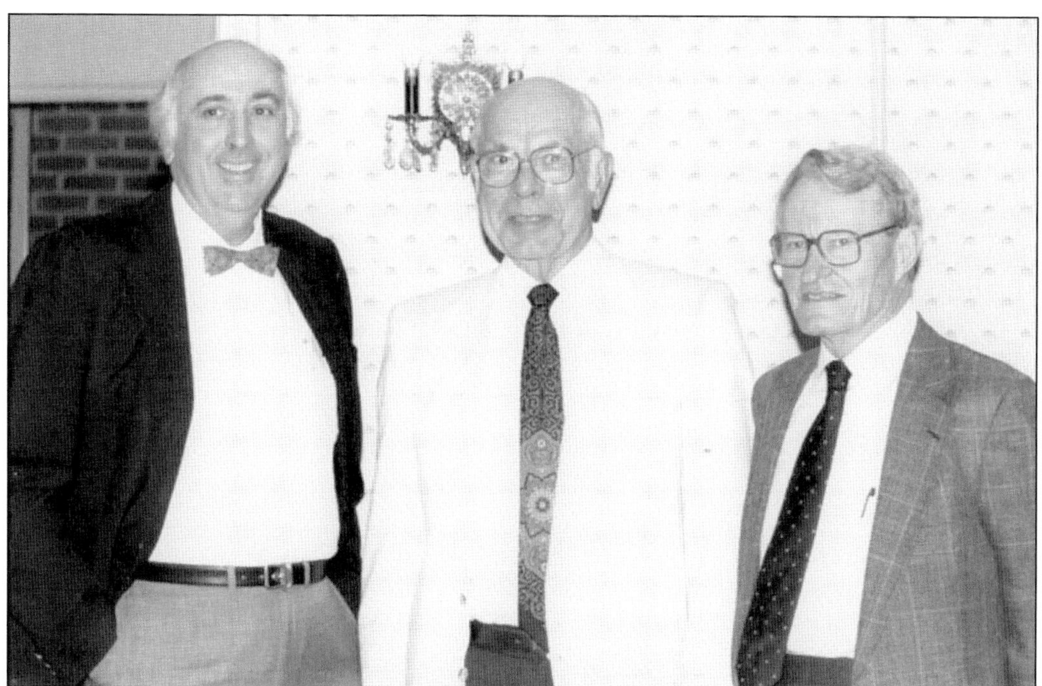

Dr. Landrum McCarrell (center) and Dr. John Holliday (right) opened offices for general practice medicine in 1951 in the old Roe Building, located at the corner of McElhaney Road and Geer Highway. They then moved their offices to the Love home on Poinsett Highway. Dr. James Barnett (left) joined the group in 1955. In 1956, the physicians moved into a new medical facility on Poinsett Highway, where they cared for the residents of the area for more than 30 years. Dr. Barnett served as mayor of Travelers Rest in the 1960s and was named Travelers Rest Citizen of the Year in 2010.

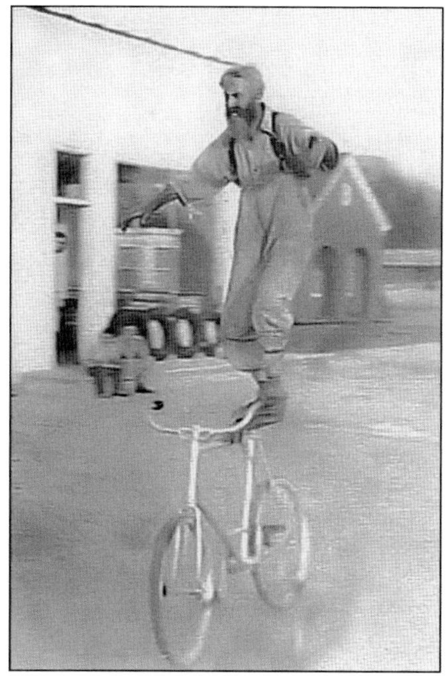

Found in the sixth volume of *Echoes* and in the *Washington Daily News* are articles about a popular mid-1900s citizen of Travelers Rest—Harry "Pop" Kramer. He was a world-famous trick bicycle rider who rode with various circuses and traveled throughout the country putting on performances. One of his most amazing tricks was when he jumped his wagon wheel up the steps of the U.S. Capitol Building. He then rode down the steps with his arms outstretched. It is said that he came down the Capitol's steps so fast that cameras could not capture his image; thereafter, he was often called the "Ghost Rider."

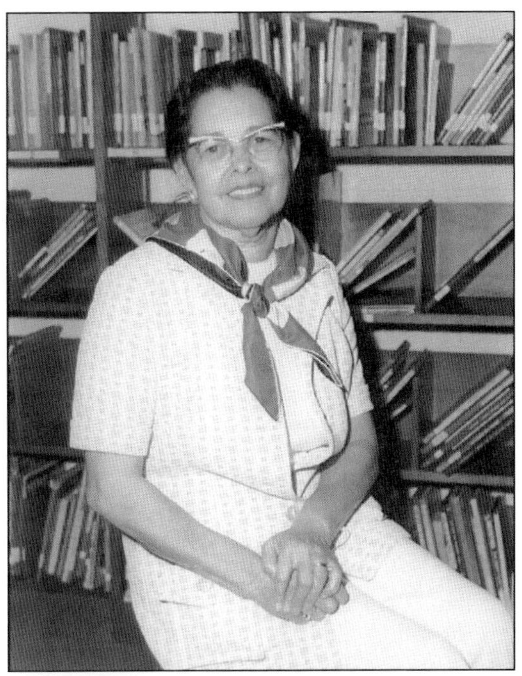

Edris Walker graduated from Hampton University and received her master's degree from South Carolina State College. She was teaching at Sullivan Street Elementary School in Greenville in 1956 when she was named principal of Athens Elementary School in Travelers Rest. Walker was known for being an excellent administrator as well as for her graciousness, dignity, and astuteness. When integration occurred in February 1970, the school became a sixth grade center. Walker remained at the school until it closed. She then served as principal of Westcliffe Elementary.

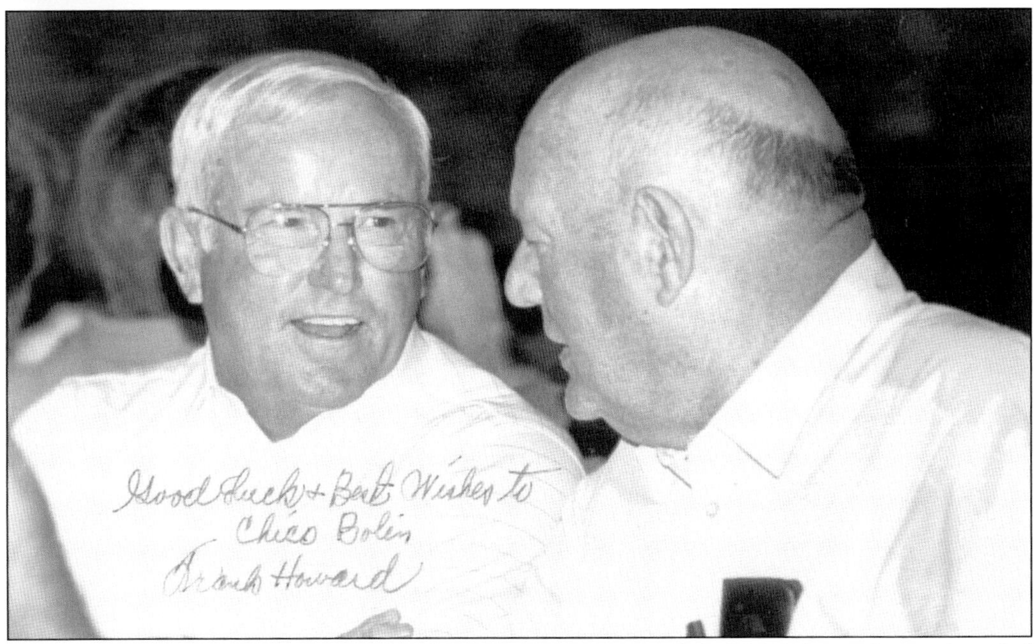

Milton Dean Bolin (left) was molded by the Great Depression and the U.S. Marine Corps. Awarded the Purple Heart after being seriously wounded multiple times in the bloody battle of Iwo Jima, Bolin returned to Furman University, where he was nicknamed "Chico." Bolin became a coach, teacher, and athletic director at Travelers Rest High School, where he would remain for 38 years. He named the athletic teams the "Devil Dogs." For the first years that he was at Travelers Rest, he coached girls' basketball, boys' basketball, baseball, softball, and football. Bolin was inducted into the South Carolina Coaches Association Hall of Fame in 1997. In the picture above, Bolin is congratulated by former Clemson University football coach Frank Howard.

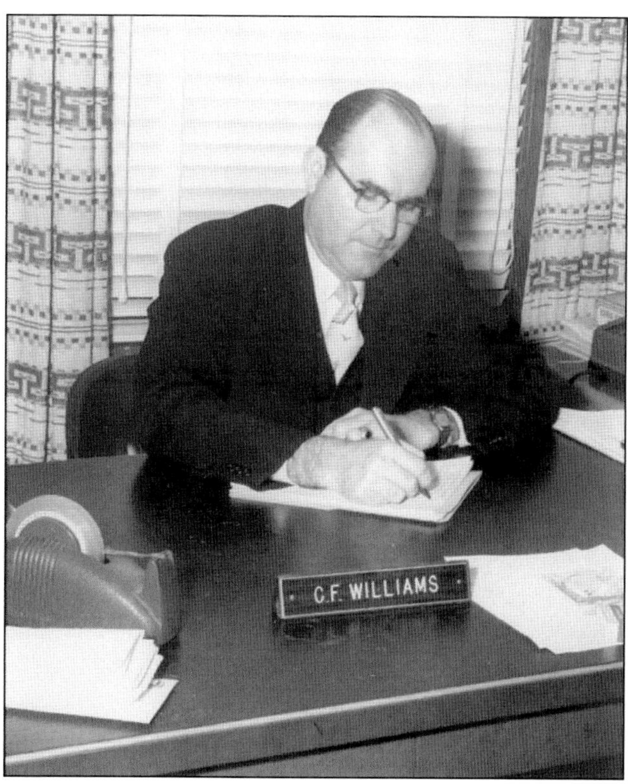

Curtis F. Williams became the superintendent of Travelers Rest area schools in 1950, responsible for Travelers Rest High School and the grammar school as well as 15 elementary schools. In 1951, Greenville County schools were consolidated into one district, and Williams became principal of Travelers Rest High and Elementary School until 1956, when a new high school was built. Williams then remained principal at what was then known as Travelers Rest Elementary School. He retired as principal in 1971 and died in 1999 at the age of 92.

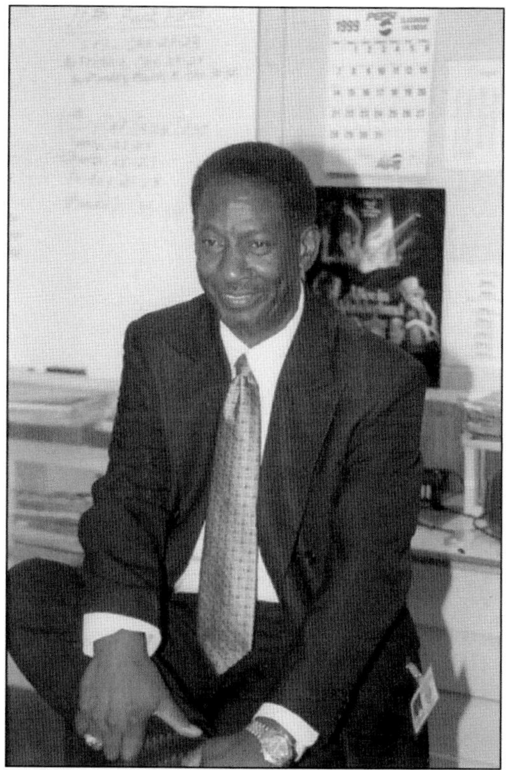

Harvey Choplin has served the Travelers Rest community in many different roles. Married to the former Vivian McCoy, he taught math and coached basketball at Travelers Rest High School for 18 years before becoming assistant principal and then principal. He has been a member of the Travelers Rest City Council for 25 years.

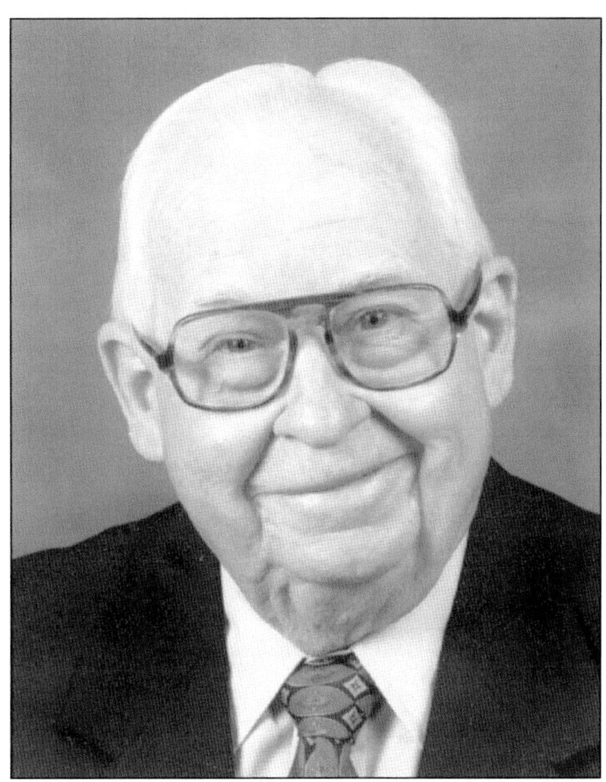

Mann Batson, born in 1925, was educated in Travelers Rest schools and at Furman University. He earned both a Purple Heart and a Bronze Star for heroic action in World War II. He taught at Travelers Rest High School and was superintendent of Dacusville Schools for 4 years before serving for 18 years as superintendent of St. George Schools in Dorchester County, South Carolina. He returned to his native hometown, owned Williams Hardware, served as mayor from 1997 to 2001, was magistrate of Travelers Rest for two years, and served as a member of Greenville County Council for 8 years. Considered to be the foremost authority of Upstate South Carolina history, he is the author of five local history books, numerous articles, and pamphlets.

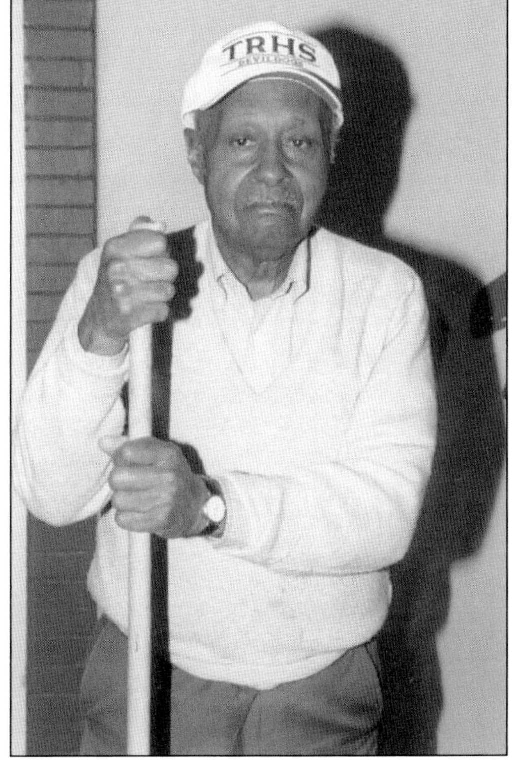

Travelers Rest High School is a family in the truest sense of the word, and a longtime member of that family was Alfonzo Brown, who worked at the high school for almost 40 years. His work ethic and loyalty set an example for the students. He walked to school every day—rain or shine—and never complained when his circumstances were difficult. His dedication to the school and community were inspirational, and the grateful community gave him a large retirement celebration.

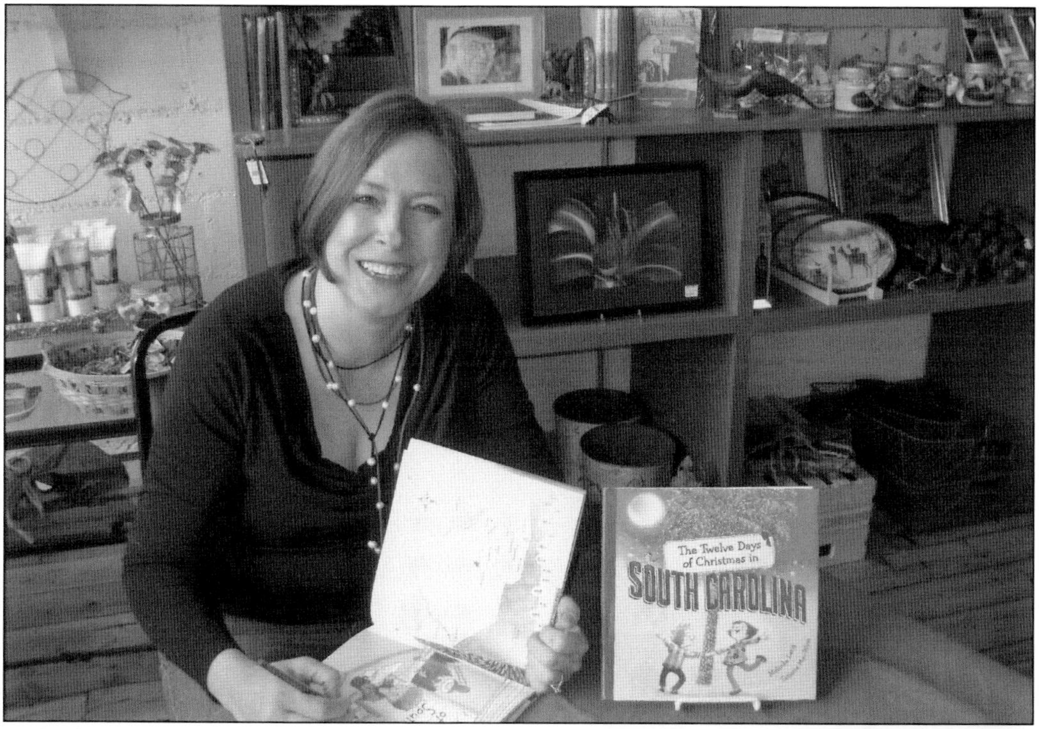

Melinda Long graduated from Travelers Rest High School and Furman University and then worked as a middle school teacher for 23 years. She is the author of six children's books. One of these books, *How I Became a Pirate,* has been translated into many languages, including Spanish, Greek, Hebrew, Norwegian, and Japanese, and has been made into a movie. Her latest book is entitled *The Twelve Days of Christmas in South Carolina*.

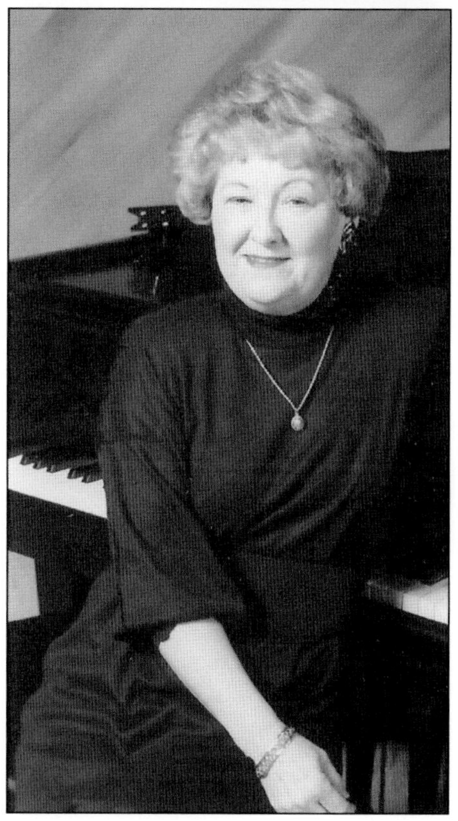

During her 41-year teaching career, Patricia Summey Hunt Fisher guided and enriched individual lives in addition to making contributions to many facets of the community. She taught for 38 years at Travelers Rest High School and was recognized three times by the local Jaycees and her fellow faculty members as Teacher of the Year. Her gentle, firm guidance aided in the merging of Slater-Marietta and Travelers Rest High Schools. Named by her students, "Hunt's Kids," the school's premier choral group, were popular performers at events and celebrations.

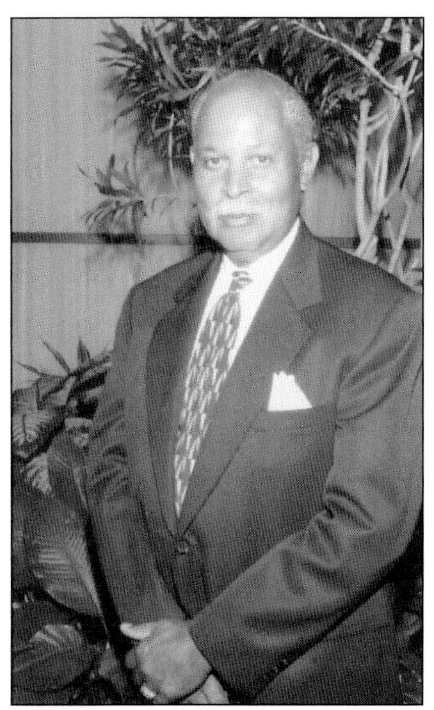

Clyde Carr is a volunteer in the Travelers Rest community, serving on boards of the North Greenville Food Crisis Ministry (NGFCM), the local YMCA, district committees of the United Methodist Church, and as an active member of St. John's United Methodist Church. In 1967, he organized a golf tournament with nine participants to help raise money for his church. In 2003, with 60 to 70 participants taking part, he started sharing the tournament's income with the NGFCM. In 2009, he was declared Citizen of the Year in Travelers Rest, and September 29 was declared Clyde Carr Day.

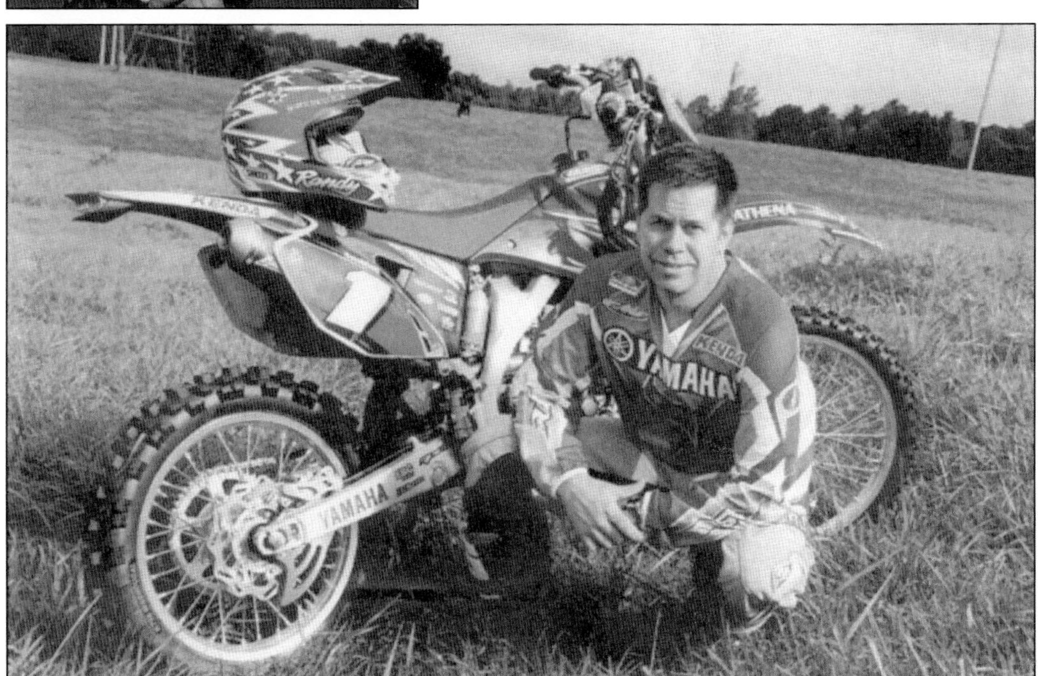

Off-road racer and Travelers Rest native Randy Hawkins first raced in a motocross event in 1976, launching a career that would see him capture a long list of American Motorcyclist Association (AMA) National victories, championship titles, and international gold medals. Between 1987 and 2004, Hawkins earned 73 AMA National race wins. He was chosen Most Popular Off-Road Rider in Japan in 1992 and has produced a DVD titled *Champions at Play*. In December 2009, he was inducted into the American Motorcyclist Association Hall of Fame.

Nine

History in the Making

Travelers Rest is located in a junction. Physically, it lies in the junction between two highways that run from Greenville, South Carolina, and across the mountains to North Carolina. Historically, it is poised between a rich history and an exciting new future. After years of relative stasis, healthy new ideas and energy are working together to bring fresh life, progress, and change to the community. A combination of new businesses, a new look to the downtown area, and the creation of the new Swamp Rabbit Trail—in tandem with a growing local appreciation of the area's history—have given Travelers Rest a new reputation as a great place to live, shop, play, and learn. In the following pages are some of the exciting new looks and faces of Travelers Rest.

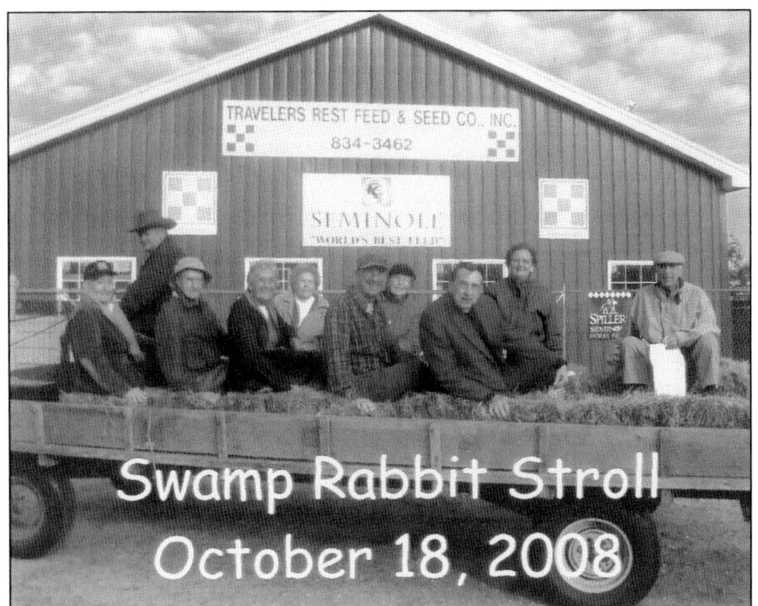

In 2008, many activities marked the celebration of the Travelers Rest bicentennial. One major event was a "Celebrity Hayride." Some outstanding senior citizens were honored by participating in the first official event on the Swamp Rabbit Trail. Seen here among those at the end of the hayride are Howard Addis, Dr. John Holliday, Ilse Holliday, Dr. Jim Barnett (far right), Birdie Harmon, Frankie Hightower, and Carroll and Katherine Smith.

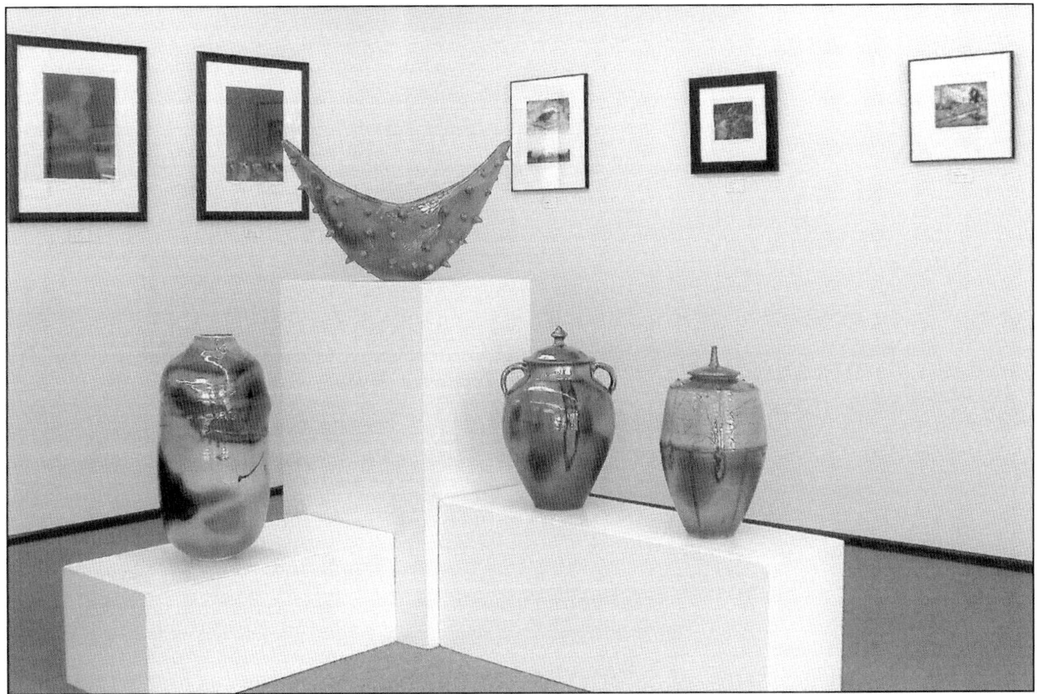

The Trillium Arts Centre was originally founded in 2005 by Travelers Rest native Nichole Livengood as the Travelers Rest Arts Mission with the purpose of bringing the arts into an underserved portion of Greenville County. As the organization expanded its scope and mission over the years, the organization was renamed the Trillium Arts Centre and moved to Main Street in Travelers Rest. Trillium Arts currently provides support services to local artists, arts education for children and adults, and produces art events for the community, including frequent exhibitions, literary events, and festivals. Trillium Arts is also deeply involved in the development of the community and hosts a welcome center for the City of Travelers Rest.

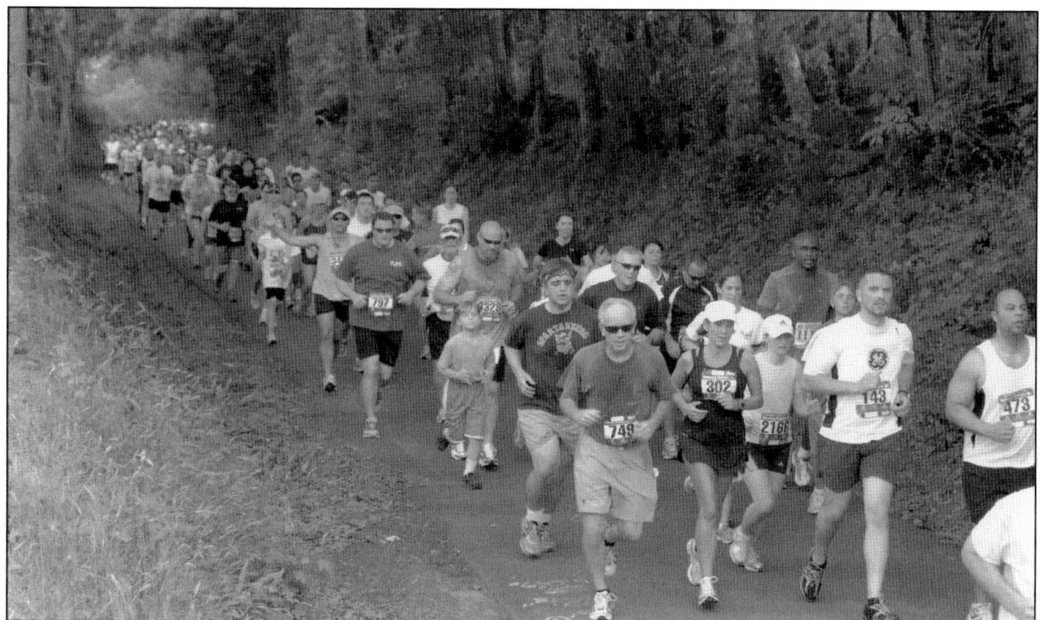

The railroad line that ran from Greenville to Marietta for almost 100 years was sold several times, and different owners would take up the tracks and replace them. In 1999, Greenville County purchased the tracks. The county's recreation department developed a walking/biking trail, the Greenville Hospital System Swamp Rabbit Tram Trail, which runs from Travelers Rest to southern Greenville County. The Travelers Rest segment of this trail is heavily used and enjoyed by hundreds of people daily. The photograph here shows runners competing in the Swamp Rabbit Run in the spring of 2010.

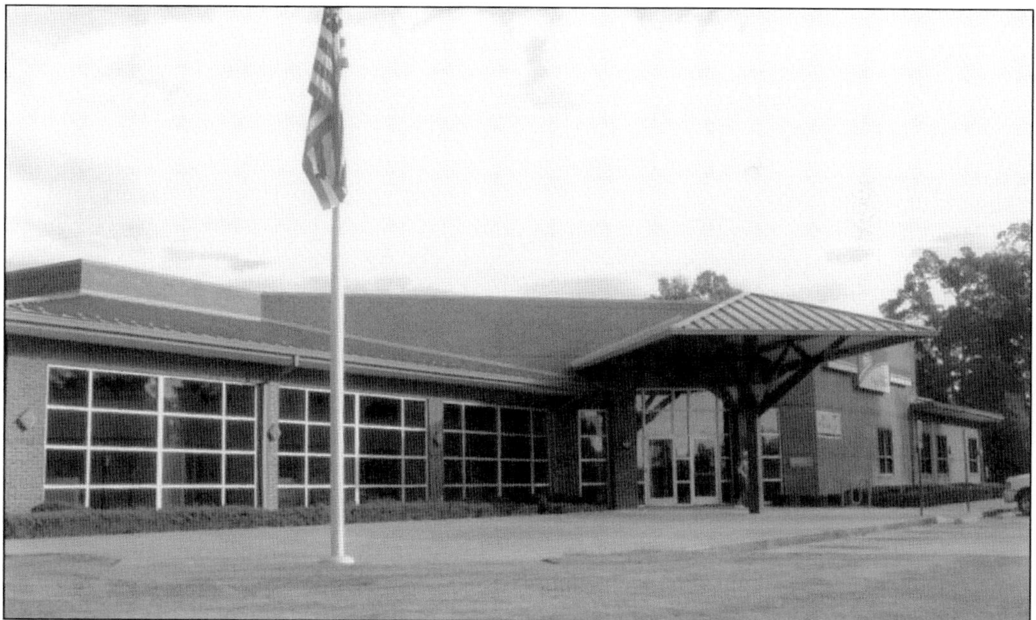

The current Travelers Rest Post Office is located on the corner of Roe Road and South Main Street on the site of the old Clarence and Nora Roe home. This building was constructed and occupied in 2001.

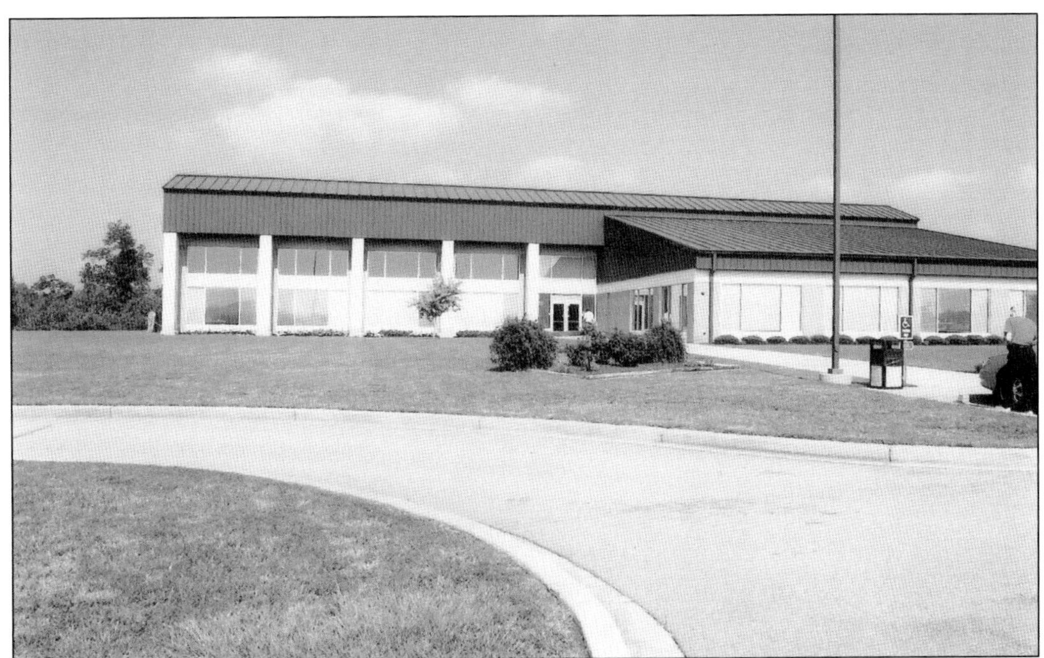

In 2002, a beautiful 12,000-square-foot facility housing the George I. Theisen YMCA opened on 95 acres of land donated by Walter Brashier. Offerings include a wide variety of fitness programs for all citizens from young children to the Senior Action Program. Sports teams, summer day camps, and summer sports camps are offered to students.

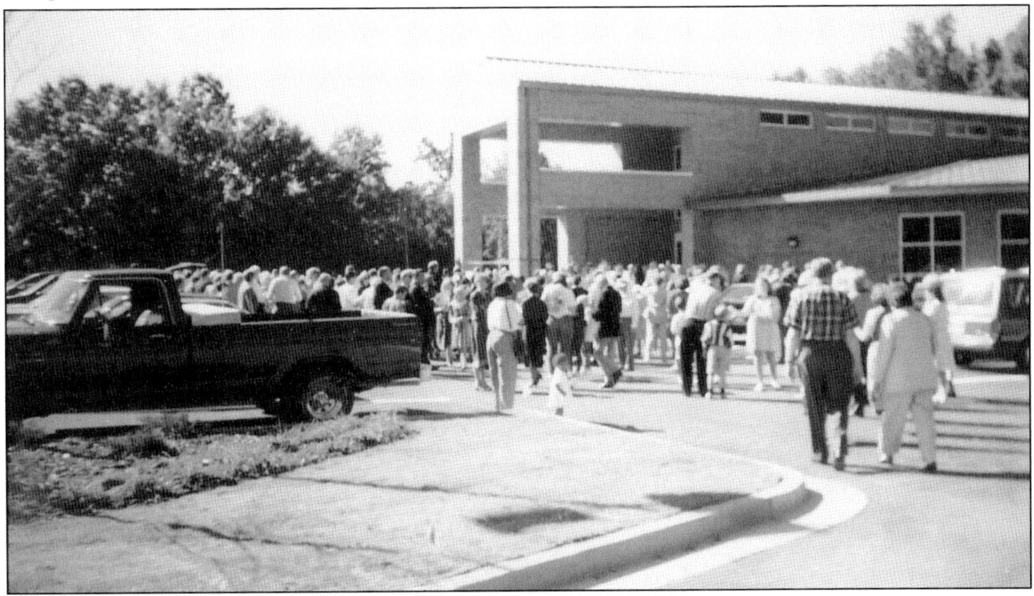

The availability of borrowed reading materials in Travelers Rest began with a small library in a home near the town and progressed to weekly trips of a bookmobile from 1927 until the early 1960s, when a small branch library opened upstairs in the savings and loan on Main Street and later relocated to a storefront on South Main Street. Pictured here in 1996 is the opening day of the beautiful, modern, well-equipped Sargent Branch Library on the site of the old Travelers Rest Elementary School. The library's Southern Reading Garden was funded by local women's clubs.

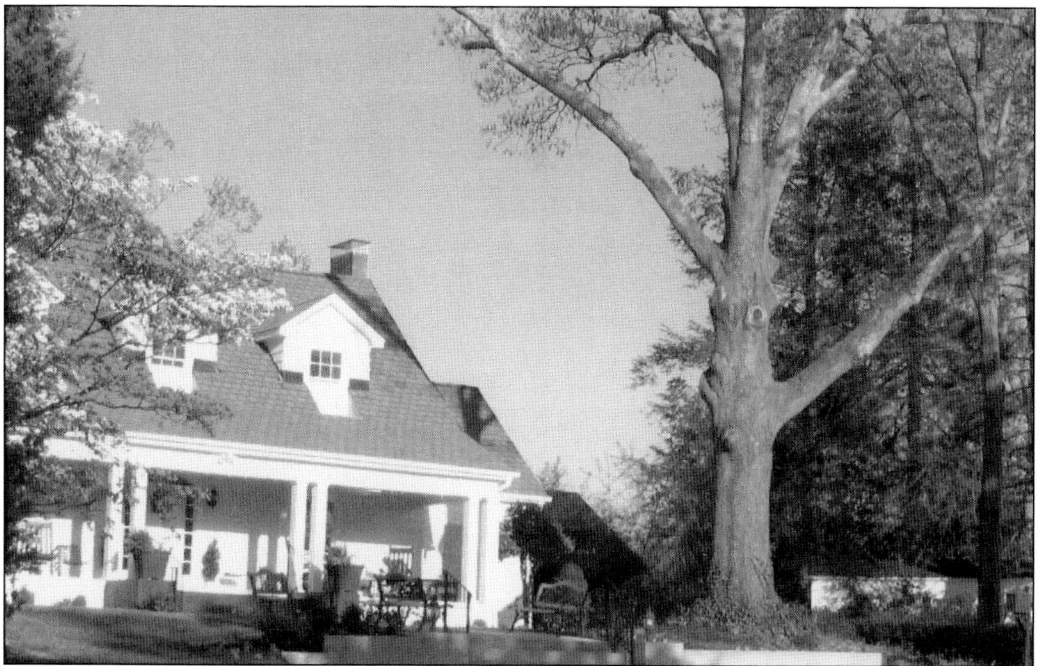

The Magnolia Inn, formerly the home of Robert and Charlotte Roe, has been lovingly restored and serves as a reminder of the glory days of the 1800s, when Lowcountry planters would stop at Travelers Rest as they traveled to the mountains to escape from the heat and mosquitoes of South Carolina's coastal areas. Magnolia Inn proudly welcomes visitors as they enter Travelers Rest on Main Street.

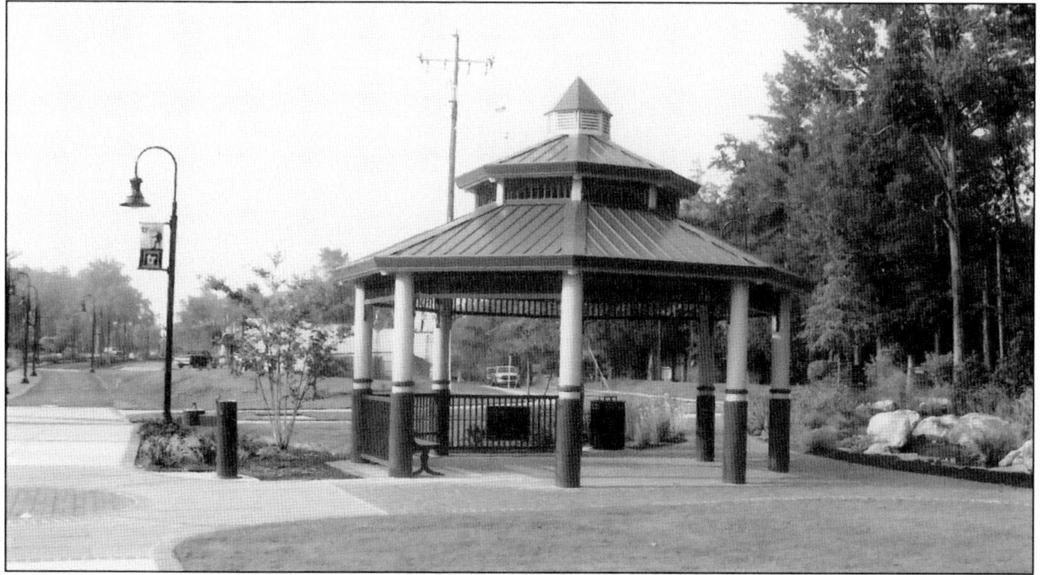

Travelers Rest City Council embarked on an exciting downtown revitalization effort with the goal of creating a vibrant, pedestrian-oriented environment in which economic prosperity and creativity can flourish. With beautiful landscaping, on-street parking, decorative streetlights, a new park, and wider sidewalks, Main Street is now a focal point of Travelers Rest rather than simply a pass-through four-lane highway to the mountains.

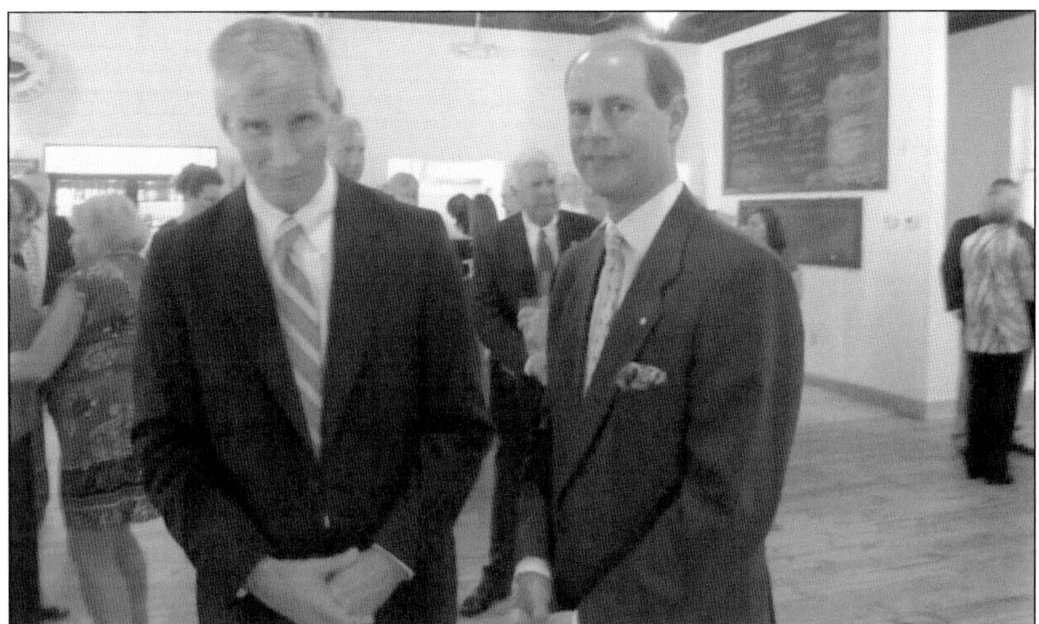

In June 2010, on the eve of the opening of the Scottish Games at Furman University, Prince Edward of England (right) was guest of honor at a drop-in and buffet dinner at Café at Williams Hardware in Travelers Rest. South Carolina state representative Harry Cato (left) hosted the affair, which included local community leaders.

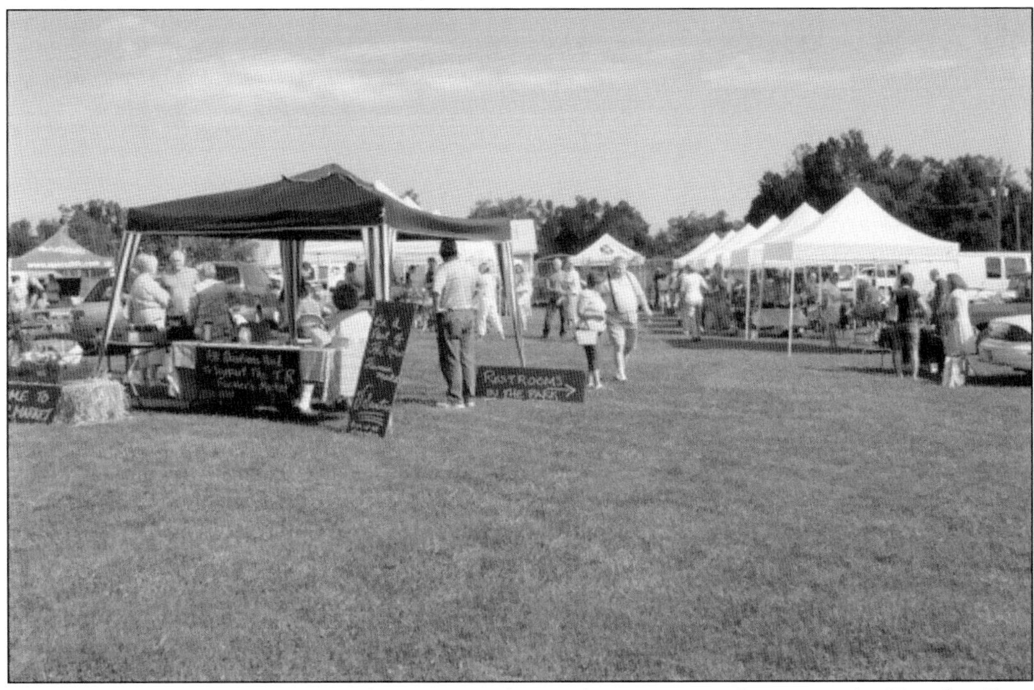

Beginning in 2009 on every Saturday morning during the summer and autumn, the Travelers Rest Community Farmers Market offers fresh, locally grown, top-quality produce, eggs, and other foodstuffs as well as plants and flowers for sale. The motto of this popular market, located behind Sunrift Adventures on Center Street, is "Supporting Our Farmers—Supplying Our Community."

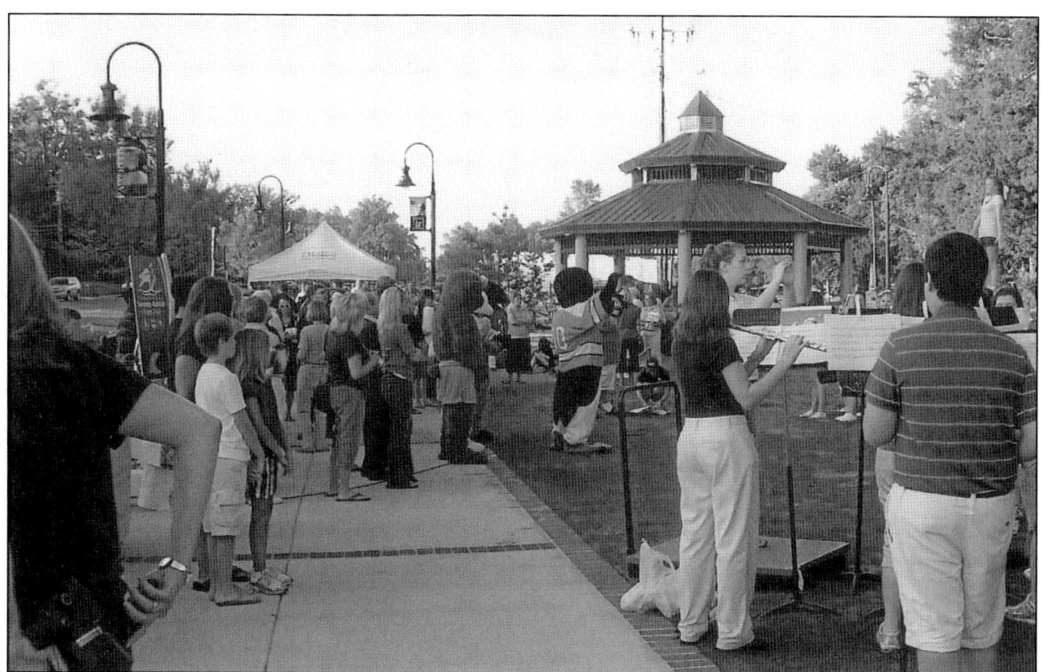

The new Main Street Park and wide sidewalks are ideal for art shows and community events. Shown here, Travelers Rest was featured in the local Fox Carolina *Town Takeover* series in June 2010. This type of event is reminiscent of the days when the Swamp Rabbit Train brought trainloads of guests to Spring Park Inn for parties, dances, picnics, ball games, and political meetings.

Founded in 2008, the Travelers Rest Historical Society has several objectives. One is to preserve and encourage others to preserve valuable historic material and property. In 2010, a local realtor donated a historic building to be used as a history museum on the condition that it be moved. The photograph shows the 1926 store being transported in August of that year to its new home on a highly visible, city-owned site that is a portion of the land given to the city by the Roe family.

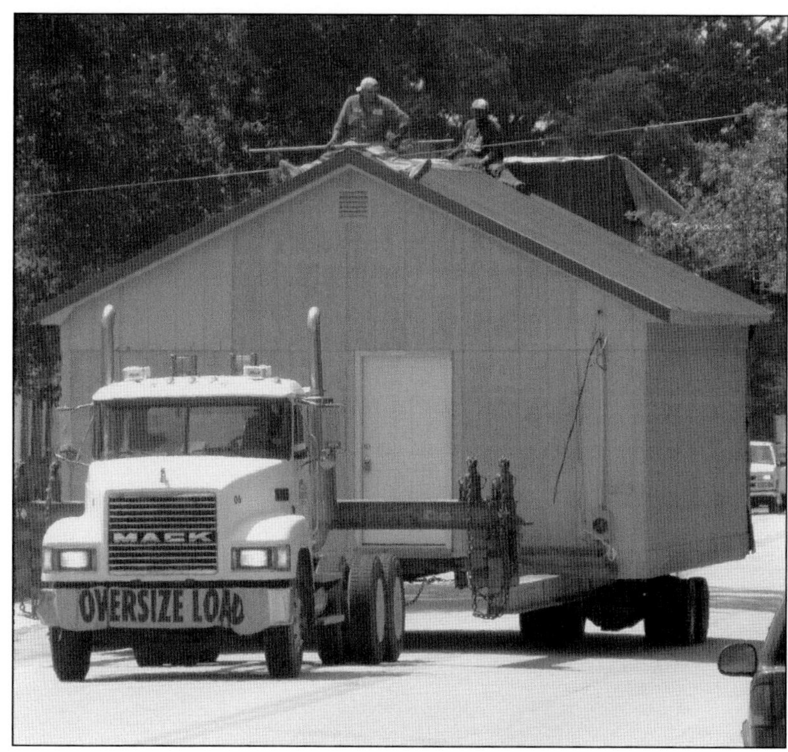

Bibliography

"An Ex-Big Wheel." *The Washington Daily News* [Washington, DC]. June 7, 1956.

Bainbridge, Judith G. *The Renfrew Community.* 1999.

Batson, Mann. *A History of the Upper Part of Greenville County, South Carolina.* Taylors, SC: Faith Printing, 1993.

———. *Early Travels and Accommodations.* Taylors, SC: Faith Printing, 1995.

———. *History of Reedy River Baptist Church.* Greenville, SC: Poinsett Printing, 1959.

———. *Water-Powered Gristmills and Owners.* Taylors, SC: Faith Printing, 1996.

Batson, Stephen M., and D. R. Whitaker, eds. *Cooper Lodge 282, Travelers Rest, SC.* 2004.

Cornell, Polly, Frances Lockaby, and Naida Lyle. *Travelers Rest United Methodist Church: 1893–1993.* Columbia, SC: South Carolina Methodist Conference, 1993.

Cottingham, Walt, ed. "Harry Kramer—Ride 'Em Grandpa!" *Echoes.* Vol. 6. Greenville, SC: Enoree Career Center, 1990.

———. "Life of the Swamp Rabbit." *Echoes.* Vol. 2. Greenville, SC: Enoree Career Center, 1986.

———. "The Burning of Travelers Rest High School." *Echoes.* Vol. 3. Greenville, SC: Enoree Career Center, 1987.

Davis, Edgar, Jr., and Katie Lee Tate Dill. *Quills.* Published monthly. Greenwood, SC: Abney Mills, 1951–1964.

"Dining Hall at Viet Nam Base Bears Batson Name." *The Greenville News* [Greenville, SC]. May 1, 1966.

Duncan, Lynn, ed. "Renfrew Mill." *Echoes.* Vol. 13. Taylors, SC: Faith Printing, 1997.

———. "The Roe House." *Echoes.* Vol. 10. Greenville, SC: Enoree Career Center, 1994.

Ellis, Joyce Howard, and Ann Pollard. *Springfield Family 1739–2001.* Vol. 1. Baltimore, MD: Gateway Press, Inc., 2001.

Gilmore, Maj. Lawrence J., and Capt. Howard J. Lewis, comps. *435th Troop Carrier Group.* Greenville, SC: Keys Printing Company, 1946.

Goodlett, Mildred W. *Travelers Rest at Mountain's Foot.* Self-published, 1966.

Trull, Elaine. "New Ownership, New Emphasis at Renfrew Bleachery." *The Travelers' Adviser* [Greenville County, SC]. Spring 1980: 1.

Watson, J. N. *A History of the First Baptist Church of Travelers Rest, South Carolina.* 1963.

About the Society

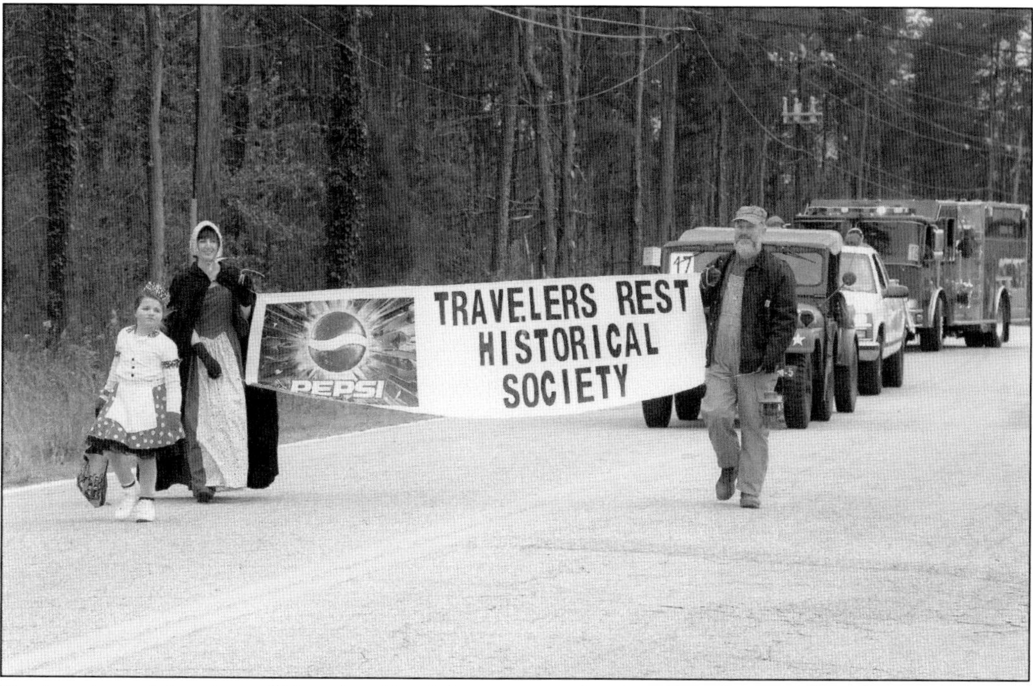

During the celebration of Travelers Rest's bicentennial, it became obvious that there is a hunger for information about the town's history as well as a great interest in preserving that history. The need for an organization to work toward gathering and preserving photographs, artifacts, properties, and stories became evident, and in June 2008, the Travelers Rest Historical Society was formed. The purposes of the society are as follows: to bring together people interested in Travelers Rest area history, to broaden historical knowledge among youth and adults, to preserve and encourage others to preserve valuable historic material and property, and to sponsor special-interest events that serve both the society and the community. Over 180 charter members joined together to learn, celebrate, and honor Travelers Rest's history so that the "old town won't lose her yesterdays." In this photograph, Brandy Hart Amidon, Randy "Country" Hawkins, and Lauren Amidon (front) represent the historical society in the 2009 Travelers Rest Christmas Parade.